Baltimore Orioles IQ:
The Ultimate Test of True Fandom

TUCKER ELLIOT

Printed in the United States of America.
Copyright © 2013 by Tucker Elliot.

All rights reserved. No part of this publication may be reproduced, stored in a retrieval system, or transmitted in any form or by any means, electronic, mechanical, recording, or otherwise, without the prior written permission of the author.

This title is part of the IQ Sports History / Trivia Series, which is a trademark owned by Black Mesa Publishing, LLC.

Cataloging-in-Publication Data is available from the Library of Congress.

ISBN: 978-0-9883648-9-9
First edition, first printing.

Front cover photo courtesy of Mark Whitt.
Back cover photo courtesy of KeithAllisonPhoto.com.
Cover design by Holly Walden Ross.

Black Mesa Publishing, LLC
Florida

admin@blackmesabooks.com
www.blackmesabooks.com

BLACK MESA IQ TITLES

Baltimore Orioles

CONTENTS

"This ain't a football game. We do this every day."
— *Earl Weaver*

INTRODUCTION

Baltimore's professional baseball scene dates back more than 125 years to the late 1800s when guys like Wee Willie Keeler and John McGraw suited it up for the old Orioles teams that played in the American Association and later in the National League. The Orioles would eventually become an American League charter franchise in 1901—but that team was destined from the beginning to move elsewhere, as the league believed long-term success was dependent upon having a franchise located in New York City. Thus the Orioles became the Highlanders, later renamed the Yankees.

As Baltimore lost its club to a couple of Manhattan businessmen another team was on the move as well—this time from Milwaukee to St. Louis, where the newly-minted Browns debuted at Sportsman's Park on April 23, 1902. For half a century the Browns were nothing short of spectacular … when it came to futility. Whatever promise or hope or grandeur dreams held by the franchise and its fans after a second place finish in its inaugural season in St. Louis was quickly replaced by this abysmal reality: the Browns were dead last in the eight-team American League ten times in 52 seasons. They were the proverbial butt of every bad baseball joke told during the first half of the 20th century. For two decades the Browns looked up in the standings as Philadelphia, Boston, New York, Chicago and Cleveland all won World Championships. The only reason the Browns had any fan-base at all was that the St. Louis Cardinals—which leased Sportsman's Park from the Browns—were just as bad. Until the 1920s.

Out of nowhere the Browns won 76 games in 1920 and placed fourth in the league for the first time since 1908. The Cardinals won 75 games and placed fifth in the National League that same year. The Browns improved again in 1921—winning 81 games and placing third in the AL. The Cardinals won 87 games and placed third in the NL. The Browns won 93 games and placed second in the league in 1922. The Cardinals won 85 games and held on to third place for the second straight year.

St. Louis fans—Browns or Cardinals—seemingly had much to be excited about.

The Cards had a kid named Rogers Hornsby and the Browns had George Sisler, Ken Williams and Baby Doll Jacobson. The Browns front office began expanding the seating area at Sportsman's Park, claiming it would host a World Series in the coming years. The Browns also had a not-yet-prominent name working behind the scenes of the organization—it was Branch Rickey. St. Louis was on the verge of baseball greatness—but there was only going to be room at the top for one team, and it was the Cardinals that won favor with the baseball gods.

The Browns let Branch Rickey go, and as fate would have it, he achieved his legendary status building World Championship teams with the Cardinals and the Dodgers.

The Browns fell to fifth place in 1923. By 1926 the team was winning barely 60 games a year and permanently dwelling in the AL cellar ... but Sportsman's Park, as had been predicted, was celebrating its first World Championship that same year.

As the Browns spiraled downward, the Cardinals reached the pinnacle of professional sports—winning five NL Pennants and three World Series titles in nine years. The Cardinals drew more than 400,000 fans to Sportsman's Park in 1939, filling those expansion seats with regularity and lining the pockets of the Cardinals owners. Only 81,000 came out that same year to see the Browns.

The franchise had one final chance to survive in St. Louis.

The Browns won 89 games and the American League Pennant in 1944.

It was simply bad luck that the in-town rival Cardinals won the NL Pennant that same year, and that the Cards won the all-Sportsman's Park World Series in six games. The Browns had won a Pennant but rather than paying homage to its talent, the team was mocked and ridiculed by sportswriters and baseball fans across the country for having lucked into a title by playing against American League teams with depleted war-time rosters. Whatever chance the Browns had at building a fan-base was gone. St. Louis belonged to the Cardinals, and the Browns began looking for a new home.

Baltimore was in the market for a Major League franchise.

Clarence Miles, a Baltimore attorney, was actively leading a group of investors who were trying to bring baseball back to the city. In 1953, Miles found enough support from investors to completely buy out Browns majority owner Bill Veeck. Miles immediately became president and chairman of the board and his first act was to request permission from league owners to move the team to Baltimore. They quickly agreed and in 1954 the franchise began play as the Baltimore Orioles.

There was a weird dynamic involved with the move.

For one thing, most MLB franchises that relocated during this time moved west—but the Orioles moved east. On the surface it's not that big a deal, but take a look at the other teams that moved—Brooklyn to LA, New York to San Francisco, Philadelphia to Kansas City to Oakland—and quickly you realize that all of those franchises embraced their origins and maintained their identities as the Dodgers / Giants / Athletics.

Baltimore wanted nothing to do with the heritage or the legacy of the St. Louis Browns.

After one year of play, and it was a painful year as the O's were terrible in 1954, Baltimore further removed itself from being associated with the Browns by making a 17-player trade with the Yankees that sent packing nearly every player who was a holdover from the club's time in St. Louis. And if you're skeptical about how important this really was to the franchise and its owners both then and in the future, then consider this: the Browns had publicly sold stock back in the 1930s, but when prominent Washington attorney Edward Bennett Williams bought the club five decades later the first thing he did was buy back every share that had been sold—a move that made the club privately owned and that permanently eradicated the Orioles last public association with the Browns.

It's not that the Orioles don't respect history.

It's that from the very beginning Baltimore was intent on *making its own* history. And to that end the franchise has been extraordinarily successful. In St. Louis, the Browns had more 100-loss seasons than any team in baseball history—in Baltimore, it barely took Earl Weaver a decade to manage the Orioles to five 100-win seasons. In St. Louis, the Browns backed into one Pennant in five decades. In Baltimore, the Orioles built a powerhouse that dominated the better part of two decades and won six Pennants.

Obviously, as with any franchise, there have been ups-and-downs and plenty of lean years to go with the championships—but with its successes and the many legends its produced since 1954, the Orioles have achieved the same "status" if you will as its division rivals New York and Boston as being one of baseball's truly great franchises. A virtual who's who of baseball royalty spent time playing in Baltimore. You can't discuss the game's greatest moments without including the Orioles. You can't tour the Hall of Fame in Cooperstown without seeing the influence of the Birds.

This is a book of trivia and history. It's meant for diehard baseball fans, but whether or not you count yourself part of Orioles fandom is irrelevant, because the history of the Birds is inextricably linked with the history of baseball.

Now sit back, reminisce, and enjoy.

Tucker Elliot
Tampa, FL
June 2013

"He [Brooks Robinson] played third base like he came down from a higher league."
— *Ed Hurley*

1 THE NUMBERS GAME

The Baltimore Orioles have retired just seven numbers in franchise history. The members of this elite group are: Earl Weaver, Brooks Robinson, Cal Ripken, Jr., Frank Robinson, Jim Palmer and Eddie Murray—along with baseball legend Jackie Robinson, who had his number 42 retired by every MLB team in 1997, the 50th anniversary of his debut with the Brooklyn Dodgers. The numbers hang inside the ballpark on orange cutout baseballs, prominently displayed beneath the railing of the upper deck above the third base side left field bleachers. The retired numbers are also on display as large monuments outside the ballpark, and most recently, the Orioles unveiled statues for each of the club's Hall of Famers in the walking zone behind the bullpens.

The club has good reason to honor its legends so prominently— they were the best in the game for their generation, and one could argue, they rank among the absolute best of the 21st century as well.

Never mind Cal Ripken, Jr. saved the game from itself in 1995.

After players and owners and league officials all but destroyed the game with the 1994 work stoppage, Ripken gave baseball fans the world over someone to root for, someone that kids could look up to and admire without parents having to worry about his morals or character. It's one thing to win a game with a base hit, or to save a game by pitching a scoreless ninth ... it's something altogether different to save our National Pastime by day in and day out showing up with the joy and passion of a kid playing Little League and the determined attitude and work ethic of a consummate professional bent on doing one thing and one thing only: his job.

The seven numbers on display at Oriole Park at Camden Yards are worthy of the greatest accolades this game has to offer—so it's fitting that we begin our look at Orioles history with a simple numbers game ... do you know which number each of these players wore for the Baltimore Orioles?

TOP OF THE FIRST

Question 1: Hall of Fame manager Earl Weaver ranks among the top 20 in managerial wins for all 20th century big league skippers. That's no small feat. He closed out 17 seasons at the helm in Baltimore with a .583 winning percentage—and that number ranks fifth best among 20th century managers with at least ten seasons guiding a big league club. That's even more impressive. In honor of his extraordinary leadership as Orioles manager, what is the number that Baltimore retired in his honor?

    a) 4
    b) 14
    c) 24
    d) 44

Question 2: Brooks Robinson was elected to the Hall of Fame in 1983, his first year of eligibility. His contributions to the Orioles franchise are so numerous that he's widely referred to as "Mr. Oriole." Robinson spent 23 seasons with the club and established numerous Major League, American League and Orioles team records. In honor of his extraordinary skills on the field of play, what is the number that Baltimore retired in his honor?

    a) 5

b) 15
c) 25
d) 45

Question 3: Hall of Fame legend Cal Ripken, Jr. is one of just eight players in Major League history to surpass 400 home runs and 3,000 hits. The others: Hank Aaron, Willie Mays, Eddie Murray, Rafael Palmeiro, Stan Musial, Dave Winfield and Carl Yastrzemski. Pretty elite company, for sure. Add to that his games played streak, his community involvement, his status as an incredibly positive role model and the numerous team and league records he set, and all total you have one of the greatest and most popular players in Major League history. What is the number the Orioles retired in his honor?
   a) 3
   b) 8
   c) 18
   d) 28

Question 4: Frank Robinson's exploits on the field of play were so great that he ranked among baseball's top ten all-time in no fewer than ten categories at the time of his retirement—to include his 586 home runs. Robinson won every major award imaginable, was a World Champion and a Triple Crown winner, and he was a pioneer as well—in 1975 he became manager of the Cleveland Indians, the first African American manager in Major League history. Robinson's number was also the first to be retired in Orioles history. What is the number retired in his honor?
   a) 12
   b) 19
   c) 20
   d) 29

Question 5: The Orioles official website at MLB.com calls Jim Palmer "the greatest pitcher in Orioles history." He spent his entire 19-year Major League career with the Orioles and won 268 games and a host of awards. Palmer was an eight-time 20-game winner— one of just six 20th century pitchers to accomplish this feat. The most amazing part? Palmer's 20-win seasons came in a span of nine years during which he flat out dominated the competition. What is the number retired by the Orioles in his honor?

    a) 2
    b) 12
    c) 22
    d) 32

Question 6: Eddie Murray was elected to the Hall of Fame in 2003, his first year of eligibility. Murray spent more than half his legendary career with the Orioles and ranks among the top five in nearly every major offensive category in team history. His most impressive stat? It's no contest: Murray, Rafael Palmeiro, Hank Aaron and Willie Mays are the only players in Major League history to reach 500 home runs and 3,000 hits—and of course Murray is the only switch-hitter in this most exclusive of clubs. What is the number retired by the Orioles in his honor?

    a) 3
    b) 13
    c) 23
    d) 33

Question 7: Roberto Alomar is another Hall of Famer who played with the Orioles—of course the majority of his career was spent with other teams, and he's enshrined in Cooperstown wearing a Blue Jays hat, but during his three seasons with the Orioles from 1996-98 he won a Silver Slugger and two Gold Glove awards and he was a three-time All-Star. What was Alomar's jersey number when he was an All-Star second baseman for the Orioles?

    a) 2
    b) 12
    c) 22
    d) 32

Question 8: Mike Mussina was a product of the Orioles' farm system and he debuted with the club in 1991. He quickly became a star, winning 18 games the following season and for the rest of the decade he consistently ranked among the league leaders for wins and in Cy Young balloting. Unfortunately, Mussina never won a Cy Young and he never won 20 games for the Orioles—though he did lead the league with 19 wins in 1995, and he won 19 games again in 1996. It wasn't until his final big league season that he won 20 games, pitching for the Yankees in 2008. Moose is one of only seven pitchers in franchise history to log more than 2,000 innings for the Orioles. What was the primary jersey number he wore during that time?

    a) 13
    b) 25
    c) 35
    d) 42

Question 9: Dave McNally was a key member of the Orioles pitching staff that led the club to the postseason six times from 1966-74. In that span he was a 20-game winner four times, led the league in wins once, and then backed up his league leading total by posting the highest winning percentage in the league the following season. What was the primary jersey number he wore during that time?

    a) 9
    b) 19
    c) 29
    d) 39

Question 10: The Orioles first-round draft pick in 2010, and the third pick overall, Manny Machado made his big league debut on August 9, 2012 as the Orioles were in a heated race to make the postseason for the first time since 1997. Machado was only 19-years-old at the time of his debut, but he provided a solid glove at third base and more than handled his own at the plate—he batted .262 with seven home runs and 26 RBIs during 51 games down the stretch, and very quickly became a fan-favorite. What was Machado's jersey number during his 2012 rookie season?

    a) 3
    b) 13
    c) 23
    d) 32

TOP OF THE FIRST ANSWER KEY

1. A

2. A

3. B

4. C

5. C

6. D

7. B

8. C

9. B

10. B

BOTTOM OF THE FIRST

Question 11: Brady Anderson came to Baltimore along with Curt Schilling in a July 1988 trade that sent longtime Oriole Mike Boddicker to the Boston Red Sox. Anderson steadily improved his play and worked his way from part time player, to platoon player, all the way to being a three-time All-Star. He took the baseball world by storm in 1996 when he blasted a career high 50 home runs, and yet somehow he managed to place just ninth in league MVP balloting that season. After 14 seasons with the club he left the game in 2002, but he remains among the top ten leaders in franchise history in numerous offensive categories, including hits, runs, total bases and home runs. Anderson wore number 16 his first season with the Orioles, but what was his primary number during the rest of his tenure with the club?

    a) 5
    b) 9
    c) 19
    d) 23

Question 12: And speaking of Mike Boddicker … he was drafted out of the University of Iowa by Baltimore in 1978, and five years later he was 16-8 with a 2.77 earned run average in his rookie campaign for the Orioles. He came back in his sophomore season to lead the league with 20 wins and a 2.79 earned run average. Boddicker was a consistent starter who hit double digits in wins five years straight for the O's before struggling to a 6-12 record midway through 1988— but that's what brought Brady Anderson to Baltimore, as the Red Sox were looking for starting pitching for the stretch run and despite his dismal record Boddicker was in high demand. And he responded nicely, posting a 7-3 record down the stretch to help the Red Sox clinch the AL East. What jersey number did he wear throughout his Orioles career?

    a) 22
    b) 32

c) 42

d) 52

Question 13: Rafael Palmeiro slugged 223 home runs in just seven seasons and 1,000 games for Baltimore. Palmeiro had two stints with the Birds—his first was from 1994-98, and he was nothing short of prolific. He hit 23 home runs in just 111 games during the 1994 strike-shortened season, and followed that with seasons of 39, 39, 38 and 43 bombs, and he surpassed 100 RBIs in all four of those campaigns. What jersey number did he wear through his Orioles career?

a) 5

b) 15

c) 25

d) 35

Question 14: Shortstop Miguel Tejada signed with the Orioles as a free agent after the 2003 season. Tejada was an All-Star his first three seasons with the O's and he was routinely among the league leaders in hits, doubles, RBIs and average. He wore number 9 during a brief second stint with Baltimore in 2010, but what number did he wear playing in his prime for the Orioles from 2004-07?

a) 4

b) 10

c) 14

d) 24

Question 15: Boog Powell was a fan-favorite and a two-time World Champion with the Orioles. And he could flat hit. Powell had nine 20-homer seasons, four 30-homer campaigns and he topped 100 RBIs on three occasions. His best years came from 1968-71 when he was an All-Star four consecutive seasons and won an MVP award. Powell wore four different jersey numbers during his 14 seasons in Baltimore—but what was his primary number during his days with the Orioles?

a) 8

b) 16

c) 26
d) 30

Question 16: Al Bumbry played all but 68 of his nearly 1,500 big league games for the Orioles. He was a speedster, and though he never led the league in steals he routinely ranked among the league leaders. Bumbry only wore one uniform number throughout his career in Baltimore—what was it?
   a) 1
   b) 11
   c) 21
   d) 31

Question 17: Mike Cuellar won 185 games during 15 big league seasons, but his most successful days came in Baltimore. The Cuban native was originally signed by Cincinnati, but after stops in the Mexican League and multiple minor league cities, he also spent time with the Tigers, Cardinals and Astros before being traded to Baltimore after the 1968 season. And then suddenly he was lights out, winning 23 games in 1969 and earning co-Cy Young honors with the Tigers Denny McLain. What was Mike Cuellar's primary jersey number with the Orioles from 1969-76?
   a) 3
   b) 5
   c) 35
   d) 53

Question 18: Rick Dempsey played with six different clubs in a career that spanned 24 Major League seasons, but he's best remembered for his success with the Orioles. A two-time World Champion, Dempsey is one of just three catchers in baseball history to play in a Major League game in four different decades (along with Tim McCarver and Carlton Fisk). What was Rick Dempsey's primary jersey number during his 11-plus seasons with the Orioles?
   a) 22
   b) 24
   c) 26

d) 28

Question 19: The Houston Astros drafted Mike Flanagan in 1971, but thankfully he elected not to sign. Instead he attended the University of Massachusetts where he was a standout pitcher and outfielder. Baltimore drafted and signed Flanagan in 1973, and two years later he earned his first call-up to the Orioles. Flanagan would go on to win a Cy Young Award and a World Series title during parts of 15 seasons pitching in Baltimore. What was Mike Flanagan's primary jersey number during his tenure with the Orioles?

  a) 40
  b) 42
  c) 44
  d) 46

Question 20: Dennis Martinez is often recognized for being the first Major League player to be born in Nicaragua. Martinez came to the attention of Orioles scouts while pitching as an amateur against Team USA in an international matchup, and one year later he was pitching in Baltimore's farm system. Martinez wore number 61 while pitching four games with the Orioles in 1976. What was his jersey number while pitching for the Orioles from 1977-86?

  a) 27
  b) 30
  c) 32
  d) 37

BOTTOM OF THE FIRST ANSWER KEY

11. B

12. D

13. C

14. B

15. C

16. A

17. C

18. B

19. D

20. B

"First in shoes, first in booze, and last in the American League."
— *Old adage about the St. Louis Browns*

2 THE REALLY BAD BROWNS

The Browns played baseball in St. Louis for five decades. At times it was really, really bad baseball. There's just no other way to describe it. In 52 seasons the club had a winning record just 11 times, but managed to lose 100 games no fewer than eight times—including three consecutive years from 1910-12 when the club lost 107, 107 and 101 games respectively. And it wasn't just a bad stretch. Losing was endemic throughout the organization. Losing was the Browns culture, if you will.

Every organization has a dry spell.

This was so far beyond being a dry spell as to be ridiculous. In baseball circles, the St. Louis Browns are the overwhelming choice for being the "worst franchise in baseball history." The Browns lost 315 games in that three-year run from 1910-12, but not to be outdone, 25 years later the Browns put together another horrid stretch in which the club lost *316 games* in three seasons from 1937-39. It's no wonder that after eight consecutive losing seasons in the 1940s and 1950s the club was sold and moved—if it had stayed in St. Louis then in all likelihood it would not have survived in any form. And while Baltimore has understandably distanced itself from its St. Louis roots, at the very least it seems important that fans should take the time to recognize and remember the players who did achieve success with the St. Louis Browns.

Hall of Famer Heinie Manush played three years for the Browns. This is a guy who batted .330 during 17 big league seasons and once robbed Babe Ruth of a batting title on the season's final day by going 6 for 9 in a doubleheader. Another Browns Hall of Famer is Goose Goslin, who had three incredible seasons in St. Louis. Bucky Harris once said of Goslin, "If they tried to sneak one by Goose, he'd tag it." Goslin was a powerful left-handed hitter who batted .316 for his career and amassed nearly 3,000 hits. Other stars in Browns history: George Sisler, Ken Williams, Urban Shocker and Jack Powell to name just a few. Here in the second we take a look at the origins, records and stars from the St. Louis era in franchise history.

TOP OF THE SECOND

Question 21: The franchise that would eventually become the Baltimore Orioles began play as an original member of the American League in 1901. That year the club was a dismal 48-89 and finished dead last, 35.5 games behind the Pennant-winning Chicago White Stockings. This can get a bit confusing because one of the eight original teams in the AL actually *was* called the Baltimore Orioles— but that team later became the New York Yankees and was a different franchise altogether from today's Orioles. Which of the eight original AL franchises later became the Baltimore Orioles beloved by its fans today?

    a) Milwaukee Brewers
    b) Washington Senators
    c) Cleveland Blues
    d) Philadelphia Athletics

Question 22: The second stop along the way to becoming the Baltimore Orioles was in St. Louis. In its first season as the St. Louis Browns the club won 78 games and placed second in the American League, just five games behind Philadelphia for the league's best record. Which season was the first in franchise history as the St. Louis Browns?

a) 1902
b) 1905
c) 1908
d) 1911

Question 23: The Browns made it to the World Series just one time, losing in six games to the St. Louis Cardinals. What year did the Browns win the only Pennant during the St. Louis era in franchise history?

a) 1942
b) 1944
c) 1946
d) 1948

Question 24: The final seasons in St. Louis were abysmal. The Browns lost 88, 95, 94, 101, 96, 102, 90 and 100 games in the final eight seasons before moving to Baltimore. The Browns were last or second-to-last in seven of those seasons—the lone exception a sixth place finish in 1948—and home attendance was almost non-existent. It was clear the team needed a fresh start, so other owners around the league gave St. Louis unanimous support to move the franchise to Baltimore. Which season did the franchise begin playing as the Baltimore Orioles?

a) 1952
b) 1953
c) 1954
d) 1955

Question 25: There have been more than 40 "managers" total during all eras in franchise history when you include those with interim tags, but there is only one who can claim to have been the very first. Who managed the club in 1901 during the first season in franchise history?

a) Jimmy McAleer
b) Hugh Duffy
c) Jack O'Connor

d) Bobby Wallace

Question 26: Of the 40-plus skippers in franchise history, 22 of them took the helm of the St. Louis Browns. Who managed the club during its first season playing as the St. Louis Browns?
a) Jimmy McAleer
b) Hugh Duffy
c) Jack O'Connor
d) Bobby Wallace

Question 27: With only one Pennant to show for five-plus decades of baseball in St. Louis, there wasn't a lot of success to be celebrated by the Browns. Who was the only manager during the St. Louis era in franchise history to guide the club to the postseason?
a) Fred Haney
b) Rogers Hornsby
c) Luke Sewell
d) Zack Taylor

Question 28: Earl Weaver managed a franchise record 17 seasons in Baltimore. Who managed a record eight seasons during the St. Louis era in franchise history?
a) Jimmy McAleer
b) Hugh Duffy
c) Jack O'Connor
d) Bobby Wallace

Question 29: Earl Weaver managed the Orioles for a full decade longer than the second-longest tenured skipper in the Baltimore era in franchise history. With seven seasons at the helm, who ranks second only to Weaver for managing the Baltimore Orioles for the most seasons?
a) Hank Bauer
b) Mike Hargrove
c) Frank Robinson
d) Paul Richards

Question 30: In St. Louis Browns history there is only one manager who was with the club for five or more seasons *and* achieved a career .500 or better winning percentage. Which of the following was the only skipper to manage better than .500 during five or more seasons guiding the St. Louis Browns?

a) Luke Sewell

b) Rogers Hornsby

c) Zack Taylor

d) Jimmy McAleer

TOP OF THE SECOND ANSWER KEY

21. A

22. A

23. B

24. C

25. B

26. A

27. C

28. A

29. D

30. A

BOTTOM OF THE SECOND

Question 31: In 1928, this member of the St. Louis Browns batted .378 and led the league with 241 hits and 47 doubles, but that was only good enough to place second in league MVP balloting behind the Athletics Mickey Cochrane who batted (a rather paltry, by comparison) .293 with 137 hits and 26 doubles. Go figure. His .378 average didn't even win him the batting title, but it does rank as the third highest on record during the St. Louis era in franchise history. This same player batted .362 overall during his career with the Browns—and that number is a franchise record. Who was this phenomenal hitter?

    a) George Sisler
    b) Ken Williams
    c) Heinie Manush
    d) Goose Goslin

Question 32: This member of the St. Louis Browns won two batting titles in a span of three years. He's the only player in franchise history to bat .400 for a season—and he did it twice. Which member of the St. Louis Browns won batting titles with season averages of .420 and .407?

    a) George Sisler
    b) Ken Williams
    c) Heinie Manush
    d) Goose Goslin

Question 33: Harlond Clift played ten seasons with the St. Louis Browns and scored 1,013 runs for the club—including seven seasons scoring 100-plus runs. His career total ranks him among the top ten for all eras in franchise history, and it's the second highest total among players who played exclusively during the St. Louis era. Who is the only player to outscore Harlond Clift with a total of 1,091 runs for the St. Louis Browns?

    a) George Sisler

b) Ken Williams
c) Heinie Manush
d) Goose Goslin

Question 34: This player won two-thirds of a Triple Crown when he batted .332 in 1922 and led the league with 39 home runs and 155 RBIs for the St. Louis Browns. His monstrous season contributed greatly to the 185 career home runs he hit for the Browns—a total that ranks first among all players from that era in franchise history. Who is this slugger that also ranked among the league's top four in home runs for seven consecutive seasons with the Browns?
a) George Sisler
b) Ken Williams
c) Heinie Manush
d) Harlond Clift

Question 35: This player had 100-plus RBIs four times in a span of five seasons for the Browns. All total he drove home a record 962 runs during the St. Louis era in franchise history. Who was this prolific run producer?
a) George Sisler
b) Ken Williams
c) Heinie Manush
d) Harlond Clift

Question 36: This pitcher set a franchise record when he led the league with 27 wins for the St. Louis Browns in 1921. He won 91 games in a four-year stretch with the Browns and his 126 career wins with the club ranks first for the St. Louis era in franchise history. Who was this successful pitcher?
a) Steve Barber
b) Barney Pelty
c) Carl Weilman
d) Urban Shocker

Question 37: This pitcher compiled a microscopic 2.06 earned run average while pitching more than 1,500 innings for the St. Louis

Browns. That is easily the best average in franchise history. In fact, it ranks among the top 100 in Major League history, but despite that, his career won-loss record is below .500 because he played for some terrible teams in St. Louis. For good measure he also played some third base and outfield for the Browns. Who was this versatile pitcher?

a) Fred Glade

b) Barney Pelty

c) Harry Howell

d) Eddie Watt

Question 38: Starting pitchers were expected to complete games when the franchise was based in St. Louis, so you didn't have specialized relief corps like you do in baseball today. With that in mind, who pitched in more games than anyone else during the St. Louis era in franchise history?

a) Elam Vangilder

b) Sammy Stewart

c) Jack Powell

d) Barney Pelty

Question 39: Who actually pitched more innings for the St. Louis Browns than any other player in franchise history?

a) Elam Vangilder

b) Sammy Stewart

c) Jack Powell

d) Barney Pelty

Question 40: Rube Waddell struck out 232 batters for the St. Louis Browns in 1908 to set a franchise record that has stood for more than a century—but do you know which pitcher struck out a record 918 career batters for the Browns?

a) Rube Waddell

b) Bobo Newsom

c) Steve Barber

d) Jack Powell

BOTTOM OF THE SECOND ANSWER KEY

31. C

32. A

33. A

34. B

35. A

36. D

37. C

38. A

39. C

40. C

"It's not luck. You don't get lucky over 162 games.
Our bullpen was really, really good."
— *Buck Showalter, on the Orioles' success in 2012*

3 THE DESTINATION

The 2012 Orioles battled the free-spending Yankees down the stretch for the Division title and then again down to the final out of the Division Series only to come up short, twice. "Next year" is the mentality that 29 of baseball's 30 teams—out of necessity, for there can only be one winner—cling to each winter, but it's not necessarily true that everyone starts on equal footing come spring. The wins column is reset, sure, but not the spending—and when the O's took the field in 2013 they were approximately $127 million in the hole to the Yankees.

In fairness it could be worse—there were multiple players on the Yankees' payroll whose individual salaries were more than the combined salaries of the entire 25-man roster of the Houston Astros.

But forget about big market teams vs. small market teams, forget about deep pockets trolling the free agent waters, forget about the unbalanced schedule that's absolutely brutal to AL East teams contending for the Wild Card and rather like a walk in the park to contending teams from other divisions (would you rather play the Rays, Yankees, Red Sox and Blue Jays 19 times each or would you rather play the Astros, Mariners, Angels and Athletics—just saying) … forget all that, and focus on just one thing: the destination.

It's all about October.

It's the same goal for every club, every spring—October baseball. And that's what makes the accomplishments for the 2012 Orioles so spectacular. The club improved a Major League best 27 games from 2011 to 2012 and ended a 14-year postseason drought. It did so with pieces put in place by former GM Andy MacPhail—guys like Adam Jones, Chris Tillman, Matt Wieters and Chris Davis. Dan Duquette, who replaced MacPhail after 2011, complemented those pieces with some shrewd moves of his own: acquiring Miguel Gonzalez and Nate McLouth, and calling up 20-year-old Manny Machado.

The 2012 O's won the inaugural AL Wild Card Game, barely came up short against the Yankees in the Division Series, and yet, despite that success, when the Orioles front office was relatively quiet during the ensuing offseason, one rival AL executive offered this rather snide if not exactly disparaging assessment, saying, "They [Baltimore] obviously plan to win sixteen straight extra-inning games again."

Buck Showalter said it best: "It's not luck. You don't get lucky over 162 games."

It doesn't matter how deep your pockets are. It doesn't matter how many big names are on your roster. You still have to play out the schedule and the only thing that matters is the destination—how you get there is irrelevant.

It is true, of course—the success of the 2012 O's was nothing short of remarkable.

And while the season ended in disappointment, there's something to be said for the experience gained by J.J. Hardy, Manny Machado, Chris Davis, Adam Jones, Matt Wieters, Nick Markakis, Jim Johnson, Chris Tillman and the rest of the O's roster, because as a team these guys got a taste for October.

Nothing breeds success quite like … success.

There are no guarantees of course—despite high expectations as the season began and plenty of remarkable achievements that fueled the O's postseason push in 2013, the club fell short in the season's final days. As the O's look beyond 2013, however, there are plenty of reasons to believe this core group of players will lead the club to October again—but for now, let's open the third by looking back on

2013 and reliving some of the great accomplishments by this current group of O's stars.

TOP OF THE THIRD

Question 41: J.J. Hardy hit his 20th home run of the 2013 season in an August matchup vs. San Francisco. That blast gave Hardy three consecutive seasons with at least 20 home runs while playing shortstop for the Orioles. Only two other shortstops in franchise history have achieved this feat: Miguel Tejada and Cal Ripken, Jr. Tejada did it three years in a row from 2004-06. Ripken holds the record though with an unbelievable number. How many consecutive seasons did Cal Ripken, Jr. hit 20-plus home runs while playing shortstop for the Orioles?
  a) 8
  b) 9
  c) 10
  d) 11

Question 42: A follow-up question ... since Cal Ripken, Jr. debuted in 1982 the Orioles have had more home runs from the shortstop position than any team in baseball. From April 1982 through August 2013, Orioles shortstops have launched more than 625 home runs. That is nearly 175 more home runs than have been hit by the team with the second most powerful shortstops in that same timeframe. Ironically, J.J. Hardy hit more than 70 homers in the Orioles total—and he also hit more than 70 homers in the total for the team that is second to the Orioles in this category. For which of the following teams did J.J. Hardy hit 75 home runs before joining the Orioles?
  a) Minnesota Twins
  b) Milwaukee Brewers
  c) Chicago Cubs
  d) Pittsburgh Pirates

Question 43: On July 31, 2013 Astros rookie pitcher Brett Oberholtzer pitched seven shutout innings vs. Baltimore in his first big league start. Oberholtzer gave up just three hits while striking out six as the Astros pummeled the Orioles 11-0. A week later, Oberholtzer pitched seven shutout innings vs. Boston in a 2-0 victory to become just the fourth rookie since baseball's expansion era began in 1960 to pitch at least seven shutout innings in each of his first two Major League starts. John Hiller did it for the Tigers in 1967 and Marty Bystrom did it for the Phillies in 1980, but the first player to perform this spectacular feat during baseball's expansion era did so while pitching for the Orioles. Who began his big league career with the Orioles in 1966 by pitching back-to-back complete game shutouts?

a) Jim Palmer
b) Tom Phoebus
c) Ed Barnowski
d) Wally Bunker

Question 44: When the Royals rallied from a 3-1 eighth-inning deficit to beat Baltimore on July 24, 2013 it was the fourth time that season the Orioles had blown a two-run lead in the eighth or ninth inning. That was the highest number in the American League, a fact which would be disappointing for any team, but especially so for Baltimore—that's because the Orioles were unbelievably good in such games as the club earned a postseason trip in 2012. What was Baltimore's record in 2012 when holding a two-run lead or better in the eighth inning or later?

a) 72-0
b) 72-1
c) 72-2
d) 72-3

Question 45: Chris Davis got off to a torrid start in 2013. After hitting 33 home runs to set a career high in 2012, Davis began 2013 with home runs in four consecutive games and in six out of nine games overall. By the time the All-Star break rolled around he'd already eclipsed his 2012 total and tied an American League record set by Reggie Jackson in 1969 for most home runs at the break. How many bombs did Davis hit during the first half of 2013?

a) 34
b) 35
c) 36
d) 37

Question 46: Another follow-up ... obviously Chris Davis was invited to join the American League lineup for the 2013 Home Run Derby at Citi Field. The guy was leading the world in home runs, after all. Davis hit eight home runs in the first round of the derby, tying the Nationals Bryce Harper for the second highest total behind the incredible 17 blasted by A's slugger and eventual derby champion Yoenis Cespedes. Davis was unable to advance to the final round, however, finishing fourth overall behind Cespedes, Harper and the Rockies Michael Cuddyer. How many home runs did Chris Davis hit all total during the 2013 Home Run Derby?

a) 8
b) 10
c) 12
d) 14

Question 47: Jarred Cosart made a spectacular Major League debut for the Houston Astros in 2013, pitching eight shutout innings and giving up just two hits vs. Tampa Bay. It was only the second time in nearly two decades that a rookie debuted by pitching eight scoreless innings while giving up no more than two hits—and the other guy did so for the Orioles. Who gave up just one hit while pitching eight scoreless innings in a 3-0 victory for Baltimore vs. the LA Angels on August 5, 2008?

a) Matt Albers
b) Chris Waters
c) Adam Loewen
d) Kameron Mickolio

Question 48: Tommy Davis was a 23-year-old outfielder for the LA Dodgers when he had a career season in 1962. He led the league with

230 hits, 153 RBIs and a .346 average, winning two-thirds of the Triple Crown while belting 27 home runs, making the All-Star team, and placing third in league MVP balloting. He also set a record for being the youngest player in MLB history to reach 125 hits before the All-Star break. A young Orioles star would later break Davis' record. Who surpassed 125 hits before the All-Star break when he was only 21-years-old?

    a) Cal Ripken, Jr.
    b) Eddie Murray
    c) Manny Machado
    d) Nick Markakis

Question 49: Mariano Rivera will enter the Hall of Fame as the greatest closer in MLB history. However, in July 2013 this Orioles star became just the second player to ever turn a deficit into a lead with a home run against Rivera in the ninth inning or later at Yankee Stadium (old or new). In fact, it was the seventh time overall that this player had hit a go-ahead home run in the ninth inning or later since 2009—a total that at the time was the highest in the majors. Who hit more clutch late-inning home runs than anyone in baseball from 2009-13?

    a) Nick Markakis
    b) Adam Jones
    c) Matt Wieters
    d) J.J. Hardy

Question 50: A's pitcher Bartolo Colon won AL Pitcher of the Month honors in June 2013 after posting a 5-0 record and 1.75 earned run average. This member of the Orioles staff nearly beat out Colon, and in fact, he had a better record, winning six consecutive starts with a 2.68 earned run average to become just the third player since 2008 (Justin Verlander and Jered Weaver) to post six wins in a single month. Who won six consecutive starts for the Orioles in June 2013?

    a) Jason Hammel
    b) Miguel Gonzalez
    c) Wei-Yin Chen

d) Chris Tillman

TOP OF THE THIRD ANSWER KEY

41. C

42. B

43. B

44. A

45. D

46. C

47. B

48. C

49. B

50. D

BOTTOM OF THE THIRD

Question 51: LA Dodgers rookie sensation Yasiel Puig had ten multi-hit games in his first 15 big league starts in 2013. Puig was just the second MLB player since 1900 to achieve this feat. The other player who began his career at such a torrid clip did it for the Orioles. Who had ten multi-hit games for the Baltimore Orioles *in his first 11 big league starts*?
   a) Manny Machado
   b) Brian Roberts
   c) Curtis Goodwin
   d) Jerry Hairston, Jr.

Question 52: Justin Verlander began the 2013 campaign with the most impressive pitching resume active in the game: two career no-hitters, AL Rookie of the Year, Cy Young and MVP Awards, three-time strikeout champion, two pitching Triple Crowns, an ERA title, and he also led the Tigers to the World Series in 2006 and 2012. There's not a hitter in the game that looks forward to facing the guy. Well, except maybe this Orioles slugger. From 2005-12, Victor Martinez (with the Indians in 2007) was the only player to take Verlander out of the yard three times in a single season, let alone in a single month—yet that's exactly what happened in June 2013 when this member of the Orioles homered three times against Verlander in his two starts against Baltimore. Who was the first player to ever homer against Verlander three times in one month?
   a) Matt Wieters
   b) Nick Markakis
   c) Adam Jones
   d) J.J. Hardy

Question 53: Manny Machado continued to impress as he joined some elite company in 2013, hitting his 30th double of the season in a June contest vs. Boston. Machado was only 20-years-old at the time. In MLB history only two other twenty-year-old players hit 30 doubles in fewer than 90 games in a season: Alex Rodriguez (86 games in 1996) and Ted Williams (81 games in 1939). Machado beat both Rodriguez and Williams. How many games did it take Machado to reach 30 doubles in 2013?

 a) 68
 b) 71
 c) 74
 d) 77

Question 54: Les Lancaster picked up a win for the Chicago Cubs in 1988, pitching three scoreless innings in relief vs. San Francisco as the Cubs prevailed 2-1 in twelve innings. Not all that spectacular by itself, but a year later Lancaster beat the Giants again with two scoreless innings in relief as the Cubs won 4-3 in eleven innings— only this time Lancaster not only earned the W, he also had the game-winning walk-off hit. As both clubs used up their bench players, manager Don Zimmer elected to let Lancaster bat with two outs and a runner on first, and he responded by lining a double down the left field line that scored the winning run. The same player beating a team on the mound and at the plate in extra-innings is a rare event, and you'd think it would be impossible in the AL because of the DH. Well, it's not impossible if it's a regular position player who earns the win as an emergency relief pitcher … and that's exactly what happened as this Orioles slugger came on to pitch in extra-innings and earned a win vs. Boston in 2012, and then in 2013 he had a walk-off hit in the thirteenth inning of a 5-4 victory vs. Boston to become the first player since Lancaster to beat a team on the mound and at the plate. Who did this for the Orioles?

 a) Adam Jones
 b) Nick Markakis
 c) Chris Davis
 d) J.J. Hardy

Question 55: Hall of Fame legend Mel Ott hit 20 home runs and 20 doubles in the Giants first 60 games in 1929. It was the fastest in history that anyone had reached both totals in a single season, and no one else was able to replicate this feat until Ivan Rodriguez did it with a pair of doubles in the Rangers 60th game in 2000. A new standard was set in 2013, however, as the Orioles Chris Davis became the first player in history to reach 20 homers and 20 doubles in fewer than 60 games. How many games did it take Chris Davis to reach the 20/20 plateau?

    a) 56
    b) 57
    c) 58
    d) 59

Question 56: A follow-up question … Chris Davis is the second fastest in Orioles history to reach 20 home runs in a season. Who set the franchise standard by hitting his 20th home run in the Orioles 49th game of the season?

    a) Frank Robinson
    b) Boog Powell
    c) Eddie Murray
    d) Brady Anderson

Question 57: And one more Chris Davis follow-up … Ken Williams took just 47 games to drive home 50 runs for the 1925 St. Louis Browns. That's the fastest any player has reached 50 RBIs in franchise history—including Baltimore and St. Louis. In 2013, Chris Davis hit two home runs and had three RBIs in a 9-6 win vs. Washington to give him 50 RBIs in Baltimore's first 53 games—becoming the second fastest to reach 50 RBIs since the club moved to Baltimore. The fastest that any player has driven home 50 runs for the Orioles is 49 games. Who achieved this remarkable feat?

    a) Frank Robinson
    b) Boog Powell
    c) Eddie Murray
    d) Brady Anderson

Question 58: When a player hits a game-tying home run in a late-inning pressure situation it's considered clutch—the same is obviously true when a player hits a walk-off home run to win a game. But what do you call it when the same player hits both a game-tying home run and a game-winning home run *in extra-innings of the same game?* It's one of baseball's most rare and spectacular feats. Who hit a game-tying home run in the tenth inning and then—with the Orioles again down a run—hit a two-run game-ending blast in the twelfth inning for a 8-7 walk-off win vs. the Angels in 1987?

a) Eddie Murray
b) Ray Knight
c) Larry Sheets
d) Mike Young

Question 59: It's a great night when a player goes 4 for 4. It's even better when one of those hits leaves the yard. But going 4 for 4 (or better) with a home run *multiple times* in the same season is pretty rare. In fact, since the franchise moved to Baltimore, only three players have done it. Don Baylor was the first in 1973. Chris Davis was the most recent in 2013. Who is the only other player to achieve this feat for the Orioles?

a) Brady Anderson
b) Eddie Murray
c) Cal Ripken, Jr.
d) Rafael Palmeiro

Question 60: When Freddy Garcia made his pitching debut for the Orioles in 2013 he did so in fine form: he didn't give up a hit until the seventh inning. It was the second consecutive year that a pitcher debuted for the Orioles by carrying a no-hitter into the seventh inning—a feat that had never happened in the previous 58 seasons of baseball in Baltimore. Who carried a no-no deep into his Orioles debut in 2012?

a) Jason Hammel
b) Miguel Gonzalez
c) Wei-Yin Chen
d) Randy Wolf

BOTTOM OF THE THIRD ANSWER KEY

51. C

52. D

53. A

54. C

55. C

56. D

57. A

58. D

59. B

60. A

"We ain't got no choice. You don't hit, you go home. It's no ifs, buts or maybes. Both teams know that."
— *Adam Jones, on playing the Texas Rangers in the 2012 Wild Card Game*

4 THE WILD CARD

Until baseball began divisional play in 1969 the AL Pennant was awarded to the team with the best overall record during the regular season. Interleague play, divisions and wild cards were nowhere to be found in the baseball lexicon of that time. It was real simple—play out the schedule and win more games than any other team. If you do, then you earn a trip to the World Series. If you don't, then it's wait until next year. In 1969, however, baseball expanded for the second time in a decade, bringing four additional teams into play: the Montreal Expos and San Diego Padres in the National League, and the Kansas City Royals and Seattle Pilots in the American League. Baseball had just 16 teams in 1960—but in 1969 the total stood at 24. And clearly it was time for a change with regard to the postseason.

Not everyone readily embraces change at the big league level— that's been true since the days of Kenesaw Mountain Landis, baseball's first commissioner—but today everyone agrees that divisional play and additional rounds to the postseason not only increased the amount of late-season drama across baseball, it also led to some of the most memorable moments of the 20th century. Just picture: Bucky Dent sticking it to the Red Sox in 1978, Dave Henderson saving the Red Sox in 1986, Chris Chambliss walking off with a Pennant-winning blast for the Yankees in 1976, Ozzie Smith saving the Cardinals in the 1985 NLCS with his first career lefty home run, or Sid Bream chugging around third and scoring the Pennant-winning run for the Braves in the 1992 NLCS.

Or, painfully for the O's, there's Jeffrey Maier and Derek Jeter in 1996.

You get the picture.

If the regular season had never increased from 154 to 162 games, if the league's had never expanded to include more teams, and if baseball had never introduced divisional play and expanded playoffs, then we'd have missed out on these and countless other great moments from the past half-century.

There's always an adjustment period when changes are made— but divisional play and an expanded postseason came pretty easy to the O's. Baltimore won the AL East and the American League Championship Series for three consecutive seasons from 1969-71. Not a bad way to begin a new era in baseball history. The ALCS at that time was a best-of-five, and it would remain that way until 1985 when television money led to the best-of-seven format. TV money had a hand in the Wild Card as well—but it's greater appeal was to fans who were more likely to stay engaged with their team if its late August and September games had meaning. And that's exactly what the Wild Card did—it gave a great deal of meaning to late season games for teams that under the previous postseason format would have been out of contention weeks earlier.

If there was any stigma at all attached to being a "second place" team going into the postseason then it quickly faded when the Florida Marlins won the 1997 World Series after finishing nine games behind the Atlanta Braves during the regular season. A fact that's annoying to Braves fans, but true: during Atlanta's incredible run of 14 consecutive Division titles the Wild Card Florida Marlins won twice as many World Series titles (1997, 2003) than the Braves (1995).

As for Baltimore, the Orioles began the Wild Card era with some strong play, though without the same results as the O's clubs that won three consecutive Pennants from 1969-71 in the early years of the divisional play era. The Wild Card was supposed to come into play for the first time during the 1994 postseason—but of course the players' strike ended the season prematurely and cancelled the playoffs. The O's were 63-49 when play stopped, good for second in the AL East behind the Yankees and fourth best in the league behind the Yankees, White Sox and Indians. Baltimore was 2.5 games behind Cleveland for what would have been the inaugural Wild Card, but the club was just getting hot when the season came to a screeching halt in early August. The Orioles had just swept the Yankees to complete a 7-3 road trip and were returning home to a favorable August schedule.

Baltimore's first full season run at the Wild Card was in 1995.

The Birds never won more than five in a row all season, suffered a huge setback by losing seven straight in early June, yet still managed to go 17-10 in July to climb into a tie with the Yankees for second place in the AL East and within striking distance of the Wild Card. Unfortunately, the Orioles won just 11 games in August and the Yankees surged ahead and claimed the first Wild Card in AL history.

You never start a season aspiring to win the Wild Card. Any manager who did so would be out of a job very quickly, and any players who voiced such aspirations would find it difficult to explain such a position to the fans—but there's something to be said for having realistic expectations, and by the time 1996 got underway the general consensus was that New York, Boston and Baltimore would battle all season long for the Division crown ... and for the Wild Card. Hey, it's not a bad fallback position, just ask the Marlins. You set a goal to win the Division, but you take whatever path is available to play in October. Of course Florida was a year away from its first title and baseball fans in general were still sorting out their feelings about a non-Division winner earning a postseason berth—but a year earlier Don Mattingly played in his only career postseason thanks to the Wild Card, and getting there without winning the AL East didn't diminish his experience. As for the O's, in 1996 the club fielded its strongest team in years and expectations were high. Like they had a year earlier, the club had a huge summer setback—this time in July— when they lost five straight and six out of seven overall to the Red

Sox and Yankees … at home. Baltimore began that home stand just five games out of first and with visions of making a run at the top of the standings, but when it was over the team and its fans were left wondering how things had gone wrong so fast. The O's fell ten games behind the Yankees.

Things began to turn around in August.

Baltimore gained a lot of ground in three short weeks and by the time the calendar turned to September the O's were only four games behind the Yankees for the Division lead and just a single game behind the White Sox for the Wild Card. For the first time in club history, thanks to the Wild Card, the O's were involved in two races down the stretch—and the White Sox were coming to town in mid-September. In the series opener Rafael Palmeiro hit a two-run bomb and David Wells pitched seven-plus strong innings as the O's won 5-1 to move into a tie for the Wild Card. In the second game of the series, it was Palmeiro who scored the winning run in the tenth inning as Eddie Murray hit a walk-off sacrifice fly to move Baltimore into first position in the chase for the Wild Card.

Was the team satisfied to finish second behind the Yankees?

Absolutely not … but was the team happy to still be playing come October?

You bet.

Baltimore not only won its first Wild Card berth that year, but the O's also became the first Wild Card team to advance to a League Championship Series after they eliminated Cleveland in the Division Series—this after the Indians had posted the best record in baseball during the regular season. If nothing else, the 1996 Orioles settled the debate as to whether or not a Wild Card team belonged in the postseason. Clearly this team belonged in October. This was validated a year later when the O's improved by ten games in the standings to win the AL East outright.

As exciting as the O's were as a team from 1994-97, every season ended in disappointment.

Lost the season to the strike.

Lost the Wild Card to the Yankees.

Lost the ALCS to the Yankees.

Lost the ALCS to the Indians.

It was all disappointing, but it also pointed to a team on the cusp of greatness … or so everyone thought. No one could have predicted the lean years to come—especially with the Wild Card in play. Surely a team that could compete for the AL East title would have a leg up on winning the Wild Card, right? Well, that's actually been true for the better part of a decade—the only problem is that the O's weren't contending. In both 1998 and 1999 the club was in contention for the Wild Card through the trade deadline at the end of July, but was unable to make any kind of move in the standings. After that, well … nothing, not for a long time, not until 2012 when the second Wild Card might have provided an additional path to the postseason, but the Orioles still had to do battle in a division with the two highest payrolls in baseball and the greatest overachieving team in baseball history.

The 2012 Orioles team achieved something remarkable when they emerged from baseball's best division to claim one of two Wild Card berths as MLB expanded the postseason format yet again. And the reward for surviving 162 games with the third best record in the league? A do-or-die road game that if you win earns you a trip to New York to face a Yankees team with the best record in the league.

And yet … it gives you a shot.

It's still October baseball, and you just never know what's going to happen. Just ask the Marlins—1997 or 2003 editions. Baltimore did win the inaugural Wild Card Game, of course, clearing perhaps the two biggest hurdles in the way of postseason success—but then suffered at the hands of New York, again.

Hey, that's baseball.

You get back up and play again. And just like 1994-97, the O's took the field again in 2013 believing they belonged in the postseason—and the club battled hard all year, but painfully the O's lost six straight (including a four-game sweep by the Rays) in late September and fell from one game back of the second Wild Card to being eliminated in the span of just seven days.

As for Wild Card trivia … here in the fourth we look at the O's 2012 postseason success against the Rangers, but first we start with some great individual performances during the club's year long quest to return to the postseason in 2013.

TOP OF THE FOURTH

Question 61: In an April 2013 matchup vs. Oakland, Nick Markakis and Adam Jones hit back-to-back home runs in the fourth inning as the Orioles rolled to a 7-3 victory. It was the 16th time that Markakis and Jones hit home runs in the same game. At that time no other current MLB teammates had homered in the same game as often as Markakis and Jones—but is it also the highest total for teammates in Orioles history? Which teammates homered in the same game more often than any other pair for the Baltimore Orioles?
   a) Cal Ripken, Jr. and Eddie Murray
   b) Frank Robinson and Paul Blair
   c) Nick Markakis and Adam Jones
   d) Rafael Palmeiro and Brady Anderson

Question 62: Matt Wieters hit a tenth-inning walk-off grand slam vs. the Rays on April 18, 2013 giving the Orioles a 10-6 victory. With that win the Orioles tied a record for the longest winning streak in extra-inning games in Major League history. How many consecutive extra-inning games did the Orioles win from 2012-13?
   a) 13
   b) 15
   c) 17
   d) 19

Question 63: A follow-up question ... Matt Wieters' grand slam vs. Tampa Bay was the third walk-off slam in Camden Yards history. The ballpark opened in 1992, but the first walk-off slam wasn't until 1996. Who hit the first-ever walk-off grand slam in Camden Yards?
   a) Chris Hoiles
   b) Rafael Palmeiro

c) Roberto Alomar
d) Bobby Bonilla

Question 64: Josh Beckett has won his share of big games over the years, but as the Red Sox imploded and missed the playoffs in 2011 it was the Orioles who beat Beckett twice in the season's final month to contribute to Boston's misery. The Orioles went on to beat Beckett five consecutive games from 2011-13. It was the first time since 1983-85 that the Orioles had a five-game winning streak against a pitcher who had won more than 100 career games. Ironically, the pitcher Baltimore beat five straight times from 1983-85 was the one guy that Orioles fans wished the team could have beaten in 1982 … that's because this same pitcher beat Jim Palmer in the 1982 season finale to win the AL East for the Brewers. Who kept the Orioles out of the 1982 playoffs with his clutch performance on the final day of the season?
a) Mike Caldwell
b) Pete Vuckovich
c) Don Sutton
d) Bob McClure

Question 65: Manny Machado's first home run of 2013 came in April at Fenway Park. It was a three-run blast in a game that saw the Orioles rally for five runs in the ninth inning to beat the Red Sox 8-5. Three months shy of his 21st birthday, Machado is the second youngest Orioles player to ever hit a home run at Fenway. Who was six months shy of his 21st birthday when he became the youngest Orioles player to ever hit a home run at Fenway?
a) Jim Palmer
b) Brooks Robinson
c) Cal Ripken, Jr.
d) Boog Powell

Question 66: When the Orioles lost back-to-back home games to the Twins by scores of 6-5 and 4-3 in April 2013, it was the first time since September 2011 that Baltimore had lost consecutive one-run games. In fact, the Orioles made the postseason in 2012 after posting the best won-loss record in one-run games in Major League history. What was the Orioles record in one-run games in 2012?

a) 27-11
b) 28-10
c) 29-9
d) 30-8

Question 67: In 1935, the Phillies Dolph Camilli had 12 RBIs during the first four games of the season, setting a record that stood nearly 80 years. With home runs in the Orioles first four games to open 2013, Chris Davis became the first player since the Yankees Bill Dickey in 1937 to have a home run *and* at least three RBIs in four consecutive games—and he also eclipsed Camilli's RBIs total from 1935. How many RBIs did Davis pick up through the first four games of 2013?

a) 13
b) 14
c) 15
d) 16

Question 68: A follow-up question … Dolph Camilli's RBIs total had previously been equaled on two occasions. Mark McGwire had 12 RBIs in four games to start 1998 for the Cardinals, and then two years later it was a member of the Orioles who drove in 12 runs in four games to start the 2000 season. Who tied Dolph Camilli's record when he got off to such a hot start for the Orioles that year?

a) Charles Johnson
b) Will Clark
c) Albert Belle
d) B.J. Surhoff

Question 69: When the Orioles faced the Rangers in the first-ever do-or-die Wild Card Game in 2012, it was a David vs. Goliath pitching matchup when the high-priced Yu Darvish took the mound for Texas to face a late-season, hardly-noticed Baltimore trade acquisition who got the surprise nod from manager Buck Showalter. After earning the win, however, the Orioles pitcher had this to say:

"We love being the underdog. When you're the favorite the pressure is on you. When you're the underdog, there's no pressure. So for us it's like Buck [Showalter] says, we were able to come in here and play with house money." Who was the winning pitcher for Baltimore?

a) Randy Wolf
b) Joe Saunders
c) Dana Eveland
d) Steve Johnson

Question 70: Baltimore won the inaugural Wild Card Game vs. Texas by a score of 5-1. Who hit a sixth-inning sacrifice fly to break a 1-1 tie and drive in the eventual game-winning run for Baltimore's first playoff win in 15 years?

a) Mark Reynolds
b) Chris Davis
c) Manny Machado
d) Adam Jones

TOP OF THE FOURTH ANSWER KEY

61. C

62. C

63. A

64. C

65. A

66. C

67. D

68. A

69. B

70. D

BOTTOM OF THE FOURTH

Question 71: After eliminating the Rangers from the 2012 postseason the Orioles were tasked with taking on the big spending New York Yankees in the Division Series. Game 1 was in Baltimore and for eight innings it was a pitcher's duel. Jason Hammel pitched well for the Orioles and CC Sabathia was dominant for the Yankees. The score was 2-2 going into the ninth, but then the floodgates opened. The Yankees scored five runs but the big spark was a home run leading off the inning against Orioles closer Jim Johnson. Who hit the game-winning shot for New York?

a) Alex Rodriguez
b) Russell Martin
c) Curtis Granderson
d) Ichiro Suzuki

Question 72: The Orioles bounced back in Game 2 of the series, holding on for a 3-2 victory thanks to some outstanding pitching and timely hitting. Wei-Yin Chen scattered eight hits over six-plus innings and gave up just two runs, including one that was unearned. Chris Davis had this to say about Chen after the game: "[He] did a good job of keeping us in the game. To hold that offense to two runs is saying something." As for the Orioles offense, it was a two-out third-inning rally that made the difference. Andy Pettitte retired the Orioles first eight batters, but back-to-back singles and a walk loaded the bases with two outs in the third—setting the stage for this slugger to get a clutch hit. Who hit a bases loaded single with two outs in the third to give the Orioles a 2-1 lead?

a) Matt Wieters
b) Adam Jones
c) Nick Markakis
d) Chris Davis

Question 73: Baltimore carried a 2-1 lead into the bottom of the ninth at Yankee Stadium during Game 3 of the series—that's when

Yankee skipper Joe Girardi made a gutsy move and used a pinch-hitter for struggling superstar Alex Rodriguez. The move paid off as the pinch-hitter belted a home run against Birds closer Jim Johnson to send the game to extra-innings—and then he belted another home run in the twelfth to give the Yankees a 3-2 victory. It was the first time in history that a player homered in the ninth to tie a postseason game and then homered in extra-innings to win it. Adam Jones was as surprised as anyone that Girardi pinch-hit for Rodriguez, saying, "It kind of caught me off-guard, hitting for a guy who's half-a-billionaire." Who came off the bench in such heroic fashion for the Yankees?

  a) Raul Ibanez
  b) Eric Chavez
  c) Andruw Jones
  d) Brett Gardner

Question 74: After the Yankees tagged Jim Johnson—the top closer in baseball during 2012—for late home runs in Games 1 and 3 of the series, the Orioles faced possible elimination in Game 4 in the Bronx. The score was tight—just like the first three games—with the clubs trading runs in the fifth and sixth, but when nine innings were in the book the score was still 1-1. It would stay that way until the thirteenth, when the Orioles broke through for a 2-1 victory. The Oriole who got the big hit said after the game, "We just kept telling ourselves, 'This is not the last night of the season.'" Who hit an RBI double to win Game 4 and even the series vs. New York?

  a) Jim Thome
  b) Adam Jones
  c) Nate McLouth
  d) J.J. Hardy

Question 75: The Orioles 2012 season finally ended with a disappointing 3-1 loss to the Yankees in Game 5 of the Division Series. CC Sabathia pitched a complete game four-hitter—and he survived some sixth-inning drama that could have affected the outcome of the game. With the Yankees leading 1-0, this Oriole batter sent a long drive that was home run distance and would have tied the game … except the umpire closest to the fence ruled it was foul. Buck Showalter asked for and got a video review, but crew chief Brian Gorman said, "There was no evidence to overturn the decision." According to the AP, however, at least one stadium usher who was standing with a perfect vantage point claimed the ball glanced off the pole and should have been a home run. Regardless, it was ruled a foul ball. Sabathia escaped his only real trouble in the eighth, and the O's went quietly in the ninth. Who nearly tied the game with a long drive that was ruled a foul ball?

a) Jim Thome
b) Adam Jones
c) Nate McLouth
d) J.J. Hardy

Question 76: The Orioles earned a 2012 Wild Card berth on the strength of 93 regular season wins—including a season high 13 at the expense of this AL East rival. Which team did the Orioles outscore 96-68 while pummeling to the tune of a 13-5 record during 2012?

a) New York Yankees
b) Boston Red Sox
c) Toronto Blue Jays
d) Tampa Bay Rays

Question 77: The Orioles were 43-29 overall against the AL East in 2012 and played .500 or better against every division opponent. Which team was Baltimore's toughest opponent (9-9 record, 92 runs scored, 90 runs allowed)?

a) New York Yankees
b) Boston Red Sox
c) Toronto Blue Jays
d) Tampa Bay Rays

Question 78: Only one team in the AL East managed to outscore the 2012 Orioles during 18 head-to-head matchups. Which team outscored Baltimore 61-56 during the 2012 regular season?

a) New York Yankees
b) Boston Red Sox

c) Toronto Blue Jays

d) Tampa Bay Rays

Question 79: The 2012 Orioles made the postseason despite being middle of the road in offense when compared to the rest of the league. The Birds were tenth in average, eleventh in on-base percentage, sixth in slugging and ninth in runs scored. Baltimore's offense could hit the long ball though, and that makes up for a lot. The Orioles ranked second in the league with 214 home runs and boasted five players to hit 20 or more on the season. One player in particular stood out, leading the club in runs, hits, doubles, steals and slugging, and earning Orioles Team MVP honors for the second consecutive season. He was also the first player in franchise history to hit four extra-inning home runs in one season. Who is this clutch offensive performer?

a) Matt Wieters

b) Adam Jones

c) Nick Markakis

d) Chris Davis

Question 80: The 2012 Orioles were third in the league with 93 wins, but only one pitcher reached double-digit victories on the season. Who led the O's with 12 wins in 2012?

a) Jason Hammel

b) Miguel Gonzalez

c) Chris Tillman

d) Wei-Yin Chen

BOTTOM OF THE FOURTH ANSWER KEY

71. B

72. D

73. A

74. D

75. C

76. B

77. A

78. D

79. B

80. D

"I'm beginning to see Brooks Robinson in my sleep. If I dropped a paper plate, he'd pick it up on one hop and throw me out at first."
— *Sparky Anderson, after Robinson's spectacular defense led Baltimore to victory vs. Cincinnati in the 1970 World Series*

5 THE TEAMS

Baltimore's history is replete with great defensive players. Brooks Robinson, anyone? Add Luis Aparicio, Bobby Grich, Mark Belanger and Paul Blair—just to name a few—alongside Robinson's name and you've got a pretty impressive list of slick fielders who plied their trade for the Orioles. Baltimore began the 2013 season with five Gold Glove winners—plus Manny Machado, who would earn his first Gold Glove in 2013—on its roster, but what these guys did, even for a franchise steeped in defensive excellence, was flat out ridiculous.

The 2003 Seattle Mariners set a Major League record by recording just 65 errors all season. Ten years later the O's got the full attention of the baseball world by recording just 34 errors through the team's first 112 games—a pace that would total just 49 errors on the season if it could be maintained. To put it in perspective, it'd be like breaking Roger Maris' record 61 home runs by hitting 70 (or 73) bombs on the season. It's just not a naturally occurring event—not possible. Oh wait. Well, never mind. The point is this: of course the Orioles defense could not maintain such a ridiculous pace ... the guys slipped up down the stretch and finished with a whopping 54 errors instead. The club actually set two fielding records—one for fewest errors and another for playing 119 errorless games. The 2013

Orioles were obviously disappointed with missing the playoffs after winning just 85 games, but the 2.3 million fans who saw this club play can legitimately say they've seen the best fielding club in Major League history. That's pretty impressive.

And what about the sluggers?

Chris Davis & Co. led the majors with 212 home runs in 2013. That's 24 more bombs than the Seattle Mariners, the club with the second highest total in baseball. Even crazier, the O's hit more home runs than the Giants and the Marlins ... *combined*. Baltimore had four guys with 20-plus home runs and eight who hit double digits—and as a team the club went yard every 26.5 at-bats, easily the best ratio in the majors. In case you're wondering, the 2013 Orioles came up well short of hitting a franchise record number of home runs. That honor goes to the 1996 Orioles who went yard an astounding 257 times and boasted *seven* players with 20-plus home runs.

Here's a look at some other notable Orioles teams.

The 1970 club won 108 regular season games and boasted three 20-game winners. It was one of baseball's all-time greatest teams, not just in franchise history, and it boasted three future Hall of Famers on its roster plus Hall of Fame manager Earl Weaver. Imagine having that pitching staff *and* leading the league in runs scored. Yeah, they did—and it was almost unfair. A lot of great teams make the postseason, but unless you win the World Series you can't really cement your place in history as one of the truly great teams. This club took care of the Reds and cemented its place in baseball history.

The 1983 club was one of the best in franchise history. Cal Ripken won the MVP and his only World Championship. Eddie Murray was on this team—and so was Jim Palmer, who incredibly played on all three of Baltimore's World Series winning teams: 1966, 1970 and 1983.

The other title winning team was the 1966 O's managed by Hank Bauer and led by Triple Crown and MVP winner Frank Robinson. The club won the Pennant by an impressive nine games over the Minnesota Twins. Keep in mind there were no divisions yet in 1966—the O's were up against nine other teams, all playing for one spot in the postseason. And they won by *nine games* over a very good second place club. And if you're not easily impressed, the 1966 O's faced a Dodgers team in the World Series that won 95 regular season games and had three future Hall of Fame pitchers in its starting rotation ... *and swept them.*

The 1969 Orioles won an incredible 109 games and finished 19 games in front of the Tigers in the AL East, but ... there's that "cementing your place" thing. Unfortunately the 1969 Orioles are best known for losing to the "Miracle Mets" in the World Series. This was an incredible ball club though. In the regular season the Orioles outscored their opponents 779-517. By comparison, the World Champion Mets won 100 regular season games but only managed to outscore their opponents 632-541.

Baltimore won another Pennant in 1979 and came within a game of another World Series title. Something about those teams with catchy monikers kept getting in the way ... first the "Miracle Mets" and then the "We Are Family" Pittsburgh Pirates. The club won 102 regular season games, demolished the AL East, romped through the ALCS and took the Pirates to seven games before falling in the World Series.

The 1980 Orioles are one of the very few teams in MLB history to win 100 regular season games and *not* make the postseason. Incredibly this club was 30-30 after 60 games, but 70-32 the rest of the way. Steve Stone won 25 games that year, becoming the first Baltimore Orioles pitcher to hit that mark in a season.

As for the trivia ... here in the fifth we look at Baltimore's World Series winners and contenders, Earl Weaver's career, and the truly great teams in franchise history.

TOP OF THE FIFTH

Question 81: It took 13 seasons after relocating to Baltimore before the Orioles finally won the AL Pennant in 1966. The Birds had placed third in the AL in both 1964 and 1965, despite winning 97 and 94 games respectively. The addition of Frank Robinson in the offseason obviously helped push the club over the top, but the manager who led the club to its first-ever World Championship had already been steering the O's in the right direction for quite some time. Who was manager of the 1966 World Champion Baltimore Orioles?

a) Jimmy Dykes
b) Paul Richards
c) Lum Harris
d) Hank Bauer

Question 82: The Los Angeles Dodgers won 95 games and the 1966 NL Pennant on the strength of a pitching rotation that featured three future Hall of Famers: Sandy Koufax, Don Drysdale and Don Sutton. In the 1966 World Series, however, it was the Orioles pitchers who dominated. The Dodgers used three different starters in the series, but used five different relievers out of the bullpen. One Dodger reliever gave up more runs by himself than did the entire Orioles pitching staff in the series. That's not a mistake—read it again if you have to. The Birds dominated on the mound, using three starters but needing to go to the bullpen just one time the entire series en route to sweeping the Dodgers in four games. After winning Game 1 of the series 5-2, how many runs did the Orioles pitching staff allow during Games 2, 3 and 4 combined?

a) 0
b) 1
c) 2
d) 3

Question 83: LA's offense was shutout by O's pitching a record 33 consecutive innings during the 1966 World Series. As a team the Dodgers set World Series records for futility in runs, average and total hits. Dave McNally made two starts for the Birds and pitched a complete game four-hit shutout to win Game 4 and clinch the series. Boog Powell was the leading hitter in the series with a .357 average. Paul Blair hit a home run for the only offense in Baltimore's 1-0 victory in Game 3. Frank Robinson and Brooks Robinson hit back-to-back home runs in the first inning of Game 1 to give the O's more offense than the Dodgers would get the entire series. So ... who was the 1966 World Series MVP?

a) Boog Powell
b) Brooks Robinson
c) Dave McNally
d) Frank Robinson

Question 84: The Chicago Cubs won an astounding 322 regular season games and three consecutive NL Pennants from 1906-08. That is the highest wins total by any MLB team in history during three consecutive seasons—and in fact, the Cubs had totals of 116, 107, 99, 104 and 104 during the five seasons from 1906-10. The AL record for most wins during a three-year stretch is 318 and is held by the Earl Weaver managed Baltimore Orioles. In what three consecutive seasons did the Orioles win 318 games and three AL Pennants?

a) 1968-70
b) 1969-71
c) 1970-72
d) 1971-73

Question 85: A follow-up question ... which NL teams did the Orioles face in the World Series during that three-year AL Pennant run?

a) New York Mets, Cincinnati Reds, Pittsburgh Pirates
b) New York Mets, LA Dodgers, Cincinnati Reds
c) Pittsburgh Pirates, LA Dodgers, Cincinnati Reds
d) Pittsburgh Pirates, New York Mets, LA Dodgers

Question 86: The Orioles made it to the postseason 11 times from 1966-2012. Earl Weaver earned more of those postseason trips than did any other manager in franchise history. How many times did Weaver guide the Orioles to a postseason berth?

a) 4
b) 5
c) 6
d) 7

Question 87: Earl Weaver won four AL Pennants managing the Orioles. How many World Series titles did he win?
a) 1
b) 2
c) 3
d) 4

Question 88: In the 1970 World Series the Orioles hit ten home runs in only five games—in fact, the Orioles had three players who each hit two home runs: Boog Powell, Brooks Robinson and Frank Robinson. Not to be outdone, pitcher Dave McNally hit a grand slam and earned a complete game victory in Game 3 of the series. So … who was the 1970 World Series MVP for the Baltimore Orioles?
a) Boog Powell
b) Brooks Robinson
c) Frank Robinson
d) Dave McNally

Question 89: Which NL team won two World Series titles vs. Earl Weaver and the Orioles?
a) Cincinnati Reds
b) New York Mets
c) Pittsburgh Pirates
d) LA Dodgers

Question 90: Which AL team defeated Earl Weaver and the Orioles in the American League Championship Series in back-to-back seasons?
a) Oakland Athletics
b) Kansas City Royals
c) California Angels
d) Minnesota Twins

TOP OF THE FIFTH ANSWER KEY

81. D

82. A

83. D

84. B

85. A

86. C

87. A

88. B

89. C

90. A

BOTTOM OF THE FIFTH

Question 91: In 1982, the Milwaukee Brewers beat Baltimore on the season's final day to win the AL East by a single game over the Orioles. In 1983, Baltimore was in a tight division race in late August with only 3.5 games separating the Brewers, Orioles, Tigers and Blue Jays, when a season-high eight-game winning streak propelled the Orioles into first place. The Orioles then faced a tough stretch of games: on the road in Kansas City, Toronto and Minnesota, then home for three vs. Boston, and then back on the road for back-to-back four-game series vs. New York and Boston. The Birds went on a rampage—winning 14 of 18 before facing the Milwaukee Brewers at home in mid-September with a chance to exact some revenge and close out the race. Baltimore did just that, sweeping all four games and eliminating the Brewers from the title chase. What was Baltimore's season record vs. Milwaukee just one year after the Brewers had caused the Orioles so much heartbreak?

a) 11-2
b) 10-3
c) 9-4
d) 8-5

Question 92: The Orioles were 56-30 during the second half of 1983 and finished first in the AL East with an overall 98-64 record. The best record in baseball however belonged to the winners of the AL West. Which formidable team did the Orioles defeat in the 1983 American League Championship Series?

a) Kansas City Royals
b) California Angels
c) Minnesota Twins
d) Chicago White Sox

Question 93: Cal Ripken, Jr. was only 22-years-old when he paced the O's offense and led the league in runs, hits and doubles in 1983. Another youngster on the Birds roster contributed to the team's success that year. This player was third in Rookie of the Year balloting—behind a player who suited it up for the O's opponent in the ALCS, no less—but he came out ahead in October, helping Baltimore win the Pennant and claiming MVP honors in the American League Championship Series. Who was this clutch player?

a) Storm Davis
b) Mike Boddicker
c) Mike Young
d) John Shelby

Question 94: Storm Davis was only 21-years-old when he got the nod to start Game 4 of the 1983 American League Championship Series. The Orioles led the best-of-five series two games to one but faced a tough task trying to clinch it on the road. Davis delivered a clutch performance, tossing six scoreless innings while giving up just five hits against an offense that led the league in runs scored during the regular season. Davis got some stellar relief help in the seventh and Baltimore finally prevailed 3-0 in ten innings. Who earned the victory and a trip to the World Series after pitching four scoreless innings in relief for the Orioles?

a) Tippy Martinez
b) Mike Boddicker
c) Sammy Stewart
d) Scott McGregor

Question 95: The Orioles won Game 4 of the 1983 American League Championship Series on a tenth inning home run off an unlikely bat. Whose home run sent the Orioles to the 1983 World Series?

a) Al Bumbry
b) Todd Cruz
c) Jim Dwyer
d) Tito Landrum

Question 96: Which team won the NL Pennant and was Baltimore's opponent in the 1983 World Series?

a) LA Dodgers
b) Philadelphia Phillies

c) St. Louis Cardinals
d) Pittsburgh Pirates

Question 97: In 1983, this Oriole was among the top ten league leaders in wins, earned run average, winning percentage, innings pitched, games started, complete games, shutouts and batters faced ... and his 18-7 record was the best on the Orioles staff and earned him the honor of starting Game 1 of the World Series. Who took the mound for Baltimore when the club hosted Game 1 of the 1983 World Series?
a) Scott McGregor
b) Mike Boddicker
c) Dennis Martinez
d) Mike Flanagan

Question 98: After losing a tight 2-1 ballgame to open the 1983 World Series, the Orioles stormed back to win four straight and claim the third World Championship in franchise history. Who hit two home runs in the Orioles 5-0 title-clinching victory in Game 5?
a) Cal Ripken, Jr.
b) Rick Dempsey
c) Dan Ford
d) Eddie Murray

Question 99: Baltimore's pitching staff held its opponents to a measly .195 batting average during the 1983 World Series. The Orioles offense didn't fare too much better, batting just .213, but the Birds hit six bombs and that was the big difference in a series where three games were decided by a single run. The miserable time had at the plate by the NL Champs was cemented by a complete game shutout in the decisive Game 5. Whose shutout clinched the 1983 World Series?
a) Jim Palmer
b) Mike Flanagan
c) Mike Boddicker
d) Scott McGregor

Question 100: Who earned MVP honors in the 1983 World Series?
a) Mike Flanagan
b) Scott McGregor
c) Rick Dempsey
d) Eddie Murray

BOTTOM OF THE FIFTH ANSWER KEY

91. A

92. D

93. B

94. A

95. D

96. B

97. A

98. D

99. D

100. C

"Pitchers did me a favor when they knocked me down. It made me more determined. I wouldn't let that pitcher get me out. They say you can't hit if you're on your back, but I didn't hit on my back. I got up."

— *Frank Robinson*

6 THE SLUGGERS

Chris Davis became just the second player in franchise history with a 50-homer season when he connected for an eighth-inning game-winning blast vs. Toronto's Steve Delabar on September 13, 2013. It was only the 43rd time in big league history that a player reached that plateau. The first to do it for Baltimore was Brady Anderson, but his total was only second best in the league behind the 52 Mark McGwire hit in 1996. Davis would finish 2013 with a franchise record and league leading 53 bombs.

For a franchise known for its sluggers and managerial strategies that relied on three-run homers, the Orioles have won precious few home run titles—only three in 60 seasons from 1954-2013: Frank Robinson (1966), Eddie Murray (1981) and Davis. Each home run title was unique in its own way. Robinson's earned him the Triple Crown. Murray won his home run title with just 22 home runs because a labor dispute shortened the season to barely 100 games. It was the lowest total to lead the league since Nick Etten won the title with 22 home runs for the 1944 New York Yankees during a season played with rosters depleted of talent by World War II—but Murray's total wasn't the only factor that made his title unique: he actually tied for the league lead in home runs with three other players. Tony Armas, Dwight Evans and Bobby Grich also hit 22 home runs in 1981—the only time in Major League history that four players have tied for the home run title.

And then Chris Davis in 2013 …

When the season began Davis had hit just 77 career home runs—and only ten players in history with fewer than 100 career home runs had ever hit 50 in one season. Coincidentally, one of those ten was Brady Anderson, who began his prolific 1996 campaign with just 72 career home runs. Davis' historic season also had a tie-in with Robinson's 1966 slugfest. Davis' final homer was on September 27 and it was his 28th of the season at home—breaking the record 27 at home hit by Robinson in 1966.

For much of the season Davis was on pace to hit 60 homers and in a July interview with ESPN he made headlines when he said that he still views Roger Maris as the single-season home run king. He went on to say, "He [Maris] was the last guy to do it clean. There's a lot of things that have been said about the guys who have come after him and have achieved the record, but I think as far as the fans are concerned they still view Maris as being the home run record holder—and I think you have to."

Davis came up short of Maris' record 61 home runs but he'll be in the Birds franchise record book forever—of course how long he'll hold the top spot remains to be seen. Frank Robinson held the record for 30 years, Brady Anderson for 17.

Jim Gentile, Rafael Palmeiro and Boog Powell all had great power seasons but like Brady Anderson they also had bad timing in terms of winning a home run title—Gentile's 46 was third in 1961 behind Roger Maris and Mickey Mantle; Palmeiro had seasons of 39, 39, 38 and 43 from 1995-98 but was never higher than fourth best in the league; Powell led the league with a .606 slugging percentage in 1964 but his 39 home runs was the league's second highest total behind Minnesota's Harmon Killebrew. Powell was the first O's player to lead the league in slugging. Frank Robinson (1966) and Reggie Jackson (1976) would later replicate that feat.

O's sluggers might own just three home run titles, but they've led the league in extra-base hits an impressive six times: Frank Robinson

(1966), Cal Ripken (1983, 1991), Brady Anderson (1996), Aubrey Huff (2008) and Chris Davis (2013).

Now back to the trivia ... some impressive slugging performances by Chris Davis, Adam Jones and Manny Machado, team MLB records, stellar pitching performances and more are all here as we head to the sixth.

TOP OF THE SIXTH

Question 101: Fritz Connally only played 58 games during parts of two Major League seasons, but he had a very memorable moment on May 17, 1985, when he hit a first-inning grand slam to score Cal Ripken, Jr., Eddie Murray and Fred Lynn. It took more than 25 years before another Orioles rookie would connect on a first-inning grand slam—but perhaps even more significant, he did it vs. Boston in the final week of the season as the O's were making their playoff push. Who did this for the Orioles in September 2012?

a) Ryan Flaherty
b) Manny Machado
c) Xavier Avery
d) L.J. Hoes

Question 102: The Orioles did something vs. Toronto in 2012 that the club had not done in more than four decades: Chris Davis, Mark Reynolds, Davis again, and Manny Machado all hit home runs with men on base during four consecutive innings. It was the first time any MLB team had done this feat in more than six years, but the last time the Orioles did it the guys who hit the bombs were Paul Blair, Ellie Hendricks, Blair again, and Boog Powell. So exactly how far back do you have to go to find those three bats in the Birds lineup?

a) 1960
b) 1963
c) 1967
d) 1970

Question 103: In baseball's modern era (since 1900), only four pitchers had ever won their first three Major League starts while recording six or more strikeouts in each of them: Larry Cheney (Cubs, 1911-12), Russ Ford (Yankees, 1910), Juan Marichal (Giants, 1960) and Randy Wolf (Phillies, 1999). In 2012, this Orioles pitcher joined this group by winning starts against Seattle and Toronto (twice). Who began his pitching career in such spectacular fashion for the 2012 Orioles?
a) Steve Johnson
b) Wei-Yin Chen
c) Chris Tillman
d) Zach Phillips

Question 104: The 2012 Orioles set a MLB record for longest road winning streak in extra-inning games during a single season. It began in April with a ten-inning victory vs. the Chicago White Sox. By the time the O's won a twelve-inning contest at Fenway Park in late September, what was the record number of road games the Birds had won consecutively in extra-innings?
a) 9
b) 10
c) 11
d) 12

Question 105: Chris Tillman was 8-2 during his first ten decisions in 2012. Tillman was the first O's pitcher under 25-years-old in more than 20 years to win at least eight of his first ten decisions in one season. Who was the last young pitcher to achieve this feat for the Orioles?
a) Ben McDonald
b) Mike Mussina
c) Alan Mills
d) Arthur Rhodes

Question 106: Adam Jones and Chris Davis both homered in a 7-2 win vs. Colorado in mid-August 2013. It was the 25th on the season for Jones and the 45th for Davis—and it was the ninth time on the season that they'd both homered in the same game, which at the time was the highest total for any teammates in MLB. The franchise season record for teammates going deep in the same game is ten. Incredibly, it's a feat that was achieved twice in one season by the same player—with both Bobby Bonilla and Rafael Palmeiro. Who homered in the same game as Bonilla ten times and also homered in the same game as Palmeiro ten times in the same season?

a) Brady Anderson
b) Cal Ripken, Jr.
c) Chris Hoiles
d) B.J. Surhoff

Question 107: Hall of Fame legend Hank Greenberg went off against the Yankees in 1938. The Tigers slugger had three two-homer games vs. New York that year—a feat that no MLB player achieved against the Yankees again until 2012, when in the midst of a torrid September race for the AL East title this Orioles slugger went deep eight times in seven games, including three two-homer games vs. New York. Who went on a home run binge vs. the Yankees as the clubs battled down the stretch in 2012?

a) Adam Jones
b) Nick Markakis
c) Mark Reynolds
d) Chris Davis

Question 108: Josh Hamilton (Rangers) and Mark Teixeira (Yankees) were among three AL players who had as many as five RBIs in three different games in 2012. The third member of this group did it for the Orioles. Who had three different games in 2012 with five or more RBIs?

a) Matt Wieters
b) Adam Jones
c) Nick Markakis
d) Chris Davis

Question 109: A follow-up question ... it was only the fifth time in Orioles history that a player had five or more RBIs in at least three

games during a season—and two of those were by the same player. Who is the only player in Orioles history with two seasons in which he had three games with five or more RBIs?
a) Eddie Murray
b) Miguel Tejada
c) Chris Richard
d) Jim Gentile

Question 110: Wade Miley was stellar during his rookie year pitching for the Arizona Diamondbacks in 2012. After 25 games (22 starts) he was 14-8 with a 2.80 earned run average. According to Elias Sports, Miley was the first rookie in three decades with 14 or more wins and an earned run average under 3.00 through his first 25 games. The last rookie pitcher to get off to such a hot start did so for the Baltimore Orioles. Who was 15-7 with a 2.58 earned run average through his first 25 games with the Orioles in 1983?
a) Storm Davis
b) Mike Boddicker
c) Don Welchel
d) Sammy Stewart

TOP OF THE SIXTH ANSWER KEY

101. A

102. D

103. A

104. C

105. B

106. A

107. C

108. A

109. D

110. B

BOTTOM OF THE SIXTH

Question 111: Manny Machado hit two home runs on August 10, 2012 vs. Kansas City—in just his second big league game. Machado was only 20 years and 35 days old at the time, making him the youngest player in MLB history with multiple home runs in his first or second big league game. Manny Ramirez had been the youngest, having done so for the Cleveland Indians at Yankee Stadium in September 1993 when he was just 21 years and 96 days old. Machado also became the youngest Birds player at any stage of his career to have a multi-homer game. Who had previously been the youngest player to hit two home runs in a game for the Orioles?
a) Cal Ripken, Jr.
b) Eddie Murray
c) Boog Powell
d) Brooks Robinson

Question 112: It took only 95 games for Orioles closer Jim Johnson to record his 30th save in 2012. Johnson, who would go on to save an MLB high 51 games, was the second fastest in franchise history to reach 30 saves in a season. Who was the fastest, reaching 30 saves in only 87 games for the Orioles?
a) Lee Smith
b) B.J. Ryan
c) Gregg Olson
d) Randy Myers

Question 113: A follow-up question … who was the first closer in franchise history to lead the AL in saves for an entire season?
a) Lee Smith
b) B.J. Ryan
c) Gregg Olson
d) Randy Myers

Question 114: From 1901-2010 there were only three players in MLB history who had four consecutive seasons with 43 or more doubles—one of which played for Baltimore. Who achieved this remarkable feat for the Orioles?

    a) Cal Ripken, Jr.
    b) Nick Markakis
    c) Rafael Palmeiro
    d) Frank Robinson

Question 115: Jim Palmer is far and away the franchise leader with 268 career wins ... but do you know who ranks second with 181 victories for the Orioles?

    a) Dave McNally
    b) Mike Mussina
    c) Mike Cuellar
    d) Mike Flanagan

Question 116: Baltimore has boasted some dominant pitching staffs and a host of 20-game winners, particularly in the 1970s and early 1980s. In 1921, Urban Shocker won a franchise record 27 games for the St. Louis Browns ... but do you know who won a Baltimore record 25 games in 1980?

    a) Scott McGregor
    b) Mike Flanagan
    c) Steve Stone
    d) Jim Palmer

Question 117: Jamie Walker set a franchise record when he pitched in 81 games for the Orioles in 2007. The career record for total appearances by a pitcher is 558. Who made more appearances for the O's than any other pitcher in franchise history?

    a) Mike Flanagan
    b) Dave McNally
    c) Tippy Martinez
    d) Jim Palmer

Question 118: With his 51 saves in 2012, Jim Johnson set a new franchise season record. Who held the previous record with 45 saves?
a) Gregg Olson
b) Jorge Julio
c) Randy Myers
d) B.J. Ryan

Question 119: Jim Johnson has already moved up to second in all-time saves with Baltimore and he's just the fourth Orioles pitcher to record 100 saves. Only one pitcher—through 2013—remains ahead of Johnson on the all-time saves list. Who is currently the Birds all-time saves leader with 160?
a) Tippy Martinez
b) Gregg Olson
c) Stu Miller
d) Jorge Julio

Question 120: The Orioles had four pitchers that each won 20-plus games in 1971: Mike Cuellar, Pat Dobson, Jim Palmer and Dave McNally. In today's game, along with 20 wins, another important benchmark for a pitcher is to be on the mound for 200-plus innings. As a staff the O's pitched more than 1,400 innings in 1971, and of those, its four 20-game winners logged an incredible 1,081 ... *an average of 270 innings each*. Talk about a rested bullpen ... the Birds starters tossed a mind-boggling 71 complete games. Since the franchise moved to Baltimore there has only been one pitcher who logged 300 innings in a season. He was part of that incredible 1971 rotation. And in fact, he logged 300 innings in four different seasons. Who was this O's workhorse?
a) Mike Cuellar
b) Pat Dobson
c) Jim Palmer
d) Dave McNally

BOTTOM OF THE SIXTH ANSWER KEY

111. C

112. A

113. A

114. B

115. A

116. C

117. D

118. C

119. B

120. C

"Cal Ripken, Jr. is a bridge, maybe the last bridge, back to the way the game was played. Hitting home runs and all that other good stuff is not enough. It's how you handle yourself in all the good times and bad times that matters. That's what Cal showed us. Being a star is not enough. He showed us how to be more."
— *Joe Torre*

7 THE SPECTACULAR FEATS

Ryan Minor was a second round pick in the 1996 NBA draft by the Philadelphia 76ers after starring at the University of Oklahoma. Minor, however, opted for baseball over the NBA. Like most professional athletes, Minor had been a multi-sport star in high school and was heavily recruited by Division I schools across the country for both basketball and baseball—and after his collegiate career both NBA and MLB scouts considered him a legitimate prospect. It's an enviable position Minor was in, but he chose baseball after the Orioles selected him in the 1996 amateur draft.

As for spectacular feats ... Minor's rise through the Orioles' farm system was pretty fast, and only two years and a few weeks after signing his first professional contract he was in Baltimore making his big league debut. His rise through the farm system isn't the spectacular feat he's known for, however—and in fact, it wasn't even his own spectacular feat that has made Minor the answer to one of baseball's great trivia questions. It was during his first big league start that Minor played a role in someone else's spectacular feat ... one of the greatest in all of sports history.

Need a hint?

Minor debuted on September 13, 1998 as a pinch-hitter vs. Anaheim, but his first big league start came five days later on September 18 vs. the New York Yankees.

Need another hint?

Minor played third base.

That's right ... it was Minor who took the field in place of Cal Ripken, who took a day off for the first time since his consecutive games played streak began on May 30, 1982. It's not a bad way to make your first big league start, taking the field for one of baseball's greatest legends. It was Baltimore's final home game of the season, and it was Ripken's decision to end the streak on his own terms. Ray Miller was the O's manager at the time. Ripken told Miller just before game time, "Today's the day." Miller later said he scratched Ripken's name off the lineup card, penciled in Minor's name, and then went to find the rookie to tell him the news. He pulled Minor aside and told him, "Cal's not going to be playing tonight. You're going to play third tonight so get ready."

And in one of the greatest lines ever, Minor said, "Does he know?"

There's been a lot written about how remarkable Ripken's streak was, but there are a couple of thoughts on it worth repeating for their significance: one, Ripken eclipsed Lou Gehrig's record in September 1995—a year after the players' strike ended the 1994 season and nearly destroyed baseball—and Ripken is rightfully given praise and credit for single-handedly giving fans across the country a reason to come back to baseball and fall in love with the game again; and two, David Cone, who was with the Yankees and witnessed the final game of Ripken's streak, said it best, "A lot of people who go to work every day can identify with Cal. The streak supersedes baseball."

As for Cal, he said, "I never set out to break a record. The significance in the streak isn't a number, but a sense of pride in knowing this is how I approach my job." When asked on the reactions from his teammates, Ripken smiled and said, "Ryan Minor had the biggest stare. I think a certain fear went through him."

You think?

There's a long list of spectacular feats in O's history, but Cal's streak is at the top. Obviously. Since it's also at or near the top of baseball's all-time list of spectacular feats as well.

Trivia about Cal's spectacular feat ... who played the most games with Ripken during the streak? Brady Anderson (1,330)—and in fact, on his "night off" against the Yankees Ripken came out before the sixth inning and made a few warm-up long tosses with Anderson and left fielder B.J. Surhoff. Prior to Minor, who was the last player to start in place of Ripken? Floyd Rayford, vs. Toronto on May 29, 1982. Probably the most staggering number ... aside from Ripken, how many players took the field for the Birds during his streak? It's an unbelievable number: 283. How many managers filled in Cal's name on the lineup card during the streak? Another crazy number: eight. Ripken's streak was at 2,216 when he made the move from shortstop to third base. Who replaced Ripken at shortstop on July 15, 1996? Manny Alexander. Who accidentally broke Ripken's nose during a photo shoot at the 1996 All-Star Game? It was White Sox pitcher Roberto Hernandez who slipped and slammed his forearm into Ripken's nose ... and then Ripken had it reset, went out and played seven innings in the All-Star Game and was back on the field for the O's two days later.

You get the point—entire books could be written about Cal's streak.

As for the trivia ... here in the seventh we turn to other spectacular feats in team history: no-hitters, impressive debuts, cycles, MLB records, hitting streaks, home run binges and more await you.

TOP OF THE SEVENTH

Question 121: There have been several no-hitters in franchise history, but Bobo Holloman threw one of the more notable no-hit gems in 1953. Most pitchers go an entire career and never notch a no-no, but Holloman tossed his no-hitter in his very first big league start. He probably would've traded his gem for some longevity, however, seeing as he made only ten starts that season and then never pitched in the majors again. There have been five no-hitters since the franchise moved to Baltimore (through 2013) and none since 1991. Who was the first pitcher to toss a no-hitter wearing an Orioles jersey?

    a) Hoyt Wilhelm
    b) Stu Miller
    c) Jim Palmer
    d) Tom Phoebus

Question 122: Another pretty spectacular feat is hitting for the cycle. The most recent player (through 2013) to achieve this for Baltimore was Felix Pie, who did it vs. the Angels in 2009. George Sisler hit for the cycle twice with the St. Louis Browns—he remains the only player in franchise history with two cycles. Who was the first player to hit for the cycle after the club moved to Baltimore?

    a) Frank Robinson
    b) Brooks Robinson
    c) Boog Powell
    d) Paul Blair

Question 123: And speaking of spectacular feats … who is the only Orioles slugger to blast three home runs in a single game on three different occasions?

    a) Boog Powell
    b) Albert Belle
    c) Frank Robinson
    d) Eddie Murray

Question 124: George Sisler hit safely in a franchise record 41 consecutive games in 1922. The longest hitting streak (through 2013) since the club moved to Baltimore is 30 games. Who hit safely in 30 straight games for the 1998 Orioles?

    a) Eric Davis
    b) Roberto Alomar
    c) Mike Bordick
    d) Brady Anderson

Question 125: The Birds have had a lot of success winning big awards ... but who is the only player in franchise history to twice claim league MVP honors?
a) Brooks Robinson
b) Frank Robinson
c) Boog Powell
d) Cal Ripken, Jr.

Question 126: Who is the only Rookie of the Year recipient in franchise history to later win league MVP honors?
a) Brooks Robinson
b) Eddie Murray
c) Cal Ripken, Jr.
d) Boog Powell

Question 127: The O's pitching staff that so thoroughly dominated the 1970s boasted six Cy Young Awards from 1969-80. How many of those were won by Jim Palmer?
a) 1
b) 2
c) 3
d) 4

Question 128: As much as he dominated on the mound, it's somewhat surprising that Jim Palmer never had 200 strikeouts in a season. His career high was 199. Palmer is, however, the Birds all-time leader with 2,212 career Ks. Who ranks second all-time with 1,535 Ks for the Orioles?
a) Mike Mussina
b) Dave McNally
c) Mike Flanagan
d) Mike Cuellar

Question 129: And speaking of Ks ... the franchise season record is 232 by Rube Waddell back in 1908. The record for the Baltimore era in franchise history is 221. Who had the highest season Ks total in Orioles history?

a) Mike Mussina
b) Erik Bedard
c) Dave McNally
d) Tom Phoebus

Question 130: And one more follow-up ... who is the only pitcher in Orioles history to record 200 or more strikeouts in three different seasons?
a) Mike Mussina
b) Erik Bedard
c) Dave McNally
d) Tom Phoebus

TOP OF THE SEVENTH ANSWER KEY

121. A

122. B

123. D

124. A

125. D

126. C

127. C

128. A

129. B

130. A

BOTTOM OF THE SEVENTH

Question 131: Only once in franchise history has a player hit safely six times in one game. Who set this club record?
a) Chris Hoiles
b) Frank Robinson
c) Jim Gentile
d) Cal Ripken, Jr.

Question 132: Another remarkable feat is hitting two grand slams in one game. It's been done three times in franchise history (through 2013). Which of the following is *not* one of the three players to hit two grand slams in a game for Baltimore?
a) Chris Hoiles
b) Frank Robinson
c) Jim Gentile
d) Cal Ripken, Jr.

Question 133: Cal Ripken, Jr. played in a Major League record 2,632 consecutive games from May 30, 1982 through September 20, 1998. He even played in a franchise record 163 regular season games in 1996. But ... is he the only player in franchise history to *twice* play 163 regular season games? Who did this for the O's?
a) Cal Ripken, Jr.
b) Paul Blair
c) Roberto Alomar
d) Brooks Robinson

Question 134: Jim Palmer is the franchise career leader with 211 complete games and 53 shutouts. Palmer led the league with 22 complete games in 1977 after finishing second the previous two seasons despite tossing 25 and 23 complete games. He led the league in shutouts twice—1970, and then again in 1975 when he set a career high and a franchise record. How many shutouts did Jim Palmer toss that year?

a) 8
b) 9
c) 10
d) 11

Question 135: Ken Williams set two franchise records with the St. Louis Browns in 1922: 39 home runs and 155 RBIs. No one has yet to surpass his RBIs total, though for a while it looked as if Chris Davis might do so in 2013. His home run record lasted the better part of four decades. Who was the first player to surpass Ken Williams in the record book when he smashed 46 home runs for the Orioles?
a) Jim Gentile
b) Frank Robinson
c) Boog Powell
d) Gus Triandos

Question 136: The Orioles season home run record fell for a second time in the 1960s when Frank Robinson hit 49 bombs in 1966. Robinson's record lasted three decades. That's when Brady Anderson came along and rewrote a number of entries in the franchise record book. Anderson's 1996 campaign was remarkable, not the least of which was the fact he only placed ninth in MVP balloting. Never mind he batted .297 with 50 home runs, 110 RBIs, 37 doubles and 21 steals—he also set franchise records with 92 extra-base hits and 369 total bases. And oh yeah, the Birds made the postseason, too. As for his team records ... in addition to his franchise best 50 bombs, Anderson set a new mark for home runs from the leadoff spot. How many times did he go deep from the top of the lineup?
a) 30
b) 32
c) 34
d) 36

Question 137: Brady Anderson also set a team record for home runs leading off a game. How many times did he go yard to start a game in 1996?

a) 6
b) 8
c) 10
d) 12

Question 138: And finally, Brady Anderson also set a club record for most consecutive games with a leadoff home run. How many games in a row did he start with a bomb?
a) 2
b) 3
c) 4
d) 5

Question 139: As you just read, Ken Williams holds the overall franchise record with 155 RBIs for the St. Louis Browns in 1922. The record for the Baltimore era in franchise history is 150 RBIs in a season. Who holds the season RBIs mark for the Baltimore Orioles?
a) Rafael Palmeiro
b) Jim Gentile
c) Miguel Tejada
d) Albert Belle

Question 140: And speaking of runs ... who scored a franchise record 132 runs in one season?
a) Cal Ripken, Jr.
b) Roberto Alomar
c) Brian Roberts
d) Rafael Palmeiro

BOTTOM OF THE SEVENTH ANSWER KEY

131. D

132. D

133. D

134. C

135. A

136. C

137. D

138. C

139. C

140. B

"I hope the last couple of years have restored the faith
of the fan base and given them something to cheer
about."
— *Chris Davis*

8 THE RECORDS AND AWARDS

Chris Davis finished 2013 with the following offensive stats: .286 average, 103 runs, 42 doubles, and he led the league with 53 home runs, 138 RBIs, 96 extra-base hits and 370 total bases—and his home runs, extra-base hits and total bases all set Orioles franchise records. For these ridiculous numbers he was voted the 2013 Louis M. Hatter Most Valuable Oriole Award. Davis received the award prior to the O's season finale against the Red Sox. Davis said, "I realize how fortunate I am, not only to be wearing this uniform but to be around the people I am. I wouldn't even have gotten close to where I was this year without Manny Machado, Adam Jones, Nate McLouth, Brian Roberts, Nick Markakis, Matt Wieters, J.J. Hardy. I could go on and on all day. It's a special group of guys." He then added: "I know it was tough to be a fan here for a long time. I hope the last couple of years have restored the faith of the fan base and given them something to cheer about."

After 14 consecutive losing seasons, Davis and his teammates won 178 games over 2012-13 and for sure gave the fan base plenty "to cheer about"—a Wild Card berth and a near-miss—and every reason to be optimistic in 2014 and beyond. Davis is the first to recognize that individual awards mean very little to players on losing teams—ultimately he'd give his team MVP, all the stats and all the records without a second thought if he could join this exclusive group of O's: Frank Robinson, Brooks Robinson and Rick Dempsey.

They are the only three members of Baltimore's World Series MVP Club. World Series MVP is a unique individual honor because with one exception—Bobby Richardson won 1960 World Series MVP honors for the Yankees, but the Pittsburgh Pirates won the Series that year—by virtue of winning the award you guarantee your teammates have won a ring.

For sure Davis would love to join that group—but he'd be just as happy if any of the teammates he thanked when receiving his team MVP award became the fourth member, because ultimately it's about the team winning.

As for the trivia ... here in the eighth we focus on award winners and record setting performances.

TOP OF THE EIGHTH

Question 141: From 1953-2013 the Baltimore Orioles made it to the postseason 11 times, won six Pennants and claimed three World Series titles. Two of those teams made the postseason as the AL Wild Card. Which year did the Orioles make the postseason as the Wild Card for the first time in team history?

    a) 1995
    b) 1996
    c) 1997
    d) 1998

Question 142: A first baseman by the name of Lu Blue set a franchise mark with 126 walks in 1929. The career record belongs to Cal Ripken, Jr., who walked 1,129 times. No surprise there. The Orioles season record on the other hand ... it might surprise you. Who holds the Baltimore era franchise record with 118 bases on balls during one season?

    a) Boog Powell

b) Bobby Grich
c) Ken Singleton
d) Mark Belanger

Question 143: Brady Anderson stole 53 bases for the O's in 1992. Can you imagine if he'd done that during his 1996 power binge? A 50/50 guy? That would have been MVP-worthy for sure. At least you'd think so. Anyway, Anderson just missed the team record for steals—57. Who set the standard for stolen bases for the Baltimore Orioles?
a) Delino DeShields
b) Luis Aparicio
c) Al Bumbry
d) Corey Patterson

Question 144: You always hear about how tough it is to come off the bench late in a game. Well, apparently this guy never got that memo. He had one season in which he was an incredible 24 for 72 (.333) as a pinch-hitter, setting a franchise record for pinch-hits and pinch-hit RBIs (18). His other splits were not nearly as impressive ... he only batted .172 as a starter that same year, and when he stayed in the game after coming on as a pinch-hitter he was only 1 for 15 in subsequent at bats. Who had such a banner year pinch-hitting for the Birds?
a) Russ Snyder
b) Earl Robinson
c) Dave Philley
d) Walt Dropo

Question 145: The O's have boasted some stellar arms over the years, obviously—but few have started their careers in such fine fashion as this rookie: he won a franchise record 19 games in his first big league season. Who did this for the Birds?
a) Bob Milacki
b) Hal Brown
c) Dave McNally
d) Wally Bunker

Question 146: The O's have posted some pretty impressive streaks on the mound. Reliever Gregg Olson pitched 41 consecutive scoreless innings over two seasons in 1989-90. The team record for consecutive scoreless innings in one season is 36. Who pitched scoreless baseball for an entire month for the Birds?
a) Bob Milacki
b) Hal Brown
c) Dave McNally
d) Wally Bunker

Question 147: One pitcher posted a 1.95 earned run average for an entire season, setting a record for the Baltimore era in franchise history. Who holds this record?
a) Bob Milacki
b) Hal Brown
c) Dave McNally
d) Wally Bunker

Question 148: And incredibly, one O's pitcher won a franchise record 17 consecutive decisions over the course of two seasons. He won his last two decisions of one season, and then won his first 15 decisions the following season. Who holds this record?
a) Bob Milacki
b) Hal Brown
c) Dave McNally
d) Wally Bunker

Question 149: The record career slugging percentage for the Baltimore Orioles is .543—if you go back to the St. Louis Browns days, then Goose Goslin (.548) and Ken Williams (.558) are at the top of the leader board. Who had the highest career slugging percentage for the Baltimore Orioles?
a) Rafael Palmeiro
b) Frank Robinson
c) Jim Gentile
d) Eddie Murray

Question 150: The highest season average (through 2013) in the Baltimore era in franchise history is .340—a feat achieved by two different players. However, one of those players did not have enough at bats to qualify for the league batting title, so it's the other player whose name is in the record books. Who batted .340 during a full season with the Baltimore Orioles?

a) Cal Ripken, Jr.
b) Roberto Alomar
c) Al Bumbry
d) Melvin Mora

TOP OF THE EIGHTH ANSWER KEY

141. B

142. C

143. B

144. C

145. D

146. B

147. C

148. C

149. B

150. D

BOTTOM OF THE EIGHTH

Question 151: Cal Ripken, Jr. and Eddie Murray won the first Silver Slugger Awards in franchise history in 1983. Ripken won a franchise record eight Silver Sluggers in his career. Who was the first player other than Ripken or Murray to win a Silver Slugger for the Birds?
a) Rafael Palmeiro
b) Roberto Alomar
c) Chris Hoiles
d) Mickey Tettleton

Question 152: Brooks Robinson was quite appropriately the first Gold Glove recipient in Orioles history. He won his first Gold Glove in 1960 and promptly put a stranglehold on it—no other AL third baseman would win the award until the 1970s. How many consecutive Gold Gloves did Brooks Robinson win for the Orioles?
a) 12
b) 14
c) 16
d) 18

Question 153: After the franchise moved to Baltimore to start the 1954 season it would still take some time before the club figured out how to win games with any consistency. Then in June a few seasons later the Orioles saw some signs that things were turning around—led by staff ace Connie Johnson the O's notched four consecutive shutouts. That's four days in a row in which the Birds staff completely blanked their opponents. Not bad. And with the improved pitching, the Orioles finished the regular season above .500 for the first time since moving east. What year did Baltimore have its first winning season?
a) 1956
b) 1957
c) 1958
d) 1959

Question 154: Jim Gentile and Brooks Robinson are two of the many great players in Orioles history. Gentile's rookie season coincided with Robinson's first All-Star appearance—and they teamed up to lead the O's to 85 wins, giving fans a glimpse of the exciting Pennant races in the club's near future. What year did Jim Gentile debut with the Birds?
   a) 1959
   b) 1960
   c) 1961
   d) 1962

Question 155: Talk about disappointing … Jim Gentile had a year in which he set 11 team records but placed third in league MVP balloting behind Roger Maris and Mickey Mantle. Worse, the O's won 95 games—surpassing the 90-win threshold for the first time in Baltimore history—and yet still finished 14 games behind the Yankees for the AL Pennant. What year was this?
   a) 1959
   b) 1960
   c) 1961
   d) 1962

Question 156: Brooks Robinson posted some incredible offensive numbers during his MVP campaign—including career highs in all of the following: .317 average, 194 hits, 28 home runs, 118 RBIs, .521 slugging percentage, and for good measure a league best ten sacrifice flies. What year was Brooks Robinson the AL MVP?
   a) 1962
   b) 1963
   c) 1964
   d) 1965

Question 157: Frank Robinson was the so-called missing piece of the puzzle that once acquired from the Cincinnati Reds enabled Baltimore to break through and claim its first Pennant. The Birds sent three players to the Reds to get Robinson—but which of the following was the centerpiece of the O's trade offer?

a) Ed Barnowski
b) Ken Rowe
c) Milt Pappas
d) Wally Bunker

Question 158: Mike Cuellar shared Cy Young honors in 1969 with Detroit's Denny McLain, but as the Birds got red hot that summer and gained separation from the rest of the league, it was a different member of the staff who reeled off 11 straight wins. Who helped Baltimore win 109 games by notching 11 straight victories in the summer of 1969?
a) Jim Palmer
b) Tom Phoebus
c) Dave McNally
d) Jim Hardin

Question 159: Baltimore famously had three 20-game winners on its way to winning a second consecutive Pennant in 1970. Who did *not* win 20 games for the O's that year?
a) Dave McNally
b) Mike Cuellar
c) Jim Palmer
d) Pat Dobson

Question 160: In 1971 the Birds unbelievably managed to do one better, boasting four pitchers who each won 20-plus games and winning a third consecutive Pennant. Who led the staff with 21 wins that year?
a) Dave McNally
b) Mike Cuellar
c) Jim Palmer
d) Pat Dobson

BOTTOM OF THE EIGHTH ANSWER KEY

151. D

152. C

153. B

154. B

155. C

156. C

157. C

158. A

159. D

160. A

"Correct thinkers think that 'baseball trivia' is an oxymoron: nothing about baseball is trivial."
— *George Will*

9 THE QUOTES

No other sport inspires quotes like baseball. Dozens of books are out there filled with nothing but quotes from the game's great players, managers and umpires, from the many talented sports writers, announcers and commentators who cover the game, from team owners and executives—and now in the age of social media, even quotes from fans who have the power to tweet their opinions directly to players crazy enough to willingly step into that spotlight.

One reason we are fascinated with baseball quotes is because they tell us the history of the game in the words of those who were there to make or witness firsthand the plays that inspire generations of fans. "The Giants win the Pennant!" anyone? Those five words immediately put an image in your mind, a black-and-white reel that replays history. "Let's play two!" is synonymous with daytime baseball, ivy laced walls and a Hall of Fame legend. "It ain't over till it's over!" evokes a laugh, because, well, it's Yogi. And who doesn't love a good Yogi quote?

Baseball has inspired more written words than any other sport, and many of the legends that inspired those words played their home games in Baltimore wearing an Orioles uniform. Cal Ripken has been written about more than any other contemporary ball player—there are more quotes about Ripken or attributed to Ripken in baseball lexicon than anyone who took the field during Cal's playing era. And that's a good thing, because we should give our sincerest praise and attention to players who have truly earned it.

We begin the ninth with trivia inspired by our love for baseball quotes—do you know which Orioles these words were spoken about?

TOP OF THE NINTH

Question 161: Who said in a Sports Illustrated interview that, "I think there should be bad blood between all clubs"?
a) Hank Bauer
b) Frank Robinson
c) Earl Weaver
d) Joe Altobelli

Question 162: Yogi Berra once said of this manager, "When he was on the field you were his enemy. Off the field he was one of the nicest guys you'd ever want to meet." Who was Yogi talking about?
a) Hank Bauer
b) Frank Robinson
c) Earl Weaver
d) Joe Altobelli

Question 163: Jim Palmer once said of this manager, "He was a players' manager. He didn't overcomplicate things. He was my first manager ... I was lucky ... you can't get in the Hall of Fame without your first chance." Who was Palmer talking about?
a) Hank Bauer
b) Lum Harris
c) Earl Weaver
d) Billy Hitchcock

Question 164: Jim Palmer once said of this manager, "The only thing he knows about big league pitching is that he couldn't hit it." Who was Palmer talking about?
  a) Hank Bauer
  b) Lum Harris
  c) Earl Weaver
  d) Billy Hitchcock

Question 165: Mike Flanagan said tongue-in-cheek that this pitcher "won [tons] of games but it took a picture of him standing in his underwear to get nationally known." Who was Flanagan talking about?
  a) Dave McNally
  b) Mike Cuellar
  c) Scott McGregor
  d) Jim Palmer

Question 166: AP sportswriter David Ginsburg said of this player, "[His] bronze bust in Cooperstown will chatter only slightly less than the man himself. The first line of text on the monument should read: He spoke rarely and carried a mighty bat." Who was Ginsburg talking about?
  a) Frank Robinson
  b) Brooks Robinson
  c) Eddie Murray
  d) Cal Ripken, Jr.

Question 167: Curt Schilling said of this player's legacy: "No one's ever had that aura like he had it. No one's ever done it the way he did it, in every way." Who was Schilling talking about?
  a) Frank Robinson
  b) Brooks Robinson
  c) Eddie Murray
  d) Cal Ripken, Jr.

Question 168: When asked about his work ethic, this player said: "If you're not practicing then somebody else is, somewhere, and he'll be ready to take your job." Who said that?

    a) Frank Robinson

    b) Brooks Robinson

    c) Eddie Murray

    d) Cal Ripken, Jr.

Question 169: This player once said of his determined attitude: "Pitchers did me a favor when they knocked me down. It made me more determined. I wouldn't let that pitcher get me out. They say you can't hit if you're on your back, but I didn't hit on my back. I got up." Who said that?

    a) Frank Robinson

    b) Brooks Robinson

    c) Eddie Murray

    d) Cal Ripken, Jr.

Question 170: Who famously said "on my tombstone just write 'the sorest loser that ever lived'"?

    a) Frank Robinson

    b) Hank Bauer

    c) Jim Palmer

    d) Earl Weaver

TOP OF THE NINTH ANSWER KEY

161. C

162. A

163. A

164. C

165. D

166. C

167. D

168. B

169. A

170. D

BOTTOM OF THE NINTH

Question 171: Earl Weaver managed the O's to the postseason five times in six seasons from 1969-74. The club won 109, 108, 101, 80, 97 and 91 games in those six successive seasons. In which season did Weaver win AL Manager of the Year for the first time?
a) 1970
b) 1971
c) 1972
d) 1973

Question 172: The Orioles returned to the postseason in 1979 for the first time in five years, thanks in large part to this pitcher who was 23-9 with 16 complete games on his way to winning the Cy Young Award. Who led the Birds to the 1979 Pennant on the strength of his arm?
a) Mike Flanagan
b) Scott McGregor
c) Jim Palmer
d) Steve Stone

Question 173: Baltimore took a three games to one lead in the 1979 World Series but were unable to put away the Pittsburgh Pirates. Baltimore lost Game 5 on the road by a score of 7-1. After a day off the O's had a chance to clinch at home, but couldn't solve lefty John Candelaria and lost 4-0. Rich Dauer homered to give the Birds an early 1-0 lead in Game 7, but things fell apart in the sixth inning. Who hit a two-run bomb—his third of the series—in the sixth inning of Game 7 to complete the Pirates comeback?
a) Dave Parker
b) Bill Madlock
c) Willie Stargell
d) Phil Garner

Question 174: What year did the O's win 100 games, boast two 20-game winners in Scott McGregor and Steve Stone, get a career year from Al Bumbry who had 205 hits and 44 steals, and still finished three games behind the Yankees for the AL East title?
a) 1976
b) 1978
c) 1980
d) 1982

Question 175: Cal Ripken, Jr. was a rookie when Earl Weaver announced it would be his last season managing the Birds. What year was that?
a) 1980
b) 1981
c) 1982
d) 1983

Question 176: What year did the Orioles begin with an abysmal 1-23 record only to be buoyed with the announcement that the Maryland Stadium Authority had agreed to a deal that would build a new home stadium for the club in time for the 1992 season?
a) 1987
b) 1988
c) 1989
d) 1990

Question 177: In Frank Robinson's first full year managing the Orioles the club improved by 32.5 games in the standings from the previous season and had a chance to make the postseason before losing back-to-back one-run games to Toronto in the final week of the season. For his efforts Robinson won Manager of the Year honors. What year was that?
a) 1987
b) 1988
c) 1989
d) 1990

Question 178: What year did Cal Ripken, Jr. became baseball's all-time "Iron Man" when he played in his 2,131st consecutive game?
a) 1994
b) 1995
c) 1996
d) 1997

Question 179: Who hit the infamous "Home Run That Wasn't" vs. Baltimore during the 1996 American League Championship Series?
a) Bernie Williams
b) Tino Martinez
c) Paul O'Neill
d) Derek Jeter

Question 180: After finishing second in the AL East to the Yankees in 1996 and then being eliminated by the Yankees in the 1996 ALCS, the O's began 1997 determined to make a statement both in the division and across baseball. Led offensively by Rafael Palmeiro and Roberto Alomar—and with five double-digit winners on the pitching staff—the Birds took control of the division early on and never let it go, winning the AL East in wire-to-wire fashion. Unfortunately, the O's were eliminated in the ALCS for the second year in a row. Who defeated the Orioles in the 1997 ALCS to claim the AL Pennant?
a) New York Yankees
b) Cleveland Indians
c) Seattle Mariners
d) Chicago White Sox

BOTTOM OF THE NINTH ANSWER KEY

171. D

172. A

173. C

174. C

175. C

176. B

177. C

178. B

179. D

180. B

"He [Earl Weaver] never gave up on me. He made
every single one of us a better player."
— *Rick Dempsey*

10 THE SKIPPERS

Much like Chris Davis would love to join Frank Robinson, Brooks Robinson and Rick Dempsey in Baltimore's World Series MVP Club, Buck Showalter would love nothing more than to join Hank Bauer, Earl Weaver and Joe Altobelli as managers who have won the World Series with the Birds. It remains to be seen what Showalter's legacy will be in Baltimore, but he took over a club that had lost 90-plus games in five consecutive seasons and in his second year won 93 games and a Wild Card berth. If that's the ceiling on Showalter's success then his tenure will be considered a disappointment, but if it's just the foundation … well, that's an entirely different story.

There are some distinctions in any franchise history that can never be wrestled away from someone simply because they were the first—way back in franchise history Hugh Duffy was manager of the Milwaukee Brewers in 1901. It's a long way from Baltimore, but he was the first skipper. Jimmy McAleer was the first skipper in St. Louis. Luke Sewell was the first manager to win a Pennant. In 1954, Jimmy Dykes became the first manager in Baltimore's franchise history. Hank Bauer was the first manager to win a World Series title. No one can replace these names in the history books—but when you discuss more subjective titles such as "best manager in franchise history" then you're wading into murky waters because it's a topic open to debate and subject to change.

Well, unless you're talking about the Orioles and Earl Weaver.

Right?

The Earl of Baltimore won 1,480 games, six Division titles, four Pennants and the 1970 World Series. He led the club for 17 seasons, easily the longest tenured manager in franchise history. Weaver was known for his wit, fiery managerial style and a complete lack of inhibition when it came to confronting umpires. He was a demanding, authoritative figure—but he got results and earned the respect and admiration of his players. You hear a lot of "love-hate" when guys describe their complicated relationships with Weaver, but you also learn a lot about the man and his influence on the game. Take Rick Dempsey for example. Dempsey had some notorious confrontations with Weaver, but looking back on his former manager's career he had this to say, "He never gave up on me. He made every single one of us a better player … we hated him a lot of the time, but at the end of the day you loved him because he was a winner."

And now the last of the trivia … here in the tenth we begin with a few managerial inspired questions, and then we close out the frame with a final look at Buck Showalter's 2013 Birds.

TOP OF THE TENTH

Question 181: What year did Ray Miller replace Davey Johnson as manager of the Baltimore Orioles?
a) 1997
b) 1998
c) 1999
d) 2000

Question 182: Mike Hargrove won two Pennants and five consecutive Division titles managing the Cleveland Indians—feats he

was never able to replicate while managing in Baltimore. In four seasons guiding the Orioles, how many times did Hargrove lead the club to a winning record?
   a) 0
   b) 1
   c) 2
   d) 3

Question 183: The Orioles and Mike Hargrove parted ways after four seasons. Who replaced Hargrove as Birds manager?
   a) Sam Perlozzo
   b) Lee Mazzilli
   c) Dave Trembley
   d) Juan Samuel

Question 184: Davey Johnson managed the O's to back-to-back appearances in the American League Championship Series in 1996-97. After Johnson, the Birds used seven different managers from 1998-2011 without earning a return trip to October baseball. In fact … in their 14-year hiatus, the O's finished last or second to last in their division an astounding 13 times. How many seasons did the Birds post a winning record from 1998-2011?
   a) 0
   b) 1
   c) 2
   d) 3

Question 185: The O's closed out 2011 dead last in the AL East with a dismal 69-93 record. How many games did the Birds improve in the standings to claim a Wild Card berth in 2012?
   a) 20
   b) 22
   c) 24
   d) 26

Question 186: Chris Davis became the most recent O's slugger to compete in the annual Home Run Derby when he entered the competition in 2013. Which two players represented the Orioles in the first-ever All-Star Home Run Derby?

a) Eddie Murray and Mickey Tettleton
b) Cal Ripken, Jr. and Mickey Tettleton
c) Eddie Murray and Cal Ripken, Jr.
d) Cal Ripken, Jr. and Fred Lynn

Question 187: Cal Ripken, Jr. was the first Orioles player to win the annual Home Run Derby. He hit an impressive 12 bombs at Toronto's SkyDome in 1991 to claim the trophy. Appropriately, Ripken also set a career high for home runs in 1991. How many did he hit on the season?

a) 33
b) 34
c) 35
d) 36

Question 188: Oriole Park at Camden Yards hosted the All-Star Game and the Home Run Derby ... but oddly enough, not a single member of the Birds was invited to participate in the derby. What year did Juan Gonzalez and Ken Griffey, Jr. tie as derby champions at Camden Yards?

a) 1992
b) 1993
c) 1994
d) 1995

Question 189: Cal Ripken, Jr. isn't the only Orioles player to win the Home Run Derby. The 2004 derby champion played for the Orioles as well. Who hit 27 home runs to win the 2004 Home Run Derby?

a) Rafael Palmeiro
b) Melvin Mora
c) Javy Lopez
d) Miguel Tejada

Question 190: From 1962-2013 a Baltimore Orioles player has won All-Star Game MVP six times. The players who have achieved this feat are: Brooks Robinson, Frank Robinson, Cal Ripken, Jr., Roberto Alomar and Miguel Tejada. One of these players won the award twice. Who is a two-time All-Star Game MVP for the Baltimore Orioles?

a) Brooks Robinson
b) Frank Robinson
c) Cal Ripken, Jr.
d) Miguel Tejada

TOP OF THE TENTH ANSWER KEY

181. B

182. A

183. B

184. A

185. C

186. C

187. B

188. B

189. D

190. C

BOTTOM OF THE TENTH

Question 191: Baltimore won its final game of the 2013 season 7-6 over the playoff bound and eventual World Champion Boston Red Sox. Jim Johnson earned the save to tie Atlanta Braves closer Craig Kimbrel for the Major League lead with 50 saves. Johnson became just the second pitcher in baseball history to lead both leagues in saves in two consecutive seasons (Rollie Fingers did it in 1977-78) and just the second in history to save 50-plus games in two consecutive seasons (Eric Gagne did it in 2002-03). With 57 team saves the O's bullpen led the AL—and Buck Showalter called on three pitchers besides Johnson who combined to earn seven saves. Who was the only pitcher on the 2013 Orioles to make more than 20 starts on the mound and also earn a save out of the bullpen?
a) Chris Tillman
b) Miguel Gonzalez
c) Jason Hammel
d) Wei-Yin Chen

Question 192: The Orioles made the 2012 postseason on the strength of a 29-9 record in games decided by just one run—but that .763 winning percentage in tight ballgames took a serious hit in 2013, and as a result the O's missed out on October baseball. In fact, Baltimore's drop in one-run games winning percentage from 2012 to 2013 was the third largest in history. What was the Orioles 2013 record in games decided by just one run?
a) 20-31 (.392)
b) 22-29 (.431)
c) 24-27 (.471)
d) 26-25 (.510)

Question 193: As the O's season was dismantled by a four-game September sweep in St. Petersburg by the Tampa Bay Rays, the club and its fans watched helplessly as young superstar Manny Machado suffered a season-ending and potentially career threatening injury.

Machado tore the patellofemoral ligament in his left leg running out an infield single in the seventh inning of the O's 5-4 loss to Tampa Bay on September 23. The scene was pretty traumatic and the initial impression was that it was a catastrophic injury. As Machado received treatment over the following days the news was somewhat better, and it was thought he could avoid surgery—but that wasn't the case and eventually he had surgery and began a long rehab, scheduled to last 4-6 months. Machado's absence the final week of the season gave someone else an opportunity to play—and his replacement did something that's happened just twice in 60 years of Orioles baseball: he had two home runs, three runs and four RBIs in a game while batting ninth in the lineup. Only Josh Bell, who did it in 2010 vs. Texas, had that kind of day while hitting ninth for the Orioles. Who filled in so admirably for Manny Machado?

a) Steve Pearce
b) Yamaico Navarro
c) Jonathan Schoop
d) Ryan Flaherty

Question 194: Chris Davis was the AL Player of the Month in April 2013 after starting the season with nine home runs and 28 RBIs in 27 games. Davis also won Player of the Week honors during 2013. He was the only O's player to be recognized with either award. How many total Player of the Week and Player of the Month awards did he earn in 2013?

a) 2
b) 3
c) 4
d) 5

Question 195: Manny Machado led the league with 51 doubles in 2013. Machado became the second youngest player in Major League history to hit 50-plus doubles in a season—he was 21 years and 70 days at the time of his 50th double. Only Alex Rodriguez at 21 years and 43 days was younger when he hit 50 doubles in a season for the first time in 1996. Machado's 51 doubles also tied him for the second

highest total in franchise history. Which of Machado's teammates holds the O's single-season record with 56 doubles?
a) Adam Jones
b) Chris Davis
c) Nick Markakis
d) Brian Roberts

Question 196: Chris Davis had such prolific numbers in 2013 that it would be easy to overlook many great accomplishments by his teammates. For example, the O's actually had two players who reached 100 RBIs in a season for the first time in 2013—Chris Davis and ... who?
a) Nick Markakis
b) J.J. Hardy
c) Matt Wieters
d) Adam Jones

Question 197: Jim Palmer set a franchise record back in 1975 when he pitched ten complete game shutouts on the season. Those days are long gone. The 2013 Orioles had only two complete games all year— *as a staff*—and for the second year in a row, the Birds pitched just one complete game shutout. Who pitched the Birds only complete game shutout of the season?
a) Scott Feldman
b) Chris Tillman
c) Miguel Gonzalez
d) Jason Hammel

Question 198: Among everyday players, who led the 2013 O's with a .286 batting average?
a) Manny Machado
b) Adam Jones
c) Nate McLouth
d) Chris Davis

Question 199: Think about the O's batting order ... now, who was the only everyday player in 2013 that did *not* receive a single intentional walk the entire season?
a) Adam Jones
b) Manny Machado
c) J.J. Hardy
d) Matt Wieters

Question 200: The O's 2012 pitching staff was third in the league in wins, sixth in earned run average and sixth in strikeouts—but in 2013 the club fell to eighth in wins, tenth in earned run average and thirteenth in strikeouts. It wasn't this pitcher's fault ... he led the club with 16 wins, a 3.71 earned run average and 179 strikeouts—and he was also the only pitcher on the staff to throw 200 innings. Who was the O's leading starter in 2013?
a) Chris Tillman
b) Miguel Gonzalez
c) Jason Hammel
d) Wei-Yin Chen

BOTTOM OF THE TENTH ANSWER KEY

191. C

192. A

193. D

194. B

195. D

196. D

197. A

198. D

199. B

200. A

ABOUT THE AUTHOR

Tucker Elliot is a Georgia native and diehard baseball fan. A former high school athletic director, varsity baseball coach and college professor, he is now a fulltime writer living in Tampa, FL.

REFERENCES

WEBSITES
Baseball-reference.com
MLB.com (and the official team sites through MLB.com)
BaseballHallofFame.org
ESPN.com
SABR.org
Baseball-Almanac.com

BOOKS
Baseball, an Illustrated History, Geoffrey C. Ward and Ken Burns
The Team by Team Encyclopedia of Major League Baseball, Dennis Purdy
The Unofficial Guide to Baseball's Most Unusual Records, Bob Mackin
The 2005 ESPN Baseball Encyclopedia, edited by Pete Palmer and Gary Gillette
100 Years of the World Series, Eric Enders
Tales from the Tribe Dugout, by Russell Schneider
The Glory of Their Times, by Lawrence S. Ritter

Visit us on the web to learn more about Black Mesa and our authors:

www.blackmesabooks.com

Or contact us via email:

admin@blackmesabooks.com

Made in the USA
San Bernardino, CA
17 December 2013

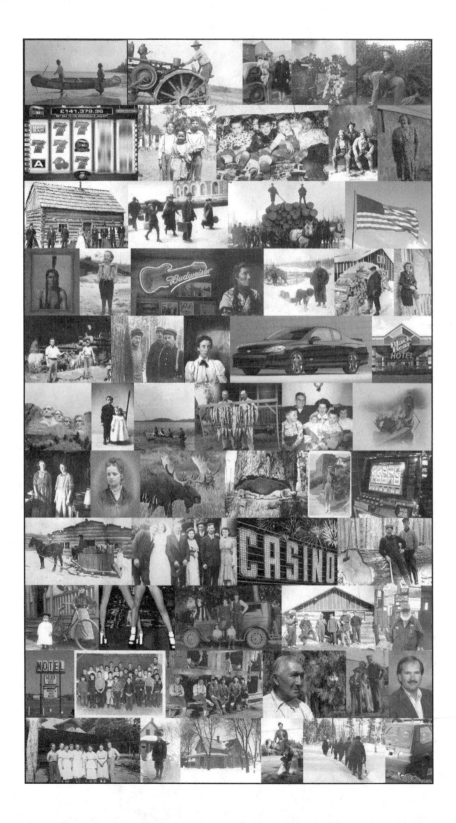

Chain of Fools
A fictional memoir by Charles Stupidnski

©2009 by Charles Sobczak

This is a first edition printing: October 2008
Printed in the United States at Whitehall Printing, Naples, Florida

Published by: Indigo Press L.L.C.
                     2560 Sanibel Boulevard
                     Sanibel, FL 33957

                     Toll free: 877-472-8900

ISBN 13: 978-0-9676199-3-4

Cover and book design by Maggie Rogers and Charles Sobczak

Acknowledgments

In October of 2003, while I was grappling with Soundex cards and microfilm at the Minnesota Historical Society in St. Paul, it was through sheer luck that I chanced upon Thomas Lanman, past president of the Minnesota Genealogical Society, while having lunch in the cafeteria. We struck up a friendship and he agreed to lend this novice genealogist a helping hand. Months later I was thrilled to receive a detailed file of young Scarface Joe's fatal misadventure at the State Reform School in Red Wing, Minnesota. I thank both Tom and the Minnesota Historical Society for all their help.

Likewise, my detailed files about my paternal grandmother, One-Eyed Maggie, would never have been discovered had it not been for the help of Joanne Sher. She is the genealogist from Duluth, Minnesota, who helped me research Maggie's jail records and the fatal house fire in the fall of 1947. I would also like to sincerely thank Janet H. Baker of Baker Freelance Editorial Services for her extensive work. Her suggestions and corrections were excellent and I greatly appreciate the extra effort Janet put forth to make this memoir a better read.

There are so many others who have helped along the way. I have to mention Maggie May Rogers of Maggie May Designs, who helped put together the cover and book design. Likewise I deeply appreciate the secondary proofing done by John Jones, Anne Bellew, Terri DeStoppelaire, Jean Heuer, Norm Zeigler, Libby Grimm and Gabriel Freedman. All of them found plenty of material to work with from the most grammatically challenged writer on the planet.

I must also thank my two sons, Logan and Blake, along with their wonderful mother and my wife, Molly Heuer, for allowing me to write this fictional memoir. Between the drinking, the strippers, the gambling, and the swearing my imaginary self partook of in this tome, I hope they can forgive me.

Thanks as well to my mother, Harriet Sobczak, for telling me the truth, and my sister Barbara Risberg and cousin Richard Contos for confirming it. Also thanks as well to Walter and Dee Plude of the Arrowhead Psychological Clinic for hours upon hours of counseling as I worked on this semi-autobiographical book.

In the end all I can say is this: I pray to God there will never be a sequel.

Charles Sobczak

The Black Bear Casino Lounge

"How's your book coming?"

"It's coming along OK. I just got started a few days ago; It's pretty rough."

"When you get a little further along, can I be in it?"

"Hell, no."

"Why not?"

"Like I've told you before, Diz, because you're a goddamned Indian, and there aren't any Indians in my family."

Diz paused for a minute, then took a long draft from his Budweiser. Charlie could see he was thinking. This wasn't good.

"Didn't you say you're half French Canadian?"

Here it comes, mused Charlie, "Yes, my mother's maiden name was LeBlanc."

"And didn't you say they shipped over here right after the French revolution?"

"Yeah, they arrived in Quebec City around 1800. What's this got to do with you getting into my book, Diz?"

"Well, Chuck...."

Charlie hated this nickname, but he let Diz get away with it. Diz and his mother, Beatrice, to whom he hadn't spoken in years, were the only two people on earth who were allowed to call him Chuck.

Diz continued "Everyone knows the French screwed around with the Native Americans a lot, and who knows? Your great, great grandfather probably had some Chippewa papoose action going on the side. You've gotta have some Indian blood mixed in. So ya see, Chuck, we're related."

"You're full of shit, Diz."

Charlie finished off his own Bud and thought about ordering another one. Maybe he'd switch to something stronger: a whiskey sour, a Black Russian, or a brandy Manhattan. It was getting to be that time.

Sensing that his Indian angle wasn't working, Diz took another tack. "But you said your family's a bunch of drunks, right? And I'm a drunk too."

"Well, that fact sure as hell comes as a big surprise! If I were going to write a book about drunks in America, it would have to be a pretty goddamned big book, don't you think?"

Diz contemplated Charlie's answer as he finished off the backwash of his Bud. Charlie was right, Diz decided; the book about drunks in America would be way too big. How could you even bind a book that big? It'd be bigger than the Bible.

"Well, Chuck, I ain't never been in no book before, and if there's any way you can squeeze in your good Indian friend, I'd be in your debt forever."

"I'll think about it."

"You want another round, or are you going back out on the floor?"

"I'll take another round if you're buying, Diz."

"I bought the last round."

"Do you want to be in my book or not?"

It was literary extortion, but Diz didn't mind. "Fine. What'll ya have?"

"Brandy Manhattan."

"Going in for the hard stuff now?"

"Might as well, the night's young."

Diz leaned forward and hollered down the bar, "Hey, Dena, can ya fix us up down here?"

Dena looked over, gave Charlie and Diz a quick nod of acknowledgment, and started winding down her conversation with the good-looking patron at the other end of the bar. Within a minute she was standing in front of them, waiting to take their next order.

"Two more Buds, you guys?"

"Nah, Stupidnski wants to start in on the hard stuff. Two brandy Manhattans, and make them doubles."

"It's mighty early for that shit, Diz."

"It's later than you think."

Dena turned around and went to work on the Manhattans. She grabbed two extra-tall glasses, scooped some ice into them, and set them on the back bar. She reached down, pulled a bottle of Petri brandy from the well, and poured two heavy-handed shots into each ice-filled glass. Then she reached for the sweet vermouth and splashed a lean half-shot on top.

"Hey, Charlie, how many cherries?"

"Four."

"How 'bout you, Diz?"

"One's fine."

Dena dropped four bright-red cherries into one of the glasses and a single cherry into the other, adding a dash of the cherry juice to each as she did. She skipped the bitters. Every bartender working the Black Bear Casino skipped the bitters. Finally, she grabbed a long-handled spoon and stirred the drinks until the vermouth, brandy, and cherry juice were thoroughly mixed. Turning around, she placed the tall ones on the bar.

"Nine bucks."

"Add it to my tab, Dena," said Diz.

"You're not allowed to run a tab anymore, Diz, and you know it."

"Shit." Diz took out his wallet, found a ten-spot and put it on the bar. "Keep the change."

"Thanks, Diz," said Dena, as she grabbed the ten-spot, turned her back on the two middle-aged drunks, and walked to the other end of the bar, where her good-looking patron was still nursing his whiskey Seven.

"She's a hell of a bartender," said Stupidnski.

"And she's got a hell of an ass," added Diz, surveying Dena's backside as she sauntered over to the young gambler, knowing they'd be watching her as she did.

"Yeah, you got that right."

"Well, here's to a night of big winnin's!" Diz raised his pinkish-colored drink up toward his lips as he made the toast.

"Ya betcha, Diz, ya betcha."

The men took long hard pulls on their cocktails and then set their glasses down in a well-rehearsed ritual. The two men hardly spoke as the misty-colored liquor began fogging them in. They loved the numbness, the mental paralysis that beer and brandy provided. They enjoyed being oblivious, ferried around in the cerebral wheelchair of liquor like inmates in some three-shot hospital ward.

Above the bar a flat screen TV carried the Minnesota Wild in an early season hockey game. The team was taking a beating from the Detroit Red Wings. It was 4 to 1, though no one at the bar except the young guy putting the make on Dena gave a damn. The TV, as always, was on mute. The only noise that could be heard was the constant din of the nearby machines—a choir of five hundred slots singing their eerie melodic refrain. Like electronic sirens, their strange soprano melodies filled the casino with the perpetual invitation to come in, sit down and start feeding them money. The money that kept them singing.

Charlie sat quietly at the bar, ignoring the call of the sirens for the moment while he reloaded his bloodstream with alcohol. They would be back out on the floor soon enough, searching for the nickel slot that was ripe, the slot that was willing to cooperate, willing to align three cherries, three sevens, or crisscross any of the three, six, or dozens of combinations that would edge the nickel meter upward toward 246, 437, or 853 coins.

They would be out on the floor gambling before their Manhattans hit empty. Chain smoking, half in the bag, and all the while systematically dropping tiny cameos of Thomas Jefferson into hungry narrow portals until the night ran out of darkness.

Chain of Fools

Chapter 1: One-Eyed Maggie

I never met One-Eyed Maggie. She died in a fire seven years and change before I was born. She died the night of November 9, 1947. Her death certificate confirmed it was a combination of extensive burns and smoke inhalation that killed her. Maggie chain-smoked, often in bed, so the odds were never in her favor—not that they are for any of us.

Maggie also drank, and drank heavily. In the end, Maggie's drinking was the major cause of her own demise. She drank bootleg whiskey, vodka, white lightning, brandy—just about anything she could get her hands on, from what I've been told. It's a bad combination, being shit-faced drunk with a freshly lit Lucky Strike while passed out on a liquor-soaked mattress.

I should explain. Magdalene Stupidnski was my grandmother on my father's side. And please don't start in about my last name, because I'm sick of it. Just remember the d is silent. It's pronounced Stupinski, not Stupidski. I was born with it, just like all the lucky assholes out there with last names like Smith, Jones, and goddamned Anderson. It's the surname lotto we all play the instant we take our first breath. I lost. I deal with it. Let's move on.

They called my grandmother One-Eyed Maggie because she only had one eye that worked. The other eye was defunct. How that happened is a story I'll get to later. I think the eye that worked was her left eye, but it might have been the other way around. The question is moot in a way, a sick, humorous way, because—let's be frank right from the start—what the hell does it matter? Maggie was your typical one-eyed, chain-smoking, bootlegging, gambling, alcoholic prostitute. Have I mentioned the prostitute thing yet? Well, I should.

The criminal record on this aspect of Maggie's miscreant career is scant, but there's plenty of hearsay. The word on the street was that Maggie Stupidnski slept around, and there was generally booze, cigarettes, or other consideration (not excluding cash) transferred to the slept arounder from the slept aroundee. My grandmother, to use a term from her own era, was a strumpet. In the end, an over-toasted strumpet.

As fate would have it, the evening Maggie checked out of the motel of life fell on a Sunday. The Fire Marshall speculated that the fire broke out around 7 p.m. and had completely engulfed Maggie's bedroom by the time the fire trucks arrived twenty minutes later. Maggie was long gone by then. Eyewitnesses say that when the flames found her bootleg stash it was all over, One-Eyed Maggie's bedroom, along with Maggie herself, went up like a Buddhist monk in Saigon during the Tet offensive.

Her roommate at the time, George Bazon, suffered from smoke inhalation and minor burns. He was treated and released the following day from Saint Mary's Hospital, the very same hospital where I was born a few years later. I don't think George had been banging Maggie the night the fire broke out. The fact that George survived the inferno leads me to speculate he was passed out drunk on the couch. It's like the blind eye thing, who cares?

In any event, by mid-century Maggie Stupidnski was getting old. At fifty-five, little Ms. One-Eye wasn't having much luck turning tricks commercially, so she had decided to settle down and shack up with George. It's the any-port-in-a- storm theory of love. Mr. Bazon, hailing from Austria but speaking only Polish and broken English, was just another lonely immigrant from the old country looking for a little warmth during those cold Minnesota winters. This particular November evening got a bit warmer than George had bargained for.

George Bazon, like my grandmother Maggie, eventually became yet another death certificate filed in the archives of the living.

He probably died from liver failure. Drinking Maggie's moonshine had serious long-term consequences.

My mother once told me that no one was shocked or even remotely surprised at Maggie's premature death. Most of the immediate family had decided she was going to drink herself to death anyway, so the fire acted as an accelerant to the inevitable.

You should be informed from the get go that One-Eyed Maggie wasn't what most people would call a looker. For starters, Maggie was short, standing just a tad over five foot two. Along with being vertically challenged, Maggie was, to put it mercifully, very, very stocky. She resembled a character from some Soviet- era newsreel depicting poor Russian laborers at a collective farm circa 1938, a farm that would once again fail to make its annual potato quota. Maggie had a compact Stalinesque build, common to proletarians of the 1930s.

Maggie also sported that round Polish face that has the word peasant permanently tattooed across the forehead. Her couture choices were modest. Nearly every photo I have ever seen depicts Maggie in the same floral shift, hanging well below her pudgy knees, its sleeves clipped just above her equally pudgy elbows. Robust describes Maggie, provided you toss the word into an adjective blender along with hefty, ornery and intoxicated and push the frappé button.

As a whore, Maggie was the kind of prostitute where—right from the moment he laid eyes on her—the guy had to ask himself why he wasn't the one getting paid to do whatever it was that needed doing. Her most appealing feature was a biological fact: She had a vagina. If there were such a thing as a discount for ugly whores, Maggie would have operated at a perpetual loss—not to mention the patch she sometimes wore over her blind eye, giving her that special burly pirate-wench look men go nuts over.

So here it is at last. If you want to keep reading, have at it. It's my memoir, sort of. It's the chain of fools, the chain of my family that got me here—Charles Bradford Stupidnski—renting this room month by month at the Golden Gate Motel in Scanlon, Minnesota. It's not the entire chain, mind you. That would make this damn story way too long. It's a brief genealogical synopsis: Rose begat Maggie begat Stanley begat me begat my three kids, ad infinitum. Just a handful of links, five generations at best. Like a snapshot in time. A lousy shot, out of focus, grainy, and overexposed, but the only shot I have.

Room 112, The Golden Gate Motel

The next morning, Charles Bradford Stupidnski lay flat on his lumpy mattress. He was awake and hung over. Not a massive, hemorrhaging hangover like the one he suffered a week ago, but enough of a throbbing blur to make him consider smoking his last joint. A joint followed by six aspirin.

He stared at the popcorn-textured ceiling above him, noting that the two large water stains had not changed in shape, color, or intensity since he'd rented this motel room months ago. He thought the shape of the large stain in the far corner looked vaguely like Africa. The stain over the front door was smaller and more symmetrical, almost circular, like Australia or Antarctica. The leaks must be fixed, he decided, as the sound of a driving October rain pounded against the cracked window beside the front door.

The television was on, as it was every minute Charlie spent in his room. The sounds of the rain mixed with the sounds of the three contestants inside the fuzzy nineteen-inch tube playing *Jeopardy*.

"Who was President Nixon?" answered an indecisive but perky brunette.

"That's correct," said Alex Trebek, just as a gust of wind threw another spray of cold rain against the windowpane.

Charlie never took his eyes off the blemished ceiling, not even for the Daily Double. He didn't care who won or lost at *Jeopardy*. He didn't care if the roof started leaking again and the shape of the two stains began changing, looking like some cheap motel version of continental drift. He stared straight up, braking only on occasion to sit upright enough to take a sip of the tall lukewarm glass of last night's parting brandy Manhattan.

He had ordered the drink just before leaving and, like the dozen other glasses scattered about his motel room, had held it tucked under his jacket when he walked out of the casino at a little past three in the morning. The ice had long since melted and the drink was the same temperature as his room, 71 degrees. Now half gone, with a washed-out pinkish hue, it looked more like contaminated well water than a cocktail. It tasted exactly the same.

This was it. This was Charlie Stupidnski's life. He was free. Free from the mortgage payments, the car lease, the utility bills, the soccer games, the help with homework, the credit cards, the wife, the dog, the hairball-puking cat, the kids, the overtime, the leaking toilets, the nagging clients, the whole motherfucking ball of wax. Free.

All he had to his name was his rusted out 1979 Ford Pinto, two suitcases, and a $487 a month motel bill, taxes and utilities included. That and $945 of working capital in his wallet. Or, as he preferred to call his gambling money, eighteen thousand, nine-hundred nickels temporarily converted into a convenient paper form. Perfect little portraits of President Jefferson that Diz referred to as nickel cameos.

As Charlie lay there, listening to a contestant say, "Who was Franz Kafka?" and Alex, with no other takers, giving the correct answer as "Who was Albert Camus?" he wondered how Diz had fared last night.

Diz was supposed to meet him back at the bar around midnight for another bump and a chance to wake up by checking out Dena's ass for the millionth time, but he never showed. Charlie suspected the worst. Diz's luck was in the toilet for the past few months and Dena said she hadn't seen him all night. He probably went back to the reservation early, having tapped out his thirty-dollar limit long before midnight.

"You've done it!" interrupted Trebek. *"It's the daily double!"*

Charlie's eyes never left the ceiling. They were surveying a section of equatorial Africa, looking for any kind of blemish or crack that might identify the Congo River weaving through. The more he looked, the more he thought the huge watermark looked more like South America and not like Africa at all. He started searching for the Amazon.

His head hurt. He sat up, finished the glass of effluent on the ring-stained night stand beside him, and opened up the single drawer just below his empty glass. There was nothing in the drawer except a lone Gideon Bible. He took out the Bible and sat there holding it on his lap for a few minutes.

Had a member of the Gideon Society walked in at that exact minute he might have relished the tableau before him: a hungover alcoholic, alone in his run-down motel, a Bible held firmly in his hands as he finds salvation at last.

Just as the contestants scribbled down their answers to Final Jeopardy, Charlie opened the Bible. He opened it to Ecclesiastes, Chapter 6, and much to God's dismay took out a half-smoked roach and a book of matches.

He quickly closed the Bible and stuffed it back in the drawer. So much for salvation.

The first three matches didn't stay lit long enough to get the joint going. The fourth match caught fire, and by the time the television screen had aired a half-dozen commercials and moved on to *The Young and the Restless*, Charles Stupidnski was stoned. He hated soap operas but not enough to turn the TV off or change the channel. It was the white noise he took comfort in, the white noise of oversexed soap opera stars getting caught screwing each other, physically or financially— husband, wife, or the family pet for that matter.

Charlie dropped what little was left of his roach into his empty highball glass. The joint sizzled for a second in the last few drops of watered-down booze. A good-looking Latino on the soap opera was trying to explain to his brother's wife that he couldn't keep having an affair with her because he had discovered he was gay. The Latino was sobbing as he spoke. So was the wife. Before the next battery of detergent commercials, she'd stab her uncloseted brother-in-law to death.

"The young and the useless," Charlie mumbled as he labored to roll out of bed and make his way to the tiny bathroom.

There was no fan in the bathroom. He needed to do two things: take a shit and eat half a dozen aspirins.

Shit first, he decided. Just before he sat down on the toilet, Charlie thought about cracking the one little frosted glass window in the shower. After thinking about it for a minute, he decided it would take too much effort, besides, the cold and the rain would get in. He knew that within minutes his motel room would be filled to capacity with the stink of his dump but he didn't give a damn. He was free. High, hung over and free.

He thought about working on his manuscript again just as his first big turd hit the calm reflective surface of the toilet bowl. He had just started it, having put it off for more than five months, struggling with where to began. This was the first book he had ever written, and he was still suffering from a dreadful case of writer's block. For the moment, the marijuana was giving him an unexpected boost of enthusiasm.

Most of his research was done. Charlie had spent countless hours pouring through the court records of Saint Louis County in search of death certificates, birth certificates, divorce papers, and court records and had already learned more than he wanted to know about his heritage. He'd taken the long drive down to St. Paul to the Minnesota Historical Society building a half dozen times, looking through the microfiche, the old newspapers, and the census records to find out what he could about his immigrant grandfather's journey to America. The stacks of documents— photocopies worth well over a hundred dollars, he had once calculated—were tucked away beside his skid-marked shorts in the bottom drawer of the room's only dresser.

He finished his business, flushed the toilet, and rifled through the small medicine cabinet in search of his bottle of aspirin. Pouring six into his hand, he tossed them into his mouth, threw his head back, and swallowed them without so much as a drop of water. It was a trick he had learned from his father, who could swallow horse pills without batting an eye.

Before he got started on the next chapter, Charlie decided he needed a pack of cigarettes. He put on the same clothes he wore the night before. The keys to his Pinto were in the right front pants pocket.

By the time he got into his Pinto, Charlie had come off his high just enough to realize that he had better put some gas in his car as well, so he started her up and drove down the street from the motel to the nearby Erickson gas station, where he pumped in three gallons before walking into the station for two packs of Kool menthols. A few minutes later he was back in his room with the used laptop computer that some unnamed Goodwill attendant had sold him a week earlier. The clerk told him that the laptop's lithium battery was shot so the machine had to be plugged in to work. It booted up: Windows 98. A damn good year, he thought.

He continued with the manuscript where he had last left off. This is what he wrote:

Chain of Fools

Chapter 2: Life Back Then

Life was different in Minnesota back then. There were no roads to speak of: no electricity, no hospitals within easy reach, no tractors, no telephones, no cell phones—hell, the list is endless. In 1892, the year little Maggie landed on the planet, Pine County was for all intents and purposes a third world country.

Infant mortality was rampant. If a newborn did manage to survive that first big squeeze through its mother's birth canal, there were plenty of other perils waiting. Smallpox, scarlet fever, influenza, infections, cholera, dysentery, wild animal attacks, Indians, forest fires, and farm accidents all took their toll. Maggie survived her childhood, save for one eye. There were plenty of stillborns, infants whose remains still rest in unmarked graves lying somewhere out in the back forty. One of Maggie's brothers lost an arm at the sawmill (fingers didn't even count), years later, two of Maggie Stupidnski's sisters died giving birth, and she lost her mother, along with two brothers, in the great Cloquet forest fire of 1918. Little wonder they leaned toward the hard stuff.

Stupidnski wasn't Maggie's maiden name. It was Myzchayp, for which there is no known Anglo-Saxon pronunciation. For convenience, therefore, Myzchayp, becomes Mishap, Magdalene Mishap. It works for me.

One-Eyed Maggie was born on March 1, 1892, in Bremen Township, Pine County, Minnesota. Think "Beware the Ides of March", only make it the first and not the fifteenth. She was one of thirteen children, a number that should have been another ominous sign, had anyone been paying attention. Her brothers and sisters had those strange foreign sounding names common at the time: George, Lawrence, Stephan, Josef, Verna, Josia, Thursa, Toffle, Clara, Clarence, Gertrude, Herbert, and of course Magdalene. Someday, someone will be looking back at an old census form from the early 2000s thinking how odd it was to be naming children Heather, Sean, Brit, Kyle, Sandra, and Taylor. Nothing really changes; we just think it does.

Maggie was born on a dirt farm, a standard government-issue homestead of 160 acres brimming with native white pine, stands of birch, and rodent-size mosquitoes. Her father, John Mishap, worked his entire life as a subsistence farmer and small-time lumber baron. They operated a sawmill on their farm, helping to deforest the nation, something no one back then thought was possible. I've heard that my great grandfather became quite wealthy with his logging enterprise, though I've not come across any evidence of it. Maggie herself never had a pot to piss in.

There can be no doubt my great-grandfather contributed to the enormous slash piles that fueled the Great Fire of 1894 in Hinckley, which flared up two years after Maggie's birth. The Mishaps were lucky to have survived that inferno, a firestorm that raged with a fire wall five miles high and wind gusts exceeding one hundred miles an hour. Miraculously, the Hinckley fire stayed just south of Bremen Township and my ancestors survived, smelling like wood smoke, covered in ash, but unscathed.

Maggie's mother's name was Rosa, though some of the historical records refer to her as Rose. They were all devout Polish Catholics, hence the truckload of offspring. Rosa had her last child, a boy named Herbert, when she was forty-eight. He had the IQ of a potato. There was no amniocentesis or prenatal care in Bremen Township circa 1892. Babies were delivered at home by anxious midwives with hot towels and a surplus of mortality.

Back then your offspring were your health and life insurance. There were no schools to attend nor any child labor laws, so your kids started working on the farm as soon as they were big enough to pick up a pitch fork or swing an ax. The children you bore took care of you when you got too old to manage the farm or when your liver finally collapsed after decades of drinking.

Maggie was the third child born to the Mishaps, two brothers having arrived before her. The first boy was born in New York City, no doubt having been conceived during the long boat ride to America. Oh, the perils of immigration!

For years I'd been told that my father's side of the family came from Poland. But on the 1910 census, Joseph and Rosa claim to be from German Bohemia. That long-lost nation, currently located in the northeast corner of present day Germany, frequently waffled between Austria, Poland, Bohemia, and Prussia throughout the 1900s so it's difficult to pinpoint their exact roots. Let's just say they were Bohemians, which may help explain Maggie's eccentric, albeit not very artistic, behavior.

Rosa Mishap had been born in 1860, the same year the civil war broke out in the States. Her maiden name was Polarczak: another ringer. John, Maggie's father, was born in 1852. They crossed the Atlantic in 1883. I never found the name of the ship that brought them here to the melting pot, nor did I spend any time looking for it. It probably departed from Bremen, Germany and docked three weeks later in the Big Apple, with Rosa having the first of many future buns in her hot little Bohemian oven.

George Mishap, their first child, was probably delivered near the notorious Five Points district of New York City, a hotbed for immigrants back then. Their second son, Lawrence, was born outside of Philadelphia in rural Pennsylvania. Maggie, the oldest daughter, was born shortly after the family had moved west to Minnesota, in search of a place to call home. By that time the Mishaps were naturalized citizens and able to secure their 160-acre grant, a homestead located along the mosquito-infested fringe of the civilized world. It's hard to fathom, but it was Abe Lincoln himself who conceived the original Homestead Act. Had he only known!

Somewhere along the long dusty wagon trail between Pennsylvania and Minnesota, Maggie was conceived. Maggie wasn't born blind in one eye. Her blindness came later, as a result of an accident. As far as I can tell, Maggie's only genetic fault was being born with a predisposition for the hard stuff. I should know. I'm carrying the same goddamn gene.

The tale of how Maggie became blind in one eye has come down to me in what can best be described as my family's tradition of dyslexic oral history. Unlike most families, my ancestral tales come in bits and pieces, with ample hearsay, innuendo, and rumor thrown in. No Uncle Jeremiah telling his nephews and nieces how his great, great grandfather came over on the *Mayflower*. No Daughters of the American Revolution in our history. No bluebloods or Founding Fathers in my seamy genealogy. The only thing that turns our blood any hint of blue is downing a bottle of Blue Caruso. That or stooping to paint thinner, tainted blue from when Uncle Herbert painted the basement and cleaned his brushes in it. That's us, laquer-based bluebloods.

No, in our family we get our histories secondhand and, even then, only after a six-pack of Budweiser or a couple of stiff shots of vodka. From everything I've been able to glean from these reluctant oral archives, Maggie was a little girl, six or seven at the time, running around outside the old homestead one fall morning with a stick in her hand.

Maggie tripped, and the stick pierced her eye.

Her younger brother, whom she was chasing, immediately took her back to the farmhouse for medical attention. Her mother, Rosa, glanced briefly at the stick in her daughter's eye, told the boy to go fetch Pa, and consoled Maggie while peeling another fifty-pound bag of potatoes for the still. Her father came in from the sawmill, pulled the stick out, and declared, "There now, Maggie, you'll be just fine."

With a half-dozen malnourished little Mishaps to feed and another brutal Minnesota winter coming on, the last thing on the Mishaps agenda was to waste money on a doctor. Maggie's eye, naturally, got infected. Then it stopped working altogether, healed up more or less, and the little girl had a new nickname: One-Eyed Maggie.

Reflecting on the calamity a few weeks later, Maggie's father added, "Who the hell needs two eyes anyway?" Dr. Spock be damned.

Back then, at least for the Mishaps, this was typical. Life was cheap, and Maggie Mishap, from the onset, was decidedly shortchanged. Sadly, Maggie was crazy enough to adopt this horrendous parenting style when she later gave birth to her own series of Mishaps, among them, my father.

But Maggie and her clan endured. The family survived by subsistence farming, selling off their own timber and sawing up everyone else's until all the forests were razed and gone. They had it all: pigs, horses, rutabagas, chickens, ducks, corn, potatoes, cows, and, of course, stills. The pine stumps and piles of slash left over from their logging and sawmill operations would come back to haunt the Mishaps in the years to come, fueling the great Cloquet fire of 1918. That firestorm killed her mother and two siblings, but by that time, Maggie was married to my grandfather, Paul, and living in Duluth.

As far as I can tell from my research there were no sexual relations with the livestock, though I wouldn't swear to it. It's pathetic to realize that the road your ancestors took was only one slippery tier above bestiality. I can only assume the various tubers and vegetables they grew were safe.

They all drank. I doubt the children drank until they hit double digits, but it's hard to say. You can rest assured they started early and stopped only when one or more internal organs failed. For all intents and purposes, vodka was the fuel my father's side of the family ran on. Hailing from Bohemia, they probably brought their potato-mash moonshine recipes with them. Lucky for them, the lowly potato thrived in the rocky glacial till of northern Minnesota. Ma and Pa Mishap soon found themselves living on what is best described as the pioneer moonshine diet. Vodka was the lubricant that allowed them to get started every morning and the sedative that put them to bed every night. Maggie, along with her dozen brothers and sisters, helped with the farm and eventually learned to work the kettle and copper coils of the family still. With a genetic disposition to alcoholism, she quickly found herself dipping her little finger in the family vat. She soon graduated to a spoon, then jumped straight to a tin cup.

Shortly after Maggie started drinking some of her own handiwork, she became sexually active. It's impossible to determine when Maggie lost her virginity, or who helped her with that loss. I can only pray it wasn't one of her brothers, but once again, I'm not taking anything off the table. When it comes to talking about a family black sheep, remember this: I own the flock.

By the time One-Eyed Maggie was betrothed to my grandfather in 1911, she had already given birth to one child out of wedlock. Bastards in my family run a close second to legitimate kids, so news of this fatherless child hardly came as a shock to me. Some neighbor kid, no doubt enjoying the liquid bounty of the Mishap's still, was reputed to be the father. Maggie was all of seventeen when she did the nasty with him. He skipped town a month later, fearing a shotgun wedding to little Miss One-Eye.

Maggie named her first child John, after her father. When his mother married my grandfather in 1911, John never adopted the

Stupidnski name, for obvious reasons. John died before I ever had a chance to meet him. I can't say whether or not he was an alcoholic but, ten to one that he was. Even so, from what I've heard, John Mishap was an OK guy. He was just dumb as bricks.

Paul Stupidnski, my grandfather, was likewise an illegitimate child, so marrying Maggie, who walked down the aisle with a second bastard on board, didn't faze him one bit.

Riverside Bar: Happy Hour 4-6

"Where the hell you been?"

"Who is this?"

"Ahh shit, Diz, it's Charlie."

There was static on the line. Charlie hardly ever used the motel room's phone, but when he did there was always static on the line. It was as if someone were giving a haircut with one of those hand-held clippers in the background of every call. Buzz-cut static.

"Oh, hey, Chuck, what's happening?" Diz's voice was bleary.

Charlie knew what was happening. Diz was coming off a bender. When Diz didn't show up at the Black Bear Casino on Saturday night, Charlie suspected the worst. When Diz didn't show up Sunday night, the jury was in. Diz had stayed on the reservation and gone on a major drunk.

How his drunk unfolded was typical. On Saturday morning his two cousins, Falling Bobby Bear and George Coyote, showed up at his mobile home with a case of ice-cold Colt 45 malt liquor and two bottles of nameless bourbon. By noon the three of them were telling tall tales and laughing like idiots at the kitchen table, so drunk they could have floated. By midnight the liquor had been joined by five joints, some little blue pills, and a liter of Popov vodka that Diz had stashed under the couch. They were no longer floating drunk but sinking drunk. After Diz threw up just before seven that night, he walked back into the mobile home and asked Falling Bobby Bear, "What the fuck were in those little blue pills?"

His cousin said he didn't know. "Rita gave them to my sister and said they would get you really screwed up, so my sister gave them to me." The offer of free pills had sounded good, so Bobby took all twenty-eight of them, stuck them in his front right pocket, and planned on downing them over the weekend. In their world, the world of the reservation, even unidentified drugs were taken. Diz, egged on by his cousins, had swallowed five of the pills around six-thirty that night, too drunk to care what the hell they were.

As it turns out, they were birth control pills. Diz's testosterone based system didn't do well with an unexpected megadose of estrogen; he became sick to his stomach within five minutes of swallowing it. Thirty minutes later there was nothing left in his stomach, not even a trace of the seven Colt 45s and the six shots of bourbon he had put away since ten that morning.

After throwing up, Diz immediately cracked another cold one to restart the oblivion machine and warned his two cousins not to take any of the little blue pills. Falling Bobby Bear agreed to steer clear of them. But his brother, George, refused to throw his seven pills away, insisting that Diz's problem might have been some kind of allergic reaction.

Just after eleven that same evening, George Coyote was retching his soul out not ten feet from Diz's pile of bile. It's an estrogen issue. Naturally, Charlie would never hear, or necessarily want to hear, about any of this. Charlie just wanted to know if Diz was OK, so the phone call continued.

"Diz, can you make Happy Hour at the Riverside?"

"Today, man? Do you mean today? I didn't think they had Happy Hour on Sunday."

It was Monday. It now became perfectly clear to Charlie that Diz had lost track of time. The last thing Diz could remember was that they were all going to drive across to Wisconsin to pick up some more booze. Minnesota, still clinging to archaic blue laws, remnants of the prohibition era that once kept One-Eyed Maggie's business booming, does not allow the sale of hard liquor on Sundays. With all three of them nursing hangovers the size of an open pit ore mine, these natives needed reinforcements and they needed them now.

George Coyote, having gone to bed around 1 a.m., still sick as a dog, was the designated driver. George would have flunked a sobriety test, but not by much. Either Diz or Bobby would have set a new state record for the Breathalyzer. So George, still slightly nauseated by the birth control pills, was conscripted to take the wheel. They drove through Jay Cooke park, down along the Saint Louis Bay and across the Arrowhead Bridge to Oliver, Wisconsin.

Oliver was a town whose economic base was deeply rooted in liquor. Maggie still had some open invoices with the bar owners of Oliver when she went up in flames in '47. The tiny town of Oliver didn't give a damn about prohibition back in the 1920s any more than it did today about Minnesota's remaining blue laws, and it was close to the reservation.

All the local cops that Sunday morning were parked beside a hundred different churches waiting to help with traffic congestion once services were out, so no one was available to pull these three derelict Indians over. They had bought sixteen dollars and twenty cents' worth of whatever liquor was on sale and drove home, polishing off seven dollars' worth of it before they pulled back into the gravel driveway of Diz's run-down trailer. The rest of the day was lost to what might best be described as annihilation. For Dismount Moose, Monday arrived unexpectedly.

"Monday, Diz, it's goddamned Monday."

"Fuck."

"Say around four?"

"Fuck."

"Are you OK, Diz?"

"Four. I'll be there around four." Whereupon Diz hung up.

Charlie knew the odds were fifty-fifty at best that Diz would show. He had known Diz for a little better than four months, and once a month, sometimes twice a month, Diz would go on a world-class bender. There wouldn't be any gambling involved. No women. No food. No water. No purpose other than anesthetizing himself. Anything to make his world, and the pain that came with it, go away.

Sometimes these drunks would last a weekend, other times a week. Charlie would usually wait them out, eventually running into Diz back at the casino bar, staring at Dena's ass, or seeing him pull up with a case of cold ones for an afternoon visit. This time Charlie couldn't wait. He wanted to talk about his book and about a new plan he had devised to win the heart of Crystal Lovelock, an exotic dancer whom Charlie felt was soon to be his new girlfriend.

So Charlie had called Diz from the static-filled phone to arrange a get-together at the Riverside Bar to have a few drinks. Then maybe both of them could head over to the casino for an early dinner. Monday nights at the casino featured the seafood buffet, Charlie's favorite.

Charlie wanted to take a copy of his fledgling manuscript along and read a section to Diz, but he didn't have a printer or any extra cash to buy one. He spent the next hour trying to memorize a couple of paragraphs so he could paraphrase his book to Diz, provided he showed.

Locking room number 112 behind him, he started walking over to the Riverside Bar around three-forty-five. To get to the Riverside, Charlie had to pass a local used car lot that displayed models he knew damn well he would never again afford to own. Cars that started. Cars that had working headlights, windshield wipers, and working heaters. As he walked by, Charlie vaguely recalled that he once drove cars like that.

Just before opening the door to the Riverside, Charlie took a look at the Saint Louis River, running wild and brilliant blue not thirty feet away. Since it was early October, the birch trees were ablaze in a stunning sunlit yellow, the red maples still hung out fistfuls of dark red leaves, and the air was so crisp and clear a man might want to capture it, making it the only air he would ever breathe again.

Charlie, long since removed from the poetry of life, saw none of this. The sound of the river cascading over the rocks made him want to take a piss. He debated between going inside or just walking off to the side of the bar to the two big propane tanks he generally pissed on. For no particular reason, he decided he'd go inside. He opened the heavy wooden front door and walked in.

"Hey, Charlie, what'z up?"

"Nothing, Carl. Just came in for a drink."

"Belly up to the bar, Charlie, Happy Hours till six."

"It's why I'm here, Carl."

Before making his way to the bar he headed back to the bathroom. As he walked inside, he noted that only one of the two urinals in the men's room was still on the wall. Where the second urinal once hung there was a capped-off water line, some ripped up Sheetrock, and an empty drain. Charlie surveyed the damage and pinned it on Saturday night's rock-n-roll crowd.

Technically, the urinal was yanked off the wall on Sunday morning, at precisely 1:15 A.M. That was when Kurt Larsen ripped the forty-pound chunk of ceramic from its anchor bolts and tried to hit Mark Anderson over the head with it for slow-dancing with his girlfriend,

Cindy Walberg. Luckily, Mark made it out of the can seconds before Kurt managed to tear the urinal off. It proved too heavy to drag back out to the dance floor, so Kurt just let it drop and shatter on the tiled floor. Cindy left with Mark before Kurt caught up with either of them. It was how things operated at the Riverside on the weekends.

After taking a long heathy piss, Charlie walked over and found a stool at the bar. He was disappointed that Angela wasn't bartending. Angela was hot. Randy was working Happy Hour tonight. Randy looked like the stereotypical northern Minnesota deer hunter minus the bright orange over-jacket and high-powered deer rifle. He weighed two hundred plus, had a long untrimmed mustache and flannel shirt, and was sporting well-worn jeans that weren't designer worn but six-years-old worn. No belt. Then Charlie remembered there was a consolation prize for not having Angela behind the bar. Randy poured twice the drink that she did.

What Charlie didn't know was that Angela was home that particular Monday afternoon, having called in sick. It wasn't the flu but a case of morning sickness that had lingered into the afternoon. It was Randy's kid, though Randy didn't know any more about that than Charlie did. Angela was carrying yet another one of Riverside's after-the-bars-close babies. Like many of the local nightclubs scattered across northern Minnesota, the Riverside Bar was a virtual illegitimate-baby factory.

"What ya havin', Stupidnski?"

Randy knew the d was silent, he didn't need reminding.

"Brandy Seven."

"You want them both at once or one after the other?"

"Both."

As Randy went about the business of making two tumblers full of ice, gunned-out 7-Up, and Petri brandy, Charlie took a studied glance around the room, wondering if by some miracle Diz had arrived before him.

There were two girls playing pool thirty feet away. They were young...cute girls. Along with them were six standard-issue Minnesota factory-town locals. They were in various stages of cell phone conversations, juke box selections or leaning over their own private brand of poison in some half-lit corner. Then there was Carl, the bouncer, who had greeted Charlie when he came in. Carl was stationed at the door, placed there to card the various high school girls and teenage punks who always tried to sneak in before the band started at eight. Monday nights at the Riverside Bar were "new band nights," notorious for attracting minors.

Diz was nowhere in sight.

"What ya up to, Charlie?" Randy set the two drinks on the shellacked wooden bar.

"I started the book, Randy. I finally started the goddamned book."

"Am I going to be in it?"

Why does everyone want to be my book? Charlie wondered.

"Hell, no. Diz ain't even going to be in it. It's about *my* relatives. It's not about you assholes."

"Shit, I ain't never been in a book."

With that comment, Randy turned his back on Charlie and walked over to talk with two regulars about how horseshit the Minnesota Wild was doing this year. That and what they thought their chances were of shooting a nice buck when deer season opened in late November.

Diz walked in a few minutes after Charlie finished off the first of his two Brandy Sevens. Diz looked like shit. His eyes were so bloodshot they looked like a miniature map of the Mississippi Delta reproduced in red. A flooded Mississippi, complete with corpses.

"You look like shit, Diz."

"I feel like shit, Chuck."

"Where you been?" Charlie didn't know why the hell he asked, because he knew damn well where Diz had been.

"I've been drinkin'."

"No shit."

"I ate some little blue pills on Saturday night and I still ain't right."

"What were they."

"Falling Bobby's sister told him she thinks her girlfriend gave us some old birth control pills. Turns out she might be pregnant. She didn't want to throw them away because she read somewhere that the estrogen ends up in the trout streams and the trout can't have babies anymore or some shit like that. Coyote and I both ate some, and we got sick as goddamn dogs, Chuck, sick as goddamn dogs."

"Maybe you and Coyote won't be able to have babies now, Diz. Such a bloody shame."

"Piss off, you asshole."

Diz turned his attention to Randy and waved him over.

"Hey, Randy, I'll have whatever Charlie's having."

"Both at once or one at a time, Diz?"

"Both at once and hurry."

Randy didn't say anything but he tacitly agreed with Charlie's assessment: Diz looked like shit. He looked like a terminally hungover, stereotypical drunken American Indian, complete with ruddy pockmarked cheeks, dark untrimmed greasy hair, a red flannel shirt, and worn jeans, stinking of barf, urine, and booze and not removed once in the past seventy-two hours.

The two tall ones were staring up at Diz within minutes. Randy collected a ten-spot from both of them and tucked both bills under a spindle full of receipts beside the cash register. He knew better than to extend credit to either of them. These were not just high-risk patrons. These were fatal accidents, multiple-fatalities risk.

Diz finished his first cocktail in one long camel-style pull. It was the first drink he had taken since skipping breakfast.

"So what's new, Charlie?"

"I'm working on the book, Diz."

"Am I in it yet?"

"Hell, no. We talked about this shit last Friday. You probably ain't ever going to be in my book, so deal with it."

"Shit."

"Don't you want to hear about it."

"Not if I ain't in the goddamn thing."

"You're a dick, Diz."

"So. What else is new?"

Ignoring his attitude, Charlie proceeded to tell Diz about the first few chapters, at least as much as he could remember. Diz thought it sounded good, even if he was disappointed for not being mentioned. As Charlie wrapped it up, Diz's eyes lit up unexpectedly.

"Ya know, Charlie, I just thought of something."

Charlie responded cautiously, dreading what was probably coming. "What?"

"Did I ever tell ya I ain't all Indian? My great-grandfather was part Norwegian. Is there any Norwegian in your blood, Charlie?"

"No."

"Damn, that angle ain't gonna work either, is it." Diz was clearly disappointed. He abandoned the conversation and took a long drink from his second cocktail. Then he continued talking without bringing up the book thing again.

"Did you go to Sugar Daddies on Saturday night to check out Crystal?"

"Of course I did. I'm in love with her."

"Did she even notice you?"

"I bought a twenty-dollar lap dance from her. It was fantastic."

"I'll bet. Did she remember your name?"

"Well, not really. She keeps calling me John. But I think I've figured out a way to win her over, Diz. I think I've finally figured her out."

"Yeah. What's your plan, Chuck?"

"I'm going to win the Monte Carlo."

"Bullshit, Charlie. You ain't gonna win the Monte Carlo any more than you won the Mustang last month or the damn Jeep Cherokee four months ago. The odds are like a billion to one, or some shit like that."

"Not for me they're not. I'm going to pull that big old handle two–three times a day until I win that car, and when I do I'm going to propose to Crystal."

"You need to take some birth control pills, Charlie. Something to clean out your system."

The conversation kept going. They both ordered two more brandy Sevens and by six o'clock, when the bell signaled the end of the official Happy Hour at the Riverside, they were pleasantly drunk. Not smashed, not angry, not unable-to-drive drunk, but comfortably drunk. Once the two-for-one special was over, it was time to leave. They were the Happy Hour crowd, and they were both very, very happy.

"Want to go to the Black Bear buffet with me, Diz?"

"That sounds great Charlie, I haven't eaten a goddamned thing except some chips and shit since Friday."

It was true. Diz had more or less committed to a liquid diet since being roused by his two cousins Saturday morning. He remembered having some buttered bread at one point, and maybe a bag of chips Sunday morning, but that was it. They bought the chips at the liquor store in Oliver. They were stale.

"It's the all-you-can-eat" seafood buffet tonight, my favorite," added Charlie, as they stumbled out of the bar into the cool gathering dusk.

Knowing Diz would head back to the reservation and Charlie

back to the Golden Gate afterward, they drove separately. Both were liable for driving-under-the-influence charges, had they been pulled over. They had driven around drunk so often they may well have been eligible for some kind of professional drunk driver designation, if such a thing existed. But neither of them were pulled over this particular Monday afternoon, and life was good.

Chain of Fools

Chapter 3: My Family's Heritage

Technically, I'm not a Stupidnski. Mine is a classic case of genealogical "too much information." Families lie; official records don't. I know damn well I'm not the first researcher to stumble upon an extra corpse or two tucked away in the family crypt. I won't be the last, either. The day I opened my crypt, one afternoon five months ago at the Minnesota Historical Society in St. Paul, I should have known some of my rotting ancestors would be leaping up from the grave, chasing me around those microfiche machines, photocopiers, and Soundex records with a bloody ax. It was bound to happen, especially given my family's heritage.

Paul Stupidnski, my grandfather, was the illegitimate son of my great-grandmother, Mary. Her maiden name was Uskiszyk, another ringer. I have no clue as to who might have knocked Mary up. She and her teenage son emigrated to America from Galicia.

Over the millennia, Galicia's been used and abused, like some geographical harlot. Dukes, grand duchies, princes, fiefdoms—a virtual laundry list of tyrants and their armies have swept across Galicia, burning villages, levying outrageous taxes, and preying on the local peasantry. It's a hilly, at times mountainous region, flanked on the south by the Carpathian Mountains. On a modern map, Galicia is located a few hundred kilometers southwest of Kracow. A century ago, the area was known for its failed potato crops and dismal poverty. It was, as Mary and my grandfather attested, a great place to get the hell out of.

So Mary sold everything she owned (including her body on several occasions), purchased two steerage tickets from a local dealer, jumped on board a freighter departing out of Gdansk in the summer of 1899, and steamed toward the promised land. No doubt Mary passed through Ellis Island with Paul, her fifteen year-old bastard, in tow and eventually landed in Minnesota, where she had relatives who'd fled their own Slovak malnutrition a decade earlier. There, near the edge of the tundra, she and my grandfather met in the winter of 1900. Speaking only Polish and unable to read or write, both immigrants felt right at home in the ethnic community that centered around Split Rock Township. Poor, hard working, and fertile, they were Catholic to a fault.

Mary Uskiszyk. married John Stupidnski in the spring of 1901. John was a dirt farmer working his 160-acre spread of boulder-riddled glacial till and mosquito-infested swamps in western Carlton County. John's first wife had died in childbirth along with the child she was hatching and, with several half-orphaned progeny already on his side of the aisle, John was in desperate need of domestic help. He put Mary to work, both on the farm and in his boudoir, that same day.

John was more than willing to take Mary's baggage, especially in light of the fact that her son Paul was seventeen when John and Mary tied the knot. Subsistence farming and hardy male teenagers are a perfect match. John not only picked up a wife but received the added bonus of a conscripted laborer, complete with no fringe benefits and an eighty-hour work week. The cows needed milking, chickens needed decapitating, fields needed to be plowed, fences mended: hell, the list was endless.

Because of the rural nature of life in northern Minnesota circa 1900, John never bothered to formally adopt Paul. Adoptions cost money and require additional paperwork. With no money and no one in the family able to read or write, filling out the necessary forms would have been a tedious ordeal. Familial consensus on the adoption idea was ultimately boiled down to "Why bother. Let's get back to bailing hay." Thinking Stupidnski was a trifle easier to pronounce than was Uskiszyk, Paul elected to use his new stepfather's name.

Granted, it's only 25 percent of the equation, but a quarter of me doesn't have a clue as to who I am. That's why I'm always 25% confused. When I'm in a semi-delusional, alcohol-induced, or reefer-wrecked state I like to think I'm related to any number of famous Poles. Who knows, my great-great-great grandfather could be Copernicus. He liked looking at the stars. I like looking at the stars.

There are others who might have sown their oats in my great grandmother, Mary. Madame Curie had a brother, Josef, who lived in Warsaw and was born in 1863. I could be related to the woman who discovered polonium. Joseph Conrad comes to mind. I like to write. He liked to write. His real name was Teodor Korzeniowski, so there's a pattern here. I could be Jewish for god's sake. Galicia held the greatest Jewish population in the world circa 1884. Maybe Mary took a tumble with the Liebowitz boy down the road. Then there's always that papacy connection. John Paul II was born in Kracow where his family has ties that run through the generations. His uncle might have knocked Mary up way back when. John Paul II certainly touted another great Polish name, Wojtyla, but I doubt the papal connection. Truth is, I'd rather the Jewish lineage. I guess I'm losing my faith.

More than likely my great-great-grandfather was just a horny stable boy. Mary probably brought a cow back to the barn a little later than usual, and you know how it went. A pile of hay, darkness descending, no one else in the barn, a bottle of mead , and two Catholic hotties. The young man, upon learning of Mary's condition, quickly stole a horse and rode off to Warsaw, where he later was shot and killed in a war everyone's forgotten. I'll never know my real lineage. It's like the blind-eye thing. What difference does it make?

There are no stories I recall hearing as to how Maggie Mishap and Paul Stupidnski met. The family farms were located near each other so chances are they could have found one another any number of ways. Maggie and Paul could have met at a church social in Kettle River, a village located about a mile from the Stupidnskis' dairy farm and less than five miles from the Mishaps' homestead. It might have been at an Oktoberfest put on by one of the Polish social clubs. Maybe they found each other at an autumnal hay ride through the back roads of Pine County. It could have been at a barn dance, a trip to the local seed store, or a friend of a friend's introduction.

What we do know is that when these two young sweethearts met, Maggie was sixteen and already saddled with her one-year-old payload of a previous liaison and Paul, exhausted and wanting nothing more than to get the hell out of his stepfather's forced labor camp, was a randy twenty-six. It was love at first sight—or partial sight for Maggie. They courted, fell in love, and decided to get hitched.

The marriage took place on a Saturday afternoon, May 13, 1911. Lucky thirteen. They tied the knot at St. Isidore's Catholic Church in Sturgeon Lake, Minnesota. St. Isidore is the patron Saint of farmers. It was springtime in the hinterlands—the lilacs were blooming, birds sang and, as the sunlight poured through the stained-glass windows of that quaint country church a century ago, love was in the air.

With Maggie's siblings and Paul's immense extended family, the church must have been filled to overflowing. Friends and relatives gathered afterward at the Mishap farm to celebrate this happy union of a whole bastard and a one-eyed woman. It was the happiest day of Maggie's life. It was the also the zenith of their relationship. By 1914, according to divorce documents filed fifteen years later, Paul would come home after an extramarital affair with an extramarital venereal disease.

Paul was never faithful, nor was Maggie. Both shared a strong genetic predisposition for the hard stuff. Over the next fifteen years of unhappy wedlock, Maggie would give birth to six additional Stupidnskis. One of those children, born in 1920, would be my father, Stanley.

Their firstborn child, Joseph Stupidnski, was a real piece of work. Born April 5, 1913, a year before Paul came home with his STD, Scarface Joe, his eventual nickname, had a whole freight train of issues. We'll get to Scarface later.

The Black Bear Buffet

The hostess at the buffet saw the two men approach her station and cringed. She knew them by name. They were what her manager referred to as buffet busters. She also knew, owing to the rules of engagement, that there was nothing she could do to stop them from skewing the profit-and-loss balance of the All You Can Eat buffet.

Diz, standing at six foot one and looking like a skinny washed-out warrior, hadn't eaten any solid food in days. Charlie, weighing in at just under 250 pounds and looking like a Caucasian sumo wrestler with health issues, was even more intimidating. It was Charlie who had masterminded this unique solution to his dietary needs. Whenever possible, Charlie ate one meal a day. That meal, day after day, week after week, was always consumed at the all-you-can-eat buffet in the Black Bear Casino restaurant.

The manager had never actually measured the volume of food these two men were capable of loading on their plates in a single pass because he didn't want to know. Whereas most patrons of these establishments use a modicum of restraint, neither Charlie nor Diz gave a rat's ass about seconds, thirds, fourths, or "farewell sucker" snacks as they called the plastic wrapped Danish pastries stuffed by the handful into their pockets and underwear before they snuck out the door. Hell, sometimes packages of Saltine crackers would come tumbling down their pant legs while they were working the slots past midnight.

About a month ago, in what he felt was a stroke of nutritional genius, Charlie had abandoned all sense of propriety. On that day, Charlie's tray became his plate. The idea came to him one afternoon during a luncheon buffet where he was growing frustrated with trying to pile the various salads and meats as high as possible onto his stupid little eight-inch plates. The plates were intentionally undersized, in hopes of containing the portions of the buffet's hungry patrons. When Charlie picked up his tray that afternoon he noted it was still warm, though a bit wet. He asked a waitress who happened to be passing by if the tray had just been washed.

"Of course," she replied. Querying the issue further, he asked if it was sanitized as were the plates, cups, and silverware.

"The state makes sure all our serving trays are sanitized," she confirmed. "It's just as clean as any of our dishes or silverware when it comes out of our dishwasher, sir."

Wrong answer. The waitress walked away, never realizing she had created a monster. The moment she was out of sight, Charlie grabbed a fistful of napkins, wiped his tray dry, and proceeded to load his food on it directly, no plates or saucers required.

This technique, much to the chagrin of the staff, allowed Charlie to virtually clean out a salad bar in a single pass. Most of the time it completely eliminated the need for seconds or thirds and, because of the half-inch lip on the tray, it cut down dramatically on the spillage that resulted from the astronomical heights of the portions he had formerly balanced there.

What was good for the carpeting was devastating for the buffet. Naturally there was a bit of a gross out factor, especially for the nice polite Minnesotans who ended up behind either of these two Huns in the buffet line. They watched in horror as Charlie plopped down a pound of mashed potatoes directly onto the plastic tray and smothered everything in gravy. They waited for the chefs to bring out more breaded shrimp as Charlie sometimes picked up the stainless warming bin and dumped the entire contents to his overflowing tray.

Once, a month ago, Charlie had tried ladling more than three bowls' worth of clam chowder onto the serving platter in a kind of volume soup experiment. It didn't go well. Although the tray held far more chowder than a standard soup bowl, the only way to transport it without excessive spillage involved dipping both of his thumbs into the hot soup and walking extremely slowly.

When he finally made it to his booth there was an unmistakable trail of white sauce, clams, and potatoes between the soup bar and his destination. Besides that, both thumb tips were badly scalded. Even worse, Charlie soon discovered that because of the flat surface, getting the chowder back up and out of the serving tray with a soup spoon took forever. As bad as the chowder experiment went, Charlie realized a chicken-noodle-soup trial would have been worse.

After the chowder disaster, he dropped the soup tray concept. If they made serving trays with slightly higher rims he would have worked it out. But they didn't.

The petite hostess knew all this as she watched the two men approach. She knew the snow crab clusters were going to be decimated. She knew the seafood Alfredo was going to be poured directly on the pasta, heaped on the skid-proof pattern of a fourteen-by-twenty-inch serving tray and she was well aware that more than a dozen patrons would gasp in disbelief as these two gourmands consumed inordinate amounts of the Black Bear's famous Monday-night buffet. But there was nothing the management could do. Two months ago, based on Charlie's consumption alone, they had raised both the luncheon and dinner buffet prices to offset his ability to gorge himself at their expense. Literally hundreds of patrons were now subsidizing Charlie's one-meal-a-day gluttony. Like water for a camel, Charlie was able to store the food in his ever-expanding stomach and survive for twenty-four hours straight on whatever they were serving. Roast beef, chicken, pork chops, Chinese night, and his all-time favorite the Monday-night-seafood spread all went down with equal resolve. Poison had crossed the manager's mind more than once, but the health department would have frowned on that solution.

"Dinner for two, please," said Charlie to the hostess, as they approached.

"Booth or table?" replied the hostess, who was thinking to herself that he should have said Dinner for eight, please.

"Booth," responded Charlie.

The seafood buffet spread was three dollars higher than the normal charge and five dollars higher than lunch. The surcharge never bothered Charlie and he seldom missed Monday nights. Diz didn't give a damn if it was seafood, barbecued ribs, or pancakes. Diz was so hungry at this point he would have eaten the napkins, provided he could ladle either gravy or maple syrup on them.

The two men sat down at their booth and within minutes the cocktail waitress came up to them. Management had learned that what they lost in food from these two barbarians they could at least partially recoup from liquor sales.

"Two brandy Sevens, please."

The waitress nodded and added, "Help yourself to the buffet." It killed her to say it to these two guys but it was part of her training. She felt like crying as she strolled away to get their cocktails.

Charlie and Diz got up, grabbed two trays, wiped them off with some table napkins, and started dumping fried fish fillets, cottage cheese, and whatever else they were serving directly onto them. The two men could hear whispered comments—"Oh, my God, will you look at that?" and "Can you believe it!"—criss-crossing the room as they ravaged the various stations. It didn't matter. Charlie and Diz, half drunk and starving, were immune to all forms of social pressure.

They dealt some fatal blows to the salad bar and piled on so many snow crab clusters that the tips of the crab legs reached their chins as they walked back to their booth. They made the clam chowder run separately—two bowls each.

After spending an hour and a half at the buffet, the men decided to head out on the floor and work the nickel slots awhile before calling it a night. Charlie had gambled all weekend and Diz, overcome with drowsiness caused by intense carbo loading, was barely able to keep his eyes open. By nine they were so tired they decided to part ways and head home.

After nearly falling asleep at one of the slots, Diz walked out of the casino without so much as saying good-bye. Twenty minutes later, Charlie followed him out.

Right beside the door, not twenty feet away, sat the Monte Carlo. It was jet black with white pinstripes running down the sides. This was it, thought Charlie. This was the key to Crystal's heart.

Charlie walked up to the car and looked inside: dark gray leather with black trim. He knew the model; it was the top of the line, limited-edition Monte Carlo Supercharged SS. The window sticker on the side told the rest of the story.

3800 Supercharged V6 with SFI, heavy duty four-speed automatic, performance suspension, 17-inch diamond-cut cast-aluminum wheels, dual exhaust, custom instrumentation with tachometer, race-inspired rear spoiler, dual-zone a/c, fog lamps, sunroof, cruise control, OnStar GPS navigation, boost gauge, tilt steering wheel, electronic traction control, AM/FM CD player with RDS and a six-speaker premium sound system with 200-watt auxiliary power, theft-deterrent alarm system with HomeLink transmitter, power steering, power seats, power mirrors, power windows....Power this, power that:

"Shit, this car has everything," Charlie mumbled to himself. "It should come with a separate bathroom, for christsake."

A lone security guard stood beside the car. He looked like he was seventy-five years old, dressed in a cheap security-guard outfit and doing his best to look official. His entire job consisted of keeping people from touching the shiny black surface of the Monte Carlo, or, if the patrons were really smashed, trying to get in and sit behind the wheel. Sometimes they'd ask him if he had the key, so they could just start her up, you know, see how she purrs. The security guard didn't have the key.

Of course, his other duty was to keep an eye on the Big Bertha slot machine that stood beside the car. They had built a special platform for Big Bertha to allow other gamblers to watch the players who were trying to win the car. When someone finally won, the machine was designed to set off all kinds of bells, whistles, and alarms to celebrate the event.

"She's a real beauty, huh?" Charlie said to the old man in the security outfit.

"Yeah, it's a nice car fer sure."

"Who won the Mustang?"

"Some gal from Hibbing. She came down with a bus load of seniors two weeks ago, put in her five dollars, pulled the handle, and up came the four cars."

"Lucky gal."

"Yeah, you can say that again."

Charlie didn't bother to say it again. He had a twenty-dollar bill—four chances—virtually burning a hole in his pocket.

"Mind if I give her a try?"

"Step right up and test your luck," answered the guard, encouraging Charlie, like he had a thousand patrons before him, to feed this Godzilla of a slot machine.

Charlie fed the twenty into the cash only slot, grabbed the

absurdly large handle, and pulled the lever down using both his arms. When the lever hit bottom, the four wheels began spinning, looking like a nickel slot under some enormous magnifying glass.

Then he waited—hoping, waiting, hoping, thinking of Crystal, waiting.

When the first wheel stopped at three cherries Charlie knew he was had. The Big Bertha was an all-or-nothing machine. You either aligned all four bars with the word car on them and walked out with the Monte Carlo, or you didn't win shit.

Long before the second wheel stopped at the number 7 or the third one at a golden-colored bell, Charlie knew his first pull was for naught. When the last wheel stopped at CAR, Charlie laughed. He'd already dumped over a hundred dollars into this one-armed bandit, and there wasn't a single pull when the word CAR didn't come up at least once. It usually came up twice, and one out of twenty times it came up on three of the four windows. It's designed to keep you hoping, Charlie said to himself.

He thought of Crystal as he pulled the giant handle a second time. Specifically, Crystal's tits, which were fake but nice. Big Bertha spit up CAR twice on the second pull, two shy of what he needed.

The third and fourth pulls were more of the same, just as they had been for the past three weeks, ever since the Monte Carlo had been parked where the Mustang once sat. Charlie couldn't have known that, on average, the casino could buy seven Monte Carlos with the amount of cash it took to get four contiguous cars aligned in the four windows of Big Bertha, on average being the operative term, because two years ago the casino gave away a brand-new Chrysler LeBaron four days after it went on display. It was, Charlie knew, a game of chance.

The security guard had been instructed to remind patrons of the Black Bear Casino of the infamous Chrysler LeBaron pull every time someone checked out the waxed-up Monte Carlo.

"She could be all yours for five bucks," he would add, as they looked at the $27,560 sticker price attached to the rear window. "That's what happened with the LeBaron, ya know."

The fourth and final pull actually got Charlie's heart racing. The first wheel stopped at car. He was in the game. The second wheel stopped at car. He thought of Crystal's tits again, this time with gusto. The third wheel stopped at a oversized lemon. He didn't even bother to wait for the fourth wheel to stop but mumbled some curse words, walked toward the front door, and, went out into the cold night air of northern Minnesota in October.

The security guard almost hollered over to him, when the last wheel said car, but he decided not to. What's the difference? the guard decided. You need all four to win.

*****

"You're going to get sick if you keep that shit up, Diz. Who the hell knows what that guy might have had."

"The alcohol kills all the germs, Charlie. That's the beauty of it."

"That's bullshit, Diz. It's just a dumb-ass thing to do. Sooner or later you're going to pay for that disgusting habit."

Charlie was referring to what Diz had just done. They were sitting at the Black Bear bar, watching the Vikings get clobbered by the Packers on TV, when the guy sitting next to them, having grown frustrated with the game, abruptly got up and walked out, calling the Viking's quarterback a "cocksucking idiot" as he left.

In his disgust he had abandoned a half-finished cocktail. With Dena blending a margarita and no one paying attention, Diz reached over, grabbed the glass, and drank it down in seconds. He then put the glass, save for a few ice cubes, back on the counter and licked his lips.

"Gin and tonic," Diz said to Charlie when their conversation resumed. "Good gin, too."

Charlie had seen Diz pull this gross stunt a hundred times before. Sometimes, after midnight, when Diz got less and less fussy, he'd pick up remnant cocktails sitting beside the slots or left for dead in the bingo room, silently making water rings on the wooden tables. Rum and Cokes, beer, white wine, red wine, unknown concoctions of various cordials, assorted call brands, and mixes would all get picked up, gulped, and set back down empty. On more than one occasion, Diz had accidentally swallowed an errant cigarette butt along with the backwash. Diz didn't mind. He swore the nicotine-soaked filters gave him a much-needed lift. Charlie didn't bother to pursue the topic any further. It was like lecturing a brick wall.

"You going to go see Crystal dance tonight? It's Saturday night. Doesn't she usually dance on Saturdays?"

"Yeah, she always dances on Saturday night. God, she's hot."

Diz didn't think Crystal was all that hot. In fact, Diz didn't even like the strip joint. He never understood why white guys found it so fascinating to watch women prance around bare naked in a smoke-filled room with rhythmic music blasting and drinks costing four times what they did just around the corner at the Riverside. Because of his dislike of strip joints, Diz never joined Charlie when he went to Sugar Daddies.

"You wanna join me?"

"Fuck, no. I can't afford the cover charge or the cost of those watered down drinks they serve. I'm broke, Chuck. I'm even thinking I might have to sell the car."

The car, thought Charlie. Whenever Diz was on a losing streak that lasted more than a couple of weeks he would start talking about selling the car. Charlie never told him it wasn't worth a pile of moose droppings.

The car was a half-rusted-out 1978, AMC Gremlin. The front window had a huge crack in it from a year ago when Diz ran into an eight-point buck. The tires were as bald as a baby's ass. The steering hadn't worked right since the collision. Not wanting to waste the venison, Diz had stuffed the mangled buck into his Gremlin; the backseat still had a funny odor, and blood-stains were everywhere. The interior had that fatal-car-wreck look to it.

To cover up the persistent odor, Diz had a dozen air fresheners hung around the inside of the vehicle. They were Christmas-tree shaped and dangled everywhere: off the inside door handles, the back of both driver and passenger seats, the rearview mirror (a total of three in that spot alone), under the backseat, and at several locations across the dashboard. The air fresheners helped to cover up the stench of the empty liquor bottles and beer cans scattered behind the driver's seat as well as the ashtray filled to overflowing with cigarette butts, roaches, and half-smoked cigars. But somehow or other, despite this onslaught of deodorants, the dead deer odor lingered, silently out-lasting Diz's host of purifiers.

Charlie knew the chances of selling Diz's vehicle for anything more than its weight in iron were nil. But that never stopped him from humoring Diz about his Gremlin's value.

"How much you figure you could get for her in today's market?" Charlie asked as though there were such a thing as a market for 1978 Gremlins.

"A lot, Chuck. She's a goddamn collectible." Diz said "Chuck" tersely, like it rhymed with muck. Which it does.

Charlie smiled at Diz in a way that easily could have been taken as a nod of reassurance but was in fact the essence of sarcasm.

"I figure at least a grand, with parts."

Most people wouldn't grasp what *"with parts"* meant, but Charlie did. The parts consisted of four other aging Gremlins, all up on blocks, located just behind Diz's mobile home on the reservation. For reasons unknown to anyone but Diz, he had been collecting broken down Gremlins since 1978, the last year of production for this misfit of an automobile, ranked fourth in the Worst Car of the Millennium contest. Diz had one classic, 73 model that had caught fire, two, 76 models, both from rollovers (only one with a fatality), and a faded red 78 model with a blown engine. All of them, except the one that was in the fire, were infested with rats, hornets' nests, and ants. Because the American Motors Corporation had gone out of business in 1987, parts for the Gremlin were all but impossible to find.

Ironically, Diz was probably right about the parts being worth something to other, equally eccentric, collectors of the infamous Gremlin, but Charlie felt the value of Diz's current car wouldn't top a hundred dollars on a good day.

"At least a grand, maybe more," Charlie repeated, dead serious, though he dared not look Diz in the eye as he said it.

"At least."

Whenever Diz spoke of selling his Gremlin, it confirmed that he had been on a losing streak. He had even resorted to the penny machines, which were incredibly tedious to play but tended to pay better than the nickel slots. It's never good when the penny slots turn on you. Diz would be low on cash until he got his monthly stipend from the tribal council, a stipend that came from money generated by the very slot machines he was addicted to. At this point, Diz didn't have enough money to buy a six-pack of Keystone beer, beer that sold for less than bottled water.

"Your luck will turn around, Diz. It always has."

"I don't know this time, Chuck. I need a change of pace. I've got the itch."

Charlie never liked it when he heard Diz say he'd got the itch, any more than when Diz called him Chuck. The itch wasn't good. It couldn't be scratched and it generally ended in hospitalization. Charlie knew Diz's history. He couldn't help but recall the story of how Diz got his first name and of how Diz's father met his untimely end.

Diz's full Indian name was Dismount Moose Nelson. His father was Eddy Wind Rider Nelson. Eddy spent most of his life attempting to live up to his name. He rode things.

He started young and he died doing it. When he was only thirteen, he bought a soapbox derby cart from a white kid in Cloquet, commandeered a dozen other teenage tribal members, sealed off all traffic in Jay Cooke Park, and attempted to ride the cart on Jay Cooke Drive from top to bottom. The vertical drop is more than six-hundred feet, complete with treacherous abutting cliffs, twisting hairpin turns, and the worst set of rapids in the Midwest running beside the road for half of its four-mile length.

Less than a mile into the run, approaching speeds of fifty miles an hour, Eddy lost control of the cart and plunged into the Saint Louis River. The brakes, designed for a quarter mile run down a gentle slope, had gone up in blue smoke half a mile earlier.

As fate would have it, Eddy plunged into a deep pool not far from where one of his friends was standing guard, keeping traffic at a standstill. His friend witnessed everything and immediately dove into the pool to retrieve Eddy. Aside from a broken arm and collar bone, multiple facial lacerations, a concussion, and a shattered kneecap, Eddy survived.

Less than two years later, Eddy was at it again. This time he was determined to ride the four major wild animals of northern Minnesota in his lifetime: the bear, the white-tailed deer, the woodland elk, and the unwieldy moose.

At fifteen, Eddy now weighed in at 110 pounds, so he decided to start with the bear. The black bear he chose to ride was familiar to him and to everyone else on the reservation. He was the local landfill bear, nicknamed Dumpy. Eddy and his friends managed to sedate Dumpy at the reservation garbage dump by using chunks of meat filled with more than enough pig tranquilizer to knock out a four-hundred pound animal. Having a little of the narcotic remaining, they conveniently divided the rest of it among themselves. Once the bear was knocked out, they duct taped his mouth shut, put multiple gunnysacks over each of Dumpy's monstrous paws, dragged him up into the bed of an old pickup, and trucked him to a small rodeo exhibition arena located just outside of Proctor, Minnesota.

Once they arrived, they dragged the sedated beast into a horse chute used by local cowboys during the summer rodeos and waited for the bear to come to enough to be able to stand up on all fours.

Eddy Wind Rider was ready. For the occasion Eddy had dressed in what he thought was a good cowboy outfit, but in all honesty, it more closely resembled that of a rodeo clown. At seven o'clock that evening, with the bear only half recovered from the pig tranquilizer and about as pissed off as any bear on earth, Eddy slid his skinny legs over the bear's massive front shoulders and told his friends to open the chute.

Hanging on to the thick neck fur of this raging animal, Eddy managed to ride him for seven terrifying seconds, which was the minimum time to qualify as a "wild ride" under the arbitrary rules established by Eddy and his group of derelict Indians. No one bothered to ask what Eddy was qualifying for.

Once thrown, Eddy realized it would only be a matter of seconds before two-inch bear claws would rip through the doubled-over gunnysacks and proceed to tear off the duct-tape muzzle, at which time this four-hundred-pound bear would immediately go about the business of trying to mutilate the kid who had just spent the last seven seconds on his back.

Eddy was right. The only problem was that Wind Rider and his friends had underestimated the amount of time it would take Dumpy to remove all their safety precautions by six of the ten seconds they had counted on. This was, no doubt, a pig-tranquilizer-inspired miscalculation.

Eddy had just made it over the wooden fence and was on his way toward the bed of the pickup when he discovered that Dumpy hadn't bothered to climb the fence; he just put his head down and ran straight through it. Had it not been for the fact that his friends were by then already in the pickup, with the motor running and the tailgate down, Eddy would have been mauled and in all probability killed by the bear.

But Eddy managed to jump into the truck bed just seconds before Dumpy arrived. As they sped away, laughing like lunatics, the bear stood up and gave out a blood-curdling growl that Eddy never forgot. He decided right them he would never take any garbage to the landfill again, just in case Dumpy recognized him.

In the end, Eddy Wind Rider died while trying to ride falling trees. He was thirty-six when he left Diz fatherless.

*****

"Don't go trying to scratch that itch, Diz. You know damn well you always end up hurt when you do."

"Ain't nothin' gunna hurt me this time, Charlie. I'm immune."

Immune my ass, thought Charlie. "Well, it's time to hit the floor, then off to Sugar Daddies to see my girl."

"She ain't your girl, Charlie. She still calls you John for christsake. All she sees in you is another twenty dollar bill stuffed down her G-string."

"Not after I win the Monte Carlo."

"Yeah. Right after the pope starts shitting rubber nickels," added Diz.

Charlie smiled that same sardonic smile and set down his empty drink. He had made sure he finished it to the last drop to prevent Diz from lapping up what was left after he walked away. Charlie said good by to Dena and started heading out toward the hundreds of one-armed sirens calling out to him.

"See you at the luncheon buffet tomorrow, Diz?"

"Maybe. My cousins are stoppin by in the morning."

"Maybe not," mumbled Charlie, knowing what usually happened next.

*****

Sunlight never penetrates the inner sanctum of Sugar Daddies strip club. It is not welcome. The last time any sunlight fell on the cement floors of the joint was just before the trusses went up seven and a half years ago. The club has no windows and the entrance to the main room is offset by a dark, narrow hallway preventing any outside light from somehow breaching the smokey interior. The club is open from five p.m. until closing but once inside, it is eternally, everlastingly, a little past midnight.

After dumping half his winnings, nearly forty dollars, into eight more pulls chasing the elusive Monte Carlo, Charlie arrived at Sugar Daddies at 10:45 p.m. Once inside, it was just a little after midnight, as always.

Crystal Lovelock was not dancing when Charlie paid the eight dollar cover and made his way to the edge of the runway. A new girl was working the pole over, and she had talent. Charlie sat down next to

- 42 -

some guys he didn't recognize and laid a stack of twenty single dollar bills along the edge of the dance floor. He had come to do business.

The new girl, although busy rubbing her ass against the brass pole like a cat in heat, was quick to note the pile of cash in front of this heavy set John who had just walked in. She started undulating toward him before Charlie had time to order a cocktail. By sheer coincidence, his waitress and the stripper arrived at the exact same time.

"Vodka seven," Charlie yelled over the blaring techno-pop music the new stripper was dancing to.

With the exotic dancer now within a few feet of him, Charlie never took his eyes off her. She was young, maybe nineteen, twenty at most. She wasn't very pretty but damn, did she have a body on her, thought Charlie to himself.

She smiled that stripper smile and kneeled down on the raised dance floor right in front of her newfound mark and his stack of singles. With her bare tits barely touching the hardwood dance floor she moved her face, her tongue extended in a licking motion, directly toward Charlie. The cash slid between her tits as her tongue came within inches of Charlie's mouth.

Charlie waited for her to retreat, grabbed three dollar bills and tucked them into the side of her g-string. She winked at him, stood up and sauntered back to her brass pole, never once losing the rhythm of the music. Homely but talented, concluded Charlie in his preliminary review of the new girl, whose introduction he had missed while coming in.

Charlie knew the rules. You should never kiss, suck on or lick them. You not supposed to touch them when they're on the floor or when you're getting a lap dance. Everyone, except the drunks, obeyed the floor rule but no one bothered with the lap dance rules, especially when it comes to their tits. No one touches them down below, unless it's after the club closes and the touching, along with additional benefits, had been previously arranged and paid for. They're not hookers, thought Charlie, they're exotic dancers.

By the time the vodka seven arrived another dancer was getting ready to take the floor. She had just been introduced by her stage name, Candy Cotton.

Candy was far and away the club's best dancer. She came out dancing to the always popular *American Woman* by the Guess Who. Candy was aptly named.

For this particular performance she walked out wearing a very, very tight secretarial outfit, complete with horn rimmed glasses and black, stiletto heels. Candy looked like a temp from Satan's Secretarial Services, Inc. The temp who leaves a trail of bloody divorces behind her. Her long, bottle-blond hair was wrapped up in a tight little bun atop her lovely head and her lipstick was a dark, blood red. She held a stenographer's pad in her left hand and a Bic pen in her right. Secretary Candy was taking dictation, so to speak.

Bypassing the pole she walked directly over toward a heavy-set lumberjack type sitting further down the runway from Charlie. She sat down along the end of the dance floor and crossed her legs, then proceeded to pretend she was taking some kind of executive memo from this paper mill employee of the week.

Wanting Candy never to leave, he immediately reached into his wallet, found his last five spot and tucked it hurriedly into her cleavage. Moving deliciously to the music, Candy immediately uncrossed her legs, and in a motion that can only be described as liquid, wrapped both her legs around the neck of this pulp worker and gave him a long, glorious look toward a lush valley he would never, ever be allowed to play in.

Then Candy got up, flung the notepad and pen to the lusting audience and strode toward the pole. At that moment in time, every man in the club wanted nothing more than to be that pole.

Candy, in her ultra-tight wool skirt, worked her pelvis up and down that cold brass until you could have swore it started to move with her. It wasn't dancing. It was some form of organic welding. The sparks Candy made were illuminating the eternal midnight with the dull glow of lust.

Tongues hit the filthy cement floor and never wanted to leave it. Dollar bills came out of shirt pockets, as reawakened men rifled through their wallets hoping they had something, anything left to tempt this harlot their way. Candy, cool and in control, started taking it off.

She slowly, almost insidiously, unbuttoned her blouse. With Burton Cummings lyrics warning everyone in the club, screaming, "gonna mess your mind," Candy threw her white blouse on the floor revealing a bra that must have been put on using a come-along. Her tits screamed to be free.

Candy left the pole, now wearing only her tight skirt and a lacy, Victoria's secret-style bra. She still wore her horn-rimmed glasses. The crowd went wild.

She slithered to the floor and got down on all fours, her ass facing

Charlie but her breasts within inches of an off duty cop from Cloquet. A cop whose wife would have shot him with his own Glock had she known he was at Sugar Daddies that night. The cop, sitting with a fair sized stack of bills, immediately put one in his mouth and invited Candy to come get it. Candy was more than willing to oblige. She rhythmically edged her tits to this officer's mouth, eventually burying his face into what must have seemed like heaven to him. When she stood back up the dollar was wedged in between her cleavage. As she sauntered away the cop had to double check his own weapon to be certain their wasn't an accidental discharge during the incident. There was.

God, Candy was sex personified, surmised Charlie. She returned to the pole, grinding it down another several millimeters, then tore off her Valcro-attached skirt revealing a tiny g-string beneath it. The bra came off next then, finally, she ditched the horn rimmed glasses. In a glorious gesture of feminine freedom, Candy pulled the hairpin out of her bun and shook her long blond hair loose with wild, almost reckless abandon. This is the kind of secretary every mid-level executive dreams of. A temp with the emphasis on TEMPtation.

Knowing Candy would probably head his way the next time out, Charlie took all but two bucks off the edge of the dance floor. Formerly an accountant, Stupidnski was a realist. Of course he wanted Candy. There wasn't a man in the club that night that didn't want Candy. There were two lesbians sitting off in a corner who wanted Candy. All the bartenders, bouncers and bar boys wanted Candy. Candy wanted Candy.

But Charlie knew it wouldn't work. Candy was nineteen and Charlie was fifty-two. Mathematically it was doable that Candy might have been Charlie's grand daughter. It just didn't sit right with Stupidnski. It reminded him too much of his heritage. Besides that, weighing in at 256 earlier that day and living in the Golden Gate Motel precluded any chance of spending any quality time with Candy. Even the Monte Carlo wouldn't impress this masterpiece of hand-carved estrogen.

So Charlie, like most of the men in the club, sipped in her exotic visuals like a fine cognac and let it go at that. Candy Cotton was too hot for an old man like Stupidnski and he knew it. He remained faithful to Crystal, though that faith was being tested as the lyrics reminded him, "American woman, stay away from me!"

With her hair loose, her tits unleashed and her undulating ass sparking against the brass like a grinding operator working overtime, men literally melted. Several of the regulars sitting in the front row took their right hands off the dance floor and God only knew where those lonely hands vanished to. Actually, God didn't want to know. Neither did Candy or the cleaning staff.

Candy left the pole for the last time. She headed straight toward Charlie. She noticed that his substantial pile of cash had mysteriously dwindled to two godforsaken dollar bills but hell, it's still money, she thought as she gyrated directly in front of him. Crouching down, working her ass back and forth, sideways and front ways in what best can be described as unfuckingbelievable, Charlie took the two dollars in his hand and, synchronizing it with the fluid motion of her glorious hips, carefully slid the money into her g-string. Candy winked at him just as the song tapered off with..."Goodbye, American woman, Goodbye American chick, Goodbye American broad..."

When the music stopped, Candy made a sweep of the dance floor, picking up any number of singles, fives and a lone ten-spot along with her clothes, threw a kiss and headed back to the dressing room via the plastic bead-covered opening. Candy knew she would pick up several hundred dollars more tonight doing lap dances for the next hour and a half until she was scheduled to come out and dance to the tune of *Wild Thing* just after twelve fifteen.

I hope Crystal's up soon, prayed Charlie. God, I love watching her.

Crystal didn't dance next. After Candy came Mercedes Bends, then came the always popular Ginger, then Cinnamon Lollipop and the new black dancer, Shariqua and as the real midnight came 'round Charlie started to wonder if Crystal hadn't called in sick.

Around 12:30 Charlie caught the eye of Ginger, who was working the dwindling crowd doing lap dances and, waving a handful of ones, flagged her down. When Ginger sat down on his knee, Charlie took out a five spot and started asking questions. Ginger wasn't surprised, knowing Charlie had a huge crush on Crystal.

"What's up with Crystal tonight?"

"She's having trouble with her costume."

"She's not doing the school girl dance tonight?"

"No, Jimmy says it's not cutting it any more, so he's asked her to come up with something new. Something original and exciting."

"Sounds hot, Ginger. Do ya know when she'll be coming on?"

"Soon, but I'm not sure her new dance is going to work out either."

"Why's that?"

"You'll see."

Ginger took Charlie's five bucks, got up, and continued stalking. Charlie scratched his head, perplexed by Ginger's comments. Still, what Ginger said didn't come as any great surprise to him.

At 38, Crystal Lovelock was the oldest dancer working at Sugar Daddies. Her once illustrious career was not what it was when she was still in her late twenties. The bloom was off the rose, and her former reputation, right along with her income and her ass, were starting to sag.

Crystal Lovelock wasn't her real name. Her real name was Lois Carlson. She was from Esko, Minnesota, not ten miles down the road from the club. Lois had wanted to be a grade school teacher, not an exotic dancer. Things happened and plans changed accordingly, or mis-accordingly as in Crystal's case.

At exactly 1:15, with Charlie losing faith and the crowd noticeably starting to thin, the DJ announced that the next dancer would be Crystal Lovelock doing an all new routine called, "It's time for sinning."

Charlie took out what was left of his stack of ones, a mere six dollars, and fixed his eyes on the bead-draped entrance, anxiously awaiting Crystal's new routine. The DJ put on Richard Palmer's *Addicted to Love,* and the stage lights dimmed.

Crystal slithered out and jaws dropped. She was dressed as a nun. She had a long, black habit complete with the coif, the scapular, the veil and a simple, hand-woven belt. Her attention to detail was impressive. Her outfit was modeled after an order called The Daughters of Mercy of the Immaculate Conception, which she had discovered on the Internet, and it had taken her weeks to order, then sew and modify all the accessories. In keeping with her Catholic theme, Crystal strutted on stage twirling two long, wooden rosaries.

The reaction from the remaining cache of local drunks was immediate and grim. A dreaded hush of sinfulness came over the club. Mens hands, where moments before had been committing lewd and lascivious acts, quickly returned into view. Lap dances grinded, literally, to a halt.

As the nun approached the brass pole some patrons grew so uncomfortable they simply got up and walked out, leaving there half-filled drinks abandoned. Diz would have loved it. Several of the bartenders asked for forgiveness, swearing they would look for other employment come Monday morning.

Crystal started working the pole in her long, black habit. She knew instinctively her new dance routine wasn't working but she was committed. Trying to save face and stir up some excitement, she whipped the two rosaries into the crowd. No one dared to lift a finger to catch them. They fell to the floor untouched and the following week a rumor spread around Scanlon they made a sizzling sound, complete with a puff of pale-blue smoke, upon landing.

As Crystal undulated and squirmed beneath her habit several fallen Catholics in the club became nauseous and left for the men's room, not to do what they usually did, but to throw up. Jimmy Cortese, the club's owner, looked on with horror as Crystal's new dance unfolded.

It got worse. Crystal, sticking to her original dance plan, loosened the front of her habit, got down on all fours and awkwardly crawled around the dance platform hoping the guys would want to look down her habit at the huge tits hidden beneath her outfit.

No one looked. There wasn't a man in the place that could muster up the courage to peer down a nuns habit without the secret fear of burning in hell. Besides, crawling around on all fours in a nuns outfit is all but impossible. Two guys sitting just across Charlie started to laugh, hesitantly at first, then hysterically as Crystal kept getting caught up in the habit's fabric as she tried to tempt the crowd into some form of unorthodox voyeurism. Crystal finally made to the nearest patron, who quickly made a sign of the cross and ran out of the strip club.

She stood up, and in a desperate attempt to save what was left of her routine, tore off her Valcro-attached outfit in a single motion. Beneath the habit she was wearing thigh high patent leather boots and a very sexy S&M outfit. But it was too late. The damage was done.

No one could work past The Daughters of Mercy of the Immaculate Conception image and no one was buying Crystal's new routine. Not even Charlie, though he had tears in his eyes out of sympathy for what Crystal was going through. He was more than half-tempted to go punch the two assholes in the face for laughing at his girl but decided it would probably only make Jimmy more upset than he already was.

Praying Crystal wouldn't dare try working the crowd for lap dances wearing her nuns outfit, Charlie didn't feel like hanging around either. He figured Crystal might be let go after this debacle and started wondering what would happen to their relationship if he couldn't find her at Sugar Daddies any more.

Crystal was still dancing as Charlie stood up to leave. Her new routine, the one she hoped would turn her aging career around, was a bomb and, if you looked closely, you could see that she was teary eyed.

Charlie tossed his six dollars out into the runway, got up and headed toward the door. He wanted to do something. If only I could win that Monte Carlo, he dreamed. Then I could save her. Then I could set us both free.

Chain of Fools

Chapter 4: Maggie's Sorry Brood

After their wedding, the next decade went as well as could be expected for Mr. & Mrs. Paul Stupidnski. Sure, there was the 1914 venereal disease that Paul brought back from one of his logging camps, but they worked through it. Then there was little Joe Stupidnski, born with some, how shall we say it politely, learning disabilities.

In 1913, the year Joe was born, no one understood the relationship between drinking, chain smoking and fetal development. Needless to say, One-Eyed Maggie loved to party and, while it's impossible to know for certain, the odds are that Joseph was born with fetal alcohol syndrome. When he did his first stretch at Redwing, the State's reform school located in Redwing, Minnesota, they tested his IQ. Young Joseph Stupidnski scored an 83.

Maggie kept drinking. Paul kept knocking her up and the children kept coming. Andrew, their second boy, was born in 1914. Lizzy, their first girl, was born in 1916. Edward, who would later become deaf, was born in 1919 and my father, Stanley, or Stauch as everyone came to call him, arrived in 1920. Irene would arrive a few years later, along with some paternity issues that linger to this day.

I can only speculate as to where the Stupidnskis resided during their first decades of marriage. The scant records indicate their first few years were spent in Pine County. They never owned a house, so searching real estate records proved useless. They probably rented out old farm houses or stayed not far from where I'm living now—in Cloquet, Carlton or Moose Lake. Paul worked as a laborer and a logger, and there were plenty of nearby forests to cut down, railroad tracks to lay and fields to clear, so he kept himself busy.

As a provider, Paul was not reliable. He had a nasty habit of vanishing, sometimes for months on end. Back in the twenties, with the roads unpaved, transportation only as fast as a horse's gallop, telephones rare, and most of northern Minnesota essentially wilderness, it would have been easy enough for Paul to fall off the grid. He had a penchant for solitude and Maggie, with her drinking and attitude, was probably impossible to live with for more than a month at a time. So Paul would just up and leave, taking whatever money they had with him and making life a financial headache for Maggie and her brood of miscreants.

Undoubtably, they kicked around various small towns and any number of low-rent properties until they moved into the thriving metropolis of Duluth sometime before 1920. That's when they show up again, counted as a family in the 14th census of the United States of America. At that time they were living in the worst part of Duluth, down below the tracks in a neighborhood known as Helm Street. Long since demolished under the auspices of urban renewal, Helm Street was a derelict assortment of tenement slums, small, poorly constructed wood frame houses, knitting mills and breweries. The perfect spot for Maggie and her litter.

The only incident that bears mention during their first ten years, aside from Paul's infidelities, is the story of Uncle Ed's deafness. Since Ed was born in 1919, I had always assumed he had come into this world born with his handicap. My mother reluctantly informed me some years ago it wasn't the case.

According to her, Ed's deafness was a result of a severe blow to the head by his father when Ed was just a toddler. Like Maggie's eye decades earlier, the deafness came about because no one bothered to bring Ed to see a doctor after the incident. No doubt there was some concern about the Minnesota Child Welfare Board asking questions as to why or how a father could hit his child so hard as to induce deafness. So they kept little Eddy at home until he couldn't hear a goddamn thing. Given the way his parents fought Eddy's deafness was a blessing.

In the end, Ed's handicap helped him escape the Stupidnski household long before my father made it out. Ed shows up at the Minnesota School for the Deaf as a pupil in the 1930 census. Although the State had tried to take uncle Ed from Maggie several times during the mid-1920s, Maggie never quite understood what they wanted him for, so he didn't get out of this household from hell until he was 10. He was one of the lucky ones. Uncle Ed has long since left this earth, having died in 1993 from cardiac arrest. He wasn't dumb though, having learned to speak aloud at the school for the deaf in Fairbault, Minnesota. He could also sign fairly well, but what I remember most about uncle Ed are the notes he and my mother used to pass back and forth across the kitchen table when I was just a child. They would talk to each other via notepad, which as a child I always thought was kind of amazing. Strangely enough, Ed Stupidnski never drank, though he had good reason to.

Despite a couple of setbacks, the first ten years of my grandparent's marriage were relatively calm. It was only after the start of prohibition that the shit hit the fan. Between 1920 and 1930 the story of One-Eyed Maggie and the chronic deserter Paul takes on a tawdry life all its own.

For Maggie, with her moonshine making skills, January 16th, 1920, the day prohibition began in America, was a godsend. As much as that date was a moment in time celebrated by the religious minority who had worked for years to banish John Barleycorn from the land, Maggie celebrated January 16th for exactly the opposite reasons. From that day forward she really didn't need Paul or his meager lumberjack earnings. Maggie was now in the bootlegging business, and business was booming. Within a year One-Eyed Maggie had forgotten all about her children and started operating an illegal blind pig out of her rented shack down on Helm Street.

If you're not familiar with the term, "Blind Pig," don't be bothered by it. The term came about in the late 1800s when certain counties across the nation started enacting county-wide prohibition. In order to sell liquor legally, proprietors could advertise the fact that you could pay $2 to come in and see a "Blind Pig", and the liquor inside was free. That's how they avoided the laws against selling booze outright.

There were other names like "Blind Tiger" used as well, but the most familiar name was "Speakeasy"—and everyone is familiar enough with that one.

There is still some doubt as to whether or not these early years included Maggie doing some after hours work on her backside but, according to some of the parole officers and welfare workers who visited the house back then, it appeared as if Maggie was for rent. From 1920 to 1930, things got progressively worse. Much, much worse.

Rendezvous Bar

"I'll tell you what I can't stand, Rudy. I'll tell you what burns my ass worse than all the other crap out there combined. It's Manifest Destiny. That's the real bullshit. Manifest fucking destiny."

Diz was drunk. Fall down drunk. Slurring your words drunk. Angry drunk.

Bruce, the bartender at the Rendezvous had heard a variation of Diz's manifest destiny discourse at least a hundred times before. Rudy, half listening, half following the muted football game on the TV hanging above the bar, had listened to it at least half that many times.

Diz continued. "Columbus didn't discover America. There were fifty million people living in the America's when he arrived. Columbus was an asshole. All the explorers were assholes."

Diz took a long, deep drink of his tap beer and went on. "Take the Arawaks. You've heard of the Arawak Indians. Right, Rudy?"

Rudy nodded. He had no idea who the Arawaks were. Sensing the outrage in Diz's tone, Rudy didn't want to get him upset. Rudy could see how plastered Diz was. Drunk, angry and Indian is a dangerous combination.

"When Colombus got off his goddamned *Santa Maria* and landed on Hispaniola in 1492 there were millions of Arawaks living on that island. Millions. They welcomed the Spanish, offering them water, fish, fruit—hell, they offered them their women. What did Colombus and his gang of thieves do to thank them? They killed them. At one point in time they had 30 sets of gallows going 24 hours a day just hanging the heathen savages. What the gallows didn't take, slavery, smallpox and diseases finished off. Fifty years later, do you have any idea how many Arawaks were left on their own island? Do you, Rudy?"

"No, Diz. How many were there?" Actually Rudy suspected the answer but played along.

"None, Rudy. Not one Arawak survived the torture, slavery, hanging and diseases all brought over by the self-proclaimed civilized people of Europe. Civilized, my ass! We offer them gifts and they bring us blankets contaminated with smallpox. Who the hell are the real savages here, Rudy. That's what I want to know."

Diz looked down at his near empty glass and started crying. He looked pathetic. One lonely drunken Indian railing against the white man's world on a solitary bar stool at the run down Rendezvous Bar on State Highway 210 in Sawyer, Minnesota on a frigid, mid-November afternoon. Rudy didn't care about manifest destiny or Diz's sad soliloquy. Rudy was wondering if the Broncos were going to pull off an upset and whether or not his wife, Linda, had remembered to take the venison roast out of the freezer in time to thaw for dinner.

Bruce, the veteran bartender, didn't give a damn about the Arawaks, the Hopi or the drunken Chippewa presently sitting at his bar. Bruce's only big concern was making sure Diz paid in advance for every tap beer he was inhaling. Nor did Bruce give a shit about the fact that he probably should have stopped serving Diz three beers ago. Bruce was used to serving the local Fond du Lac tribesman more than they should. Half of the tribe drank, and drank excessively.

Alcoholism, substance abuse, poverty, rage, suicide, despair, dropping out, crime, sex, violence, gangs, spouse abuse, child neglect, anger, imprisonment, depression, juvenile delinquents... these were the engines that freighted the 21st century Native Americans to nowhere. It was the same here as it was in Bad River, Red Lake and Pine Ridge. Five hundred years after Columbus, the systematic genocide of the Native Americans was still underway, only the strategy had changed. It was no longer necessary to eradicate the Indians so long as they were able to take on the task themselves. Diz was no exception to this sad equation.

Bruce liked Indians well enough, and he knew they suffered more than they should. Even the casinos didn't help all that much. They helped some, but only a handful of the tribe derived any real benefits from the gaming boom. Most lived in the same squalid conditions that existed before the casinos arrived and Bruce knew all too well Diz was one of them.

"I'll tell you what I'd like to do, Rudy. I'd like to piss on them. I'd like to piss on Columbus, piss on DeSoto, piss on Washington and piss on all of 'em."

Upon saying it aloud, Diz realized he needed to take a piss.

Rudy wasn't listening to Diz, instead watching the Saints conduct a brilliant goal line stand against the Broncos with less than 15 seconds left in the game. Rudy didn't think the Broncos were going to make it in.

Diz slid down off his bar stool and stumbled a bit on his feet before regaining his balance. He headed toward the john, walking past the silent juke box, the fake neon signs displaying the dancing blue waters of a Hamms beer ad and the generic, Formica-topped tables and black vinyl chairs that sat empty this wintry afternoon.

The bathroom reeked of urine and hadn't been cleaned in a week. Diz stood, wobbling, and worked to undo his fly to take a leak. His head was spinning, so he leaned it against the wall as he urinated. It felt unbelievably good to piss out some of the excess liquid the beer had drowned him in. As the piss ran down the drain he started thinking about ordering another draft. He wasn't sure he had any more money, so he thought he should check first.

Finishing up, with some urine still dribbling out, Diz zipped up and walked over to the sink to wash his hands. The mirror above the sink reflected a face he hardly recognized. It was his face but it wasn't his face. It was the face of too many contemporary Indians. The face of something broken.

His ruddy, dark complexion was typical of many of the northern Chippewas. Deeply pocked from teenage acne, Diz's skin wasn't red but a sand-colored brown. His hair was dark black, greasy and uncut, hanging down in tangled strands that almost touched his shoulders. He had on a plaid cotton shirt, dirty jeans and a ratty jean jacket. His eyes were dark—sad, half-tear-filled and as brown as the soil of Carlton County. His teeth were bad. Years of neglect had left them deeply yellowed or missing altogether. He was gaunt. Thin but not a healthy thin. At 46 years old, Diz looked to be pushing 60. He hadn't weathered well.

Diz washed his hands without using any soap and splashed some water on his face in an effort to wake up enough to keep drinking. Then he remembered to check to see if he had any money left. He reached into his pants pocket only to find the un-smoked stub of an old ditch-weed joint, some rolling papers that were all glued together from sweat and some chewing gum. He tried his other pocket.

In that pocket he found 37 cents in change, an old rubber johny that had been in his pocket for years, half a pack of Camel straights, and no cash. Diz realized he would have to head back to his trailer to see if he had any liquor stashed away somewhere or other. He knew that was unlikely.

For an instant, Diz thought about lighting up the ditch-weed roach but knew Bruce would get pissed off at him if he had. Bruce doesn't like the customers walking into a john that reeks of marijuana, even if you'd have to smoke a bale of Diz's shit to get high.

Diz realized he'd have to go out to his Gremlin, hope like hell it would start, and drive north past Big Lake along a lonely county road and head home. He wouldn't make the Sunday night buffet line as he had promised Charlie the day before. He would be passed out by six p.m. and sleep through mid-morning on Monday. He went out to say good-bye.

"I've got ta go."

"Drive careful, Diz. Sorry about Columbus and shit," said Rudy sympathetically.

"Me too. Later, Rudy. Later, Bruce."

Diz threw down his 37 cents as a tip and walked toward the door. He looked up at the ten point buck hanging above the doorway and smiled. His dad had ridden a ten point buck once, but that was long, long time ago.

Mercifully, the Gremlin started and Diz backed out of the parking lot without checking to see if anyone was coming. No one was. It they were, they would have t-boned Diz's rusty Gremlin in a heartbeat. Diz didn't give a shit one way or the other.

He drove exactly the same as he walked, stumbling drunk but much, much faster. Diz never passed any police officers on his ten mile drive home. With his Gremlin all over the roadway, they would have arrested him and slapped another DUI onto his record. He didn't need another DUI. It would have been his fourth.

There was no one in his trailer when he pulled in. Sometimes his sister would come over and stay at his place when her husband took to beating her. Sometimes his cousins would hang out and drink at his place for a change of scene. Today, his trailer sat empty.

He opened the unlocked front door, turned the propane heater up a notch and headed toward the couch. He lay down on it and fell asleep within minutes, dreaming of the days when Indians hunted elk and harvested wild rice along the northern shore of Lake Superior. Dreamed of days gone by, days that only dreams could hope to find.

*****

Charlie hadn't been out of his room for more than a few minutes at a time over the last 72 hours. At that the only trips he had made were to the nearby One Stop Liquor store or the Erickson Gas Station for cigarettes and candy bars. He was in a funk.

After Diz failed to join him for his buffet dinner at the Black Bear Casino on Sunday, Charlie started descending into what he, and his ex-wife, referred to as, "the blacks." He had pulled into the One Stop on Sunday evening at seven and purchased a full 1.75 liter of Petri vodka. Never a good sign. Charlie Stupidnski knew what was coming.

A third of the bottle was gone by nine o'clock. No mix, no ice needed. He was drinking it straight out of the bottle, staring down the $11.99 day-glow price tag every time he took another slug. As he became more and more drunk Charlie became more and more depressed. Thinking the booze could somehow cure him of his depression he kept drinking until he passed out. This occurred just past eleven that night.

When Charlie woke up the following morning, hung over and alone, he tried to sober up. He sat down and turned on his laptop and tried working on his memoir. Nothing happened. As he stared at his laptop screen it stared back. He rifled through his notes in hopes of finding something, anything that would inspire him and found nada. His files, filled with death certificates, ancient newspaper clippings, and old census forms meant nothing to him. When he fell into the blacks, everything meant nothing.

An hour later he cracked the vodka back open and restarted the annihilation machine. By noon the bottle was nearing empty. Lying on his bed, looking up, he noticed the continents were back in motion. A week earlier a fierce winter storm had pushed through, mixing rain with snow, shoving its moisture up and under the eaves, inadvertently changing the shape of the stains. South America was getting bigger. Antarctica remained the same. If the roof kept leaking the two continents would touch each other within a month, quietly reforming a part of Pangea. Ceiling cartography. It meant nothing, thought the drunken, desolate alcoholic lying beneath the damp ceiling. Absolutely nothing.

Charlie remembered he was hungry, drunk and hungry. Missing Monday nights seafood buffet was killing him but driving to the casino in his present condition was impossible. The One-Stop was just around the corner. He could take a crap, a shower and sober up just enough to stumble over to the liquor store and reload.

The television was on. Always on. Ironically, it was blaring the Jerry Springer Show to the lonely drunk lying there, staring at a stained ceiling and thinking about getting up and taking a crap. Charlie might well have been a deaf mute for all the impact the show was having on him.

He didn't hear the estranged wife pleading with her husband to take her back after stabbing him 23 times with a kitchen fork. He didn't hear about her husband sleeping with one of the tenants at their mobile home park, collecting in flesh what this poor, not-very-attractive black woman could not come up with in cash.

"How can I forgive you?" asked the husband. "After this." He lifted up his shirt to display hundreds of tiny scars where the fork tines had penetrated his pale white flesh time and time again.

"But I love you, and I've always loved you." Pleaded his wife, now kneeling before him in a wretched, pitiful display of atonement.

Springer intervened, announcing he had a surprise for both of them. Moments later, the black woman whom the husband was banging when his wife walked into the double wide walked on the set. Upon seeing her, the wife went ballistic. So did the ratings.

"You bitch, you lousy (bleeping) whore!" His wife screamed as she lunged at the homely black woman. Her husband, still not able to forgive her for the multiple stab wounds, heroically stepped between them, trying to avoid the unavoidable cat fight. His wife kicked him in the balls, then viciously grabbed hold of the black woman's hair with her left hand and started punching her in the face with her right hand clenched in a angry fist.

Springer's security crew jumped into action, putting the wife into a stranglehold and pulling the two women apart just as Charlie flipped the bathroom light on. As he sat down on the toilet, a toilet forever straining beneath Charlie's obesity, the Jerry Springer show broke for commercials. Jerry had just enough time to inform his television viewing audience to stick around because, unbeknownst to the wife, the husband or the battered black woman, they were about to bring in the couples two teenaged children to see how all of this violence has effected them.

Charlie could have been one of those kids, though he paid no attention at all to the noise emanating from the perpetual cable TV. He could have explained the cost of all those sleepless nights he spent as a child listening to his parents rage against one another through the hot air duct of one of the many low-rent homes they lived in over the years. He could have told Jerry that the damage was done. That he, in turn, had left his wife and three kids seven years ago after waking up one morning in a bedroom located in a house built in a neighborhood in a country on a planet he felt utterly disconnected to.

Charlie could tell the lowlife-loving audience about how he got into his car that morning, kissed his wife goodbye as always, petted their golden retriever, turned on the ignition and started driving to his CPA firm like he had every morning for sixteen consecutive years. Then, he likewise could explain that, instead of turning onto the Lake Avenue exit as he had ten thousand times before, he simply pointed the car down Interstate 35 and drove, without sleeping, all the way to Dallas, Texas.

The audience would have been fascinated with the fact that he never bothered to pick up the phone to let his wife and kids know he was still alive until two horrid weeks had passed. Weeks of missing persons reports, rumors of murder, suicide and a police investigation that led nowhere. When he did call, all he told his wife was that he wouldn't be coming back. No discussion needed.

He didn't have the courage to even talk to his three kids, nor has he spoken with any of them since that morning seven years ago. He could not give her, or himself for that matter, his reason for walking out. All he knew is that he needed to be free. Whatever free meant.

Springer's voyeuristic audience would have loved to boo and jeer at this obese loser from Duluth, Minnesota, but they would never have the chance to do so. Jerry Springer himself knew that even if he lived to be a hundred thousand years old, the pathetic procession of dysfunctional families would never stop e-mailing or writing him about their tragic tales of infidelity, desertion, abuse or neglect. Springer knew his show could run on every station, twenty-four seven and there would still be an excess of material complete with chairs flying across the room, tears shed in shame and fingernails digging into flesh with unbridled passion.

Everyone had their story, their fifteen minutes of infamy, thought Charlie. He sought none of it. If Jerry Springer thrived in a world filled to overflowing with people's dirty laundry, it mattered not at all to Stupidnski. After all, his family owned the Laundromat.

As he sat there, his brain swimming in a pool of cheap vodka, he took inventory of his life. He knew he had been dumping too much of his working capital into the Big Bertha in hopes of winning the Monte Carlo. His plan was simple; first win the Monte Carlo, then go on to win the heart of Crystal Lovelock. But Charlie was a realist and both scenarios were unlikely.

His battle with Big Bertha had brought his nickel inventory down to $567.50. His rent was due in six days, bringing him dangerously close to having to do something else with his life aside from drinking, chain-smoking, falling in love with exotic dancers, eating and gambling. He had one friend in the world, an alcoholic Indian with the unlikely name of Dismount Moose Nelson. True, he had his Pinto, but that wasn't worth more than scrap value. Sadly, contemplated Charlie while sitting on the stool, it was probably worth less than Diz's Gremlin in the end.

He had his laptop, but it was so old that it still had a slot for a floppy disc and he doubted the pawn shop where he bought it would dare to buy it back. He had the clothes on his back and tattered variations of them stuffed in the three drawers in his motel room. A sorry assortment of well-worn clothes complete with sweat stains under the armpits, pilled collars and splitting pants seams. Clothes the Salvation Army would refuse.

But he smiled as he wiped his ass and started undressing to take a shower. He smiled because he was free and it was all worth it. They were all a bunch of assholes. The guys at the CPA firm, the wife, the kids, the golden retriever, all a bunch of suck ass losers.

Within the hour, sober enough to walk the three blocks to the One-Stop, Charlie Stupidnski was purchasing a second bottle of Petri vodka using another 160 nickels worth of his currency, plus tax. Being sober for the past two hours was like a tedious layover on a long flight to nowhere.

He wrapped the liter of vodka in a brown paper bag and walked across the street to the Erickson gas station. Having survived on nothing other than liquor for the past 24 hours he realized he needed to eat something. He ordered four jumbo hot dogs and ate them while standing by himself in the back corner of the store. The clerk, who recognized him from months of buying Kool menthols, felt sorry for him.

"Take care, Charlie," said the attendant as Charlie walked out of the gas station.

"I will. You guys make a mean hot dog," Charlie added as the automatic door closed behind him. Within fifteen minutes he would be back at the Golden Gate drinking again. Oprah would replace Jerry Springer on the television screen. Other people—older, younger, angrier, sadder would parade their sad lamentations across the cabilized landscape of America. Charlie paid no attention to any of it. He drank until he was numb.

Eventually, Charlie's drinking binge would end. When it was over, on Wednesday, Charlie started working on his manuscript again. He didn't know why.

Chain of Fools

Chapter 5: Scarface Joe

No one knows where Joe's scar came from. It was a good-sized scar, located just below his cheek bone on the right side of his face and extending down to just above his jaw. From the look of it, the scar could have been the result of a knife fight, a farm accident or another of Paul's devastating blows. Whatever the cause, the scar ultimately gave young Joseph Stupidnski his nickname—Scarface Joe.

My mom never knew him and my father was eight when Joe died so he remembered very little about his older brother. The only story I can remember being told about Joe as a child was that he was a big kid when he departed this earth. So big they had to break his shoulders to fit him into his coffin. That always struck me as cruel, even if the fifteen year old was already deceased when they broke his broad collar bones with a mortician's hammer. I'm told Joe's buried in the Oneida Cemetery, up on top of the hills overlooking West Duluth. No one visits the lonely grave of Scarface Joe these days. No one visited his grave back then, either. He was a troubled kid.

Until his arrest in 1922 for stealing a horse and carriage, little is recorded about the boy. There are some comments written by the parole officer as well as by a State agent investigating the family to determine what might have caused this nine year old to stray, but both reports focus on the home conditions and say nothing about Joe.

The home conditions were, surprise, surprise, deplorable. Paul was gone half the time, Maggie was running a blind pig out of her house and the clientele were best defined as immigrant white trash—Poles, Norwegians and Slavs with a penchant for the hard stuff. As a parent, Maggie didn't give a damn if her kids attended school or not and had more or less written them off. The comments coming out of the official reports all echo the same lamentable theme, "subnormal intelligence," "squalid living conditions," "the mother used very coarse and vulgar language." That was Maggie's style, if you dare use the term style when describing her.

According to the police reports found at Redwing, on September 9th, 1922, Scarface Joe and a friend of his stole a horse and buggy from Mrs. Ellingson. She was an elderly woman who lived down the street from them in Helm Street neighborhood. Duluth, like many other cities of that era, was a curious mix of horses, trolleys and automobiles so having a horse and buggy in town wasn't unusual. The two boys were soon caught driving recklessly around town and promptly arrested. It was on a Saturday, so at least the two kids hadn't skipped school to take their first of many future joy rides.

Seeing that Joe was only nine and still in the 4th grade at Adams School, Judge Bert Fesler, ordered both of these juvenile delinquents to the State Training School for Boys at Red Wing, then suspended the sentence and put them on probation. Judge Fesler was naturally reluctant to send a nine-year-old off to reform school. Joseph Stupidnski was the youngest criminal he had ever encountered.

Scarface lasted a month on probation. Over the next thirty days he took a pair of gloves, a flashlight and a camera from someone's car. The owner of the car, stunned by how young this kid was, elected not to press charges but his robbery spree was far from over. Joe then stole $6 from the cash register at the nearby Penny Arcade and another $40 from a car parked down on Lake Avenue in the heart of downtown Duluth. Neither of these parties were as inclined to see past his freckled youth and asked the court that justice be served.

As the police searched for this extraordinarily young punk, Joe proceeded to steal a bike and sell it for cash, then dipped his paws into yet another cash register for $1.50 at an undisclosed grocery store in the small shopping district located on Superior Street in the West End. At this point in time Joe was clearly on the lam and had stopped attending the Adams school or coming home altogether. The cops arrested him in the Bowery district near the old Orpheum Theater on the evening of October 5th, 1922.

The judge's sympathies toward the boy had worn thin. The probation order was revoked and on October 7th, 1922, nine-year-old Joseph Stupidnski headed to Goodhue County, Minnesota, and the reform school located in Redwing. Maggie didn't really give a shit "cause the kid ain't nothin' but trouble," she told the arresting officer. Maggie was maternal love personified.

Joe spent his next two years at Redwing. Sharing a dorm with hardened young criminals who were sometimes twice his age wasn't the best environment for an impressionable boy. By the time he was released in September of 1924 he was destined to become an eleven-year-old career criminal. His moral compass pointed straight to hell.

Once on the outside, Joe lasted a month. They released him back to Maggie but she later told the cops that since returning from Red Wing, Joe was impossible to discipline. Maggie had lost all control over him. She was busy with her bootlegging and prostitution operations so she had little time to deal with a boy who kept messing with the very same law she was trying her damndest to avoid.

Within the first week, Maggie shipped Joe off to a farm in Hawthorne, Wisconsin. Once there, Joe would be kept in a form of indentured servitude for an unspecified length of time. That didn't sit well with him. He ran away the following week and hoofed it back to Duluth. Once there, he hung out in the Bowery district on the western edge of downtown doing petty crime. He broke into cars, stealing whatever he could find, dipped into open cash registers when the clerk wasn't looking and stole cigarettes and candy to resell for cash. Finally, he stole two bicycles and sold them to an undercover policeman. Still on parole, Joe was sentenced back to Redwing via the next train out of town.

His loving mother was glad to see him gone. One-Eyed Maggie was busy dodging bootlegging raids, drunk and disorderly conduct charges, and resisting arrest. Paul, Joe's defecting father, was busy screwing whores and young girls (as fate would have it, he liked young girls, very, very young from what I've been told) somewhere in the north woods of St. Louis County. The rest of the kids were trying to find something to eat and drink in Maggie's brothel beside cigarettes, chewing tobacco and grain alcohol.

In 1922, Joe's older half-brother, John, was still stuck in the 4th grade at the Adams school. At fifteen years of age he must have looked just a trifle out of place. Most of the other kids his age were in the ninth or tenth grade. A year later, John left Maggie's wretched household altogether and went off to work at his uncle's farm in Willow River. John never returned home. Like Maggie cared.

To get the full picture you have to toss in second troubled son, Andrew, a helpless deaf kid, my toddler father, a steady stream of booze-buying patrons, any number of johns and a swearing, alcoholic, chain-smoking one-eyed proprietor working out of a run-down tenement slum. It was a social worker's Armageddon. Scarface, noted the social worker, was better off in Redwing.

On Oct. 14th, 1924 the State of Minnesota ordered the street-hardened eleven-year-old back to the slammer. He did another two-year stint, released at 13 years of age on September 2nd, 1926. Thinking ahead, this time they kept Scarface on parole. Joe told his parole officer he was determined not the head back to Redwing in such record time.

Joe arrived home just in time to witness first hand the nasty divorce Maggie and Paul were neck-deep in that September of 26. Shit was flying everywhere, but we'll do the divorce later. Let's stick to Scarface's story for now.

Joe bounced around a while after his release. He worked at this farm or that farm, doing odd jobs and making a half-hearted attempt to come clean. He was already a big kid at 13 and had spent most of the past four years in reform school. A Miss Harms, from the Child Welfare Board, visited the house to meet with Joe on January 1st, 1927 to see how he was getting along.

Not well. According to her notes it took Miss Harms a half an hour to gain entrance into the apartment Maggie was living in. On that particular morning, according to Miss Harms copious notes, Maggie was harboring a woman with a broken leg in her kitchen by the name of Rosie McGraw. Rosie was with a friend of hers, a Mr. Andrews, and she had just gotten out of prison for bootlegging. No doubt they were enjoying some of Maggie's home brew when the welfare agent arrived. It was nine in the morning, a great time of the day to be drinking moonshine.

Maggie was recently divorced from Paul at this point and had been shacking up with another Pollack, a Mr. Krashiski. It's a name I'm particularly fond of because it starts with Krash. Krashnburnski would have been a better spelling. We'll get back to all these sordid characters later, but the end result of the visit was that the welfare worker left the home in a kind of catatonic stupor. She had never seen anything quite like the Stupidnski household before and reported to her superiors that there was more than likely bigger trouble brewing for the teenaged Scarface. A monstrous understatement.

A few weeks later, during one of the rare times Joe attended school, he was accused of trying to assault a fellow student named Alice Olsen. At this point Joe was a randy 14-year-old and, even though Alice was 12 at the time, she must have caught his wandering eye. He wanted her to come over to his mother's house to visit but she wisely ran away from the horny little Scarface. According to the report, Alice stumbled, cutting her knee badly but attracting the attention of some bystanders in the process. Joe was arrested and later questioned. He denied everything. He was just trying to have Alice meet his aunt, he told the investigating detective. Funny name for what he really wanted her to meet.

Joe was a ticking time bomb and, so long as he remained with Maggie, his chances of recovery were nil. Maggie, Paul, his half-brother John and even Andrew were all having trouble with the law at this point and this was not exactly the kind of familial safety net parole officers long for. In that regard it more closely resembled a gill net, wherein the progeny would get their own heads stuck in the coarse weave of catastrophic dysfunction.

Following up, another welfare agent was sent to the home in early February of 1927 looking to check up on Scarface for a second time. Probably thinking it was a paying customer, Maggie opened the door at the first knock. The agent noted that Maggie had been badly beaten and her face was covered in dried blood. Her bed, where the beating had occurred, was likewise covered in blood but still held a young girl sleeping in it. That child would have been my aunt, Irene, who was born in 24.

Maggie didn't volunteer as to who had beaten her bloody, not that it mattered. After the report the parole officer decided it was probably better for Joe to go back to Redwing than to remain at home. On Feb. 4th, 1927, without any due cause aside from trying to get the poor kid out of Maggie's pig sty, they sent Scarface back to Redwing. This time not to the reform school located there, but to a nearby farm that served as kind of a half-way house for troubled juveniles.

Maggie had enough on her plate and she was glad to see the little son-of-a-bitch out of the house, never quite grasping the fact that she was the bitch in question. So Joe returned to a farm in Red Wing and started anew. That didn't last either.

Scarface went back to school and, by this time, Joe was in the sixth grade, 'though he wasn't exactly a model student. His teacher, Miss Swanson, complained to Joe's parole officer that Scarface smoked cigarettes in the building and was a bad influence on her other pupils. The parole officer reprimanded Joe for smoking and Joe promised to stop.

He didn't stop. In fact Joe soon got fed up with the school, the farm, the whole pile of bullshit and ran away on Feb. 14th, 1928. He was fourteen years old. Joe headed back to Duluth but never moved back in with One-Eyed Maggie. He hung around the Bowery, doing odd jobs and petty crime interchangeably until June of that same year.

Then, on June 9th, 1928, Scarface Joe, along with another boy, stole a car and went for a joy ride. They got caught on June 10th and because Joe was still on probation, he was immediately sent back to Redwing for a third and final time.

That's where he died. He arrived at the school on June 23rd, 1928 with an attitude that resembled distilled juvenile delinquency, similar to some of Maggie's elixirs. At 15-years-old Scarface Joe was a career criminal who looked forward to a life in and out of jails, work farms, reform schools and prisons for the rest of his life.

Young Joe had contracted Tuberculosis Meningitis from one of the other inmates at Redwing and died on August 1st, 1928 in the school's infirmary. He was fifteen years, three months and twenty-six days old. He had spent five of the last six years of his life incarcerated, one way or the other.

They shipped the dead body back to Duluth for a proper burial. Define proper. Maggie and Paul, along with the other kids, were all there the day they lowered him and his broken shoulders into the ground. The first-born child of Maggie and Paul was gone. I want to use the word 'tragedy' here but I just don't know how to use it.

Eddy Wind Rider

The Chippewa Indians have been snaring deer for centuries. Using hemp ropes, dangling from stout limbs and set on well established deer trails in heavy cover, deer are no harder to snare than snowshoe rabbits. They are simply larger. The best time to snare them is early summer, when their antlers are covered in velvet and not so large as to become entangled in the rope, a situation that sometimes allows the larger bucks to escape. Generally speaking most snared deer are still alive when their trapper comes upon them. Using a firearm, such as a 30/30 caliber rifle or a handgun, the Indian puts the deer down then harvests the meat, hide and other usable parts of the animal accordingly. Little is wasted.

So that became their plan, to snare a buck, then ride it. Just after the war, years before Diz was born, Eddy Wind Rider and his gang had come to a decision. They knew two things: 1) riding a whitetail deer was going to be incredibly dangerous and 2) it would have to be a very large deer to support Eddy for the seven terrifying seconds he would have to hang on.

In the spring of 1947, amidst swarms of mosquitos in wet, soggy brush near the edge of a large tamarack swamp, they started setting the snares for the deer Eddy would ultimately ride. The plan was simple. Snare the biggest velvet-antlered buck in the State beneath a tree limb sturdy enough for Eddy to climb out onto, have Eddy cut the hemp rope off with his buck knife and drop onto the back of the deer before he managed to high tail it away. That and be three quarters drunk the entire time.

The plan had its flaws. Most of the time the snares would capture does or yearlings, neither of which would support the spindly 138-pound Eddy. Because of that, some of the smallest deers would be set free, while others would be shot and butchered on the spot. But on the wet, windy morning of June 27th, 1947, Eddy and his cohorts snared the biggest damn buck they had ever seen.

A big Minnesota whitetail rarely tops 200 pounds, but over the years far, far bigger deer have been taken. This particular deer, looking from its growing rack to be a magnificent 12 point buck by the fall, pushed 300 pounds. Strong, powerful and hopelessly entangled in the snare, when Rain Stops Falling, one of Eddie's cohorts, stumbled upon it that Friday morning, he knew this was Eddy's deer. Luckily a small part of the hemp line had become wrapped around a portion of the right antler, so the deer was in no danger of strangling itself before Rain Stops Falling could hike a mile back to his car and drive to the reservation to get Eddy and the rest of the crew.

By noon everything was set. The boys were sufficiently liquored up, Eddy had his knife on him and all that was needed to be done was for Eddy to carefully scale out along the edge of the large Norway pine limb where the rope was attached, cut the line and drop two feet onto the back of a very pissed-off buck.

Knowing that there was a good chance he might have to kill the deer if things got too weird, Eddy wisely elected to keep his knife with him when he fell onto the bucks huge shoulders. After the black bear incident, Eddy decided he could never be too careful. Besides, Eddy knew this deer wasn't going to be sedated when his ass hit the saddle.

Aside from the frantic kicking and strange noises made by the buck as Eddy scaled up the Norway pine not ten feet from him, the first part of the endeavor went well. With the deer mustering the biggest deer-in-the-headlights pair of eyes ever seen, the animal kept constant track of this skinny Indian with a buck knife held firmly between his teeth as he climbed out on the limb above him. Naturally the deer didn't understand the bizarre rules of Wind Rider's contest.

Eddie had no intention of killing this trophy buck. All he wanted to do was to ride it. Trying fruitlessly to calm the deer down the rest of Eddie's entourage sang any number of Indian chants and popular songs while Eddy made his way further and further out on the limb, both physically and metaphysically speaking. Naturally these attempts to soothe the animal fell on deaf ears. The massive buck was totally freaked out by what was going on, being the only creature there who wasn't inebriated.

Rain Stops Falling had a gun with him. It was a rusty 30/30 with one bullet in the chamber and four in the clip. Everyone was in agreement that once Eddy dropped down on the deer using the gun would be a decision of last resort. If Eddy were to get thrown and the buck started trampling him, or goring him with his dull, velvet covered antlers or a dozen other possibilities might determine if and when Rain Stops Falling would pull the trigger. No one in the group dared consider the fact that what they were doing was completely insane.

With the 300-pound buck terrified, Rain Stops Falling pointed the 30/30 in the general direction of Eddy and the Norway pine branch he was sitting on while the rest of the crew sang the recently released *Fools Rush In*. Reaching a point directly above the deer, Eddy sprang into action. In one smooth motion he sliced through the hemp line that was keeping the buck tethered to the pine, grabbed the rope in his hand, quickly slid his knife back into the sheath on his belt and dropped down onto the back of this trophy whitetail.

For the first full second of the randomly chosen seven seconds required by Eddy's rules of wild animal riding, the buck stood perfectly motionless. Some of the crew had placed bets as to whether or not a deer's front legs could support Eddy and those bets were lost. The deer's legs held.

The next six seconds were impossible to describe. It was as if the deer and Eddy had somehow triggered a landmine that was secretly buried directly beneath the deers naval. The buck, to state it mildly, went ballistic. Eddy crouched down and wrapped his arms around the long, slender neck of the deer and held on. The deer jumped and spun, bucked and whirled, kicked and shook like a rodeo horse on crystal meth. Somewhere around the six second mark the deer sprung up five feet off the ground and Eddy hit his back against an overhanging pine branch. He heard the sound of ribs cracking as he hit. Specifically, his ribs.

Then, upon landing, the deer buckled. His two front legs, as powerful as they might have appeared, were really never designed to carry a drunken Indian, even a skinny one. The hind legs held, but before you could blink Eddy was tumbling, head over heals, up and over the velvet antlers and spilling across the boggy path. Eddy made one small mistake. He forgot to let go of the rope.

With Eddy off his back the deer decided to make another run for it. When Eddy fell, the rope had become hopelessly entangled around his right arm. Rain Stops Falling, noting the precarious situation Eddy was in, and seeing that Eddy was clear of the buck, decided it was time to take a shot.

He missed, probably alcohol related. Understandably, the buck responded very unfavorably to the crack of a 30/30 not twenty feet from him and started bolting toward the nearby tamarack swamp. Eddy, while no longer technically on top of the deer, was in for the ride of a lifetime. Chester Yellowhair, who had been manning the stopwatch for the event, clicked the button just as Eddy hit the dirt. Seven point .329 seconds. Ride number two was now official. Official to whom was never defined.

Because the snare line was short, Eddy was now half-running, half being dragged along side the animal. Rain Stops Falling lifted the rifle up for a second shot but realized that a through and through might well put the slug smack into Eddy Wind Rider's chest.

Eddy was on his own. The buck wasn't accustomed to dragging an Indian alongside him when he ran so progress was slow and tumultuous. Within the first fifty yards Eddy had been kicked at least thirty times, his arm was killing him and the deer was becoming more and more hysterical. At a hundred yards the deer fell over, leaving the two of them in this tangled, frenzied wrestling match on the edge of the swamp. The spectators had left their viewing spot and ran down the path following Eddy and his ill-leashed deer.

Taking another shot at this point was out of the question. These two animals were now in some kind of bizarre scuffle unlike anything ever witnessed. It was best described as a deer vs. man wrestling competition. Horns, arms, legs and fur flailing together.

This scenario was exactly why Eddy had brought along his skinning knife. While being bit, kicked, scratched and generally damaged by this wailing ungulate, Eddy had to make a decision. He could either try to kill the deer with his knife, a rather unsightly and difficult concept at this point, cut his arm off, which did occur to him, or cut the rope. Killing a 300 pound buck with a hunting knife while tumbling around on a spongy bog is not pretty. Cutting his arm off might prove easier but in the end Eddy did the right thing, he sliced through the hemp line and extricated himself from this rabid quadruped. Eddy got up and ran toward his friends faster than they thought humanly possible. The deer, realizing Eddy was gone, got up seconds later and broke for the swamp.

Rain Stops Falling raised the gun up to finish off the buck but Eddy screamed, "Don't shoot him!" just in the nick of time. The deer got away, none the worse for wear except for ferrying a five foot piece of rope with him until his antlers shed the following winter. Eddy felt the deer had earned its freedom.

Eddy Wind Rider had succeeded. Eddy had two broken ribs and uncountable lacerations, bruises and Yellowhair's stop watch to prove it. All that was left to ride were the elk and the moose, neither of which Eddy cared to think about for the rest of that summer.

Of course, Diz had told this story before. It was as much a part of who Diz was as was his vintage Gremlin collection. Charlie understood this, so when Diz, half-tanked as always, told Charlie his father's deer riding tale that night, Charlie didn't bother to interrupt him. It would have been rude, despite the fact that Charlie had heard the story a dozen times before.

Charlie Stupidnski wasn't the only one listening. A handful of the regulars had gathered at the Black Bear Casino Lounge to get out of the December cold and share each other's company that particular Saturday evening. Some of the patrons were regulars, patrons who where there so often they should have been on payroll. Others were new, unfamiliar faces.

There was David Larson, the quiet one with the sad story who seldom spoke, and Mark Knudsen, who owned a hobby farm down near Willow River, as well as Susan Voytek, the three-time divorced, overweight welfare mother who had a gambling problem, to put it mildly.

Then there was Dena, as always, behind the bar along with a dozen locals sitting at the nearby tables nursing cocktails and draft beers until they mustered enough courage to get back out on the floor and give it another go. Because it was a Saturday night, Dena had a cocktail waitress on staff to give her a hand.

It was, by and large, a typical weekend night at the Black Bear. The sirens were singing their familiar chorus, luring the patrons into the rocks of their personal addictions. Almost every slot machine in the joint held a coin carrying hostage. The cigarette smoke hung thick in the air as the Bingo hall filled up with the strange, assorted crowd who loved their paper-thin Bingo cards and oversized magic markers. The Texas

Hold'em players were arriving, taking their seats and, like always, doing their best to keep sober enough to count cards.

The Monte Carlo sat near the front entrance, black and polished as ever. The managers of the casino were thrilled. While they had taken a beating on an early winner for the last vehicle, the laws of chance were making up for it on the Monte Carlo. Big Bertha wasn't going to give this car up prematurely and they had already tripled their money. Charlie Stupidnski was a major contributor to their current statistical success.

"Great story, Diz," said Knutson as Diz's tale concluded.

"That's bullshit, Diz, your dad never rode no damn deer," quipped Susan as she lifted her cocktail to her cherry-red painted lips. She had just gotten divorced again and her lips confirmed it.

"He sure as hell did. He rode them all, the black bear, the whitetail and the moose. My dad could ride anything. Hell, as a kid they used to take a sheet, stretch it between two poles and go out on Big Lake just after the first good freeze on a pair of hockey skates and ride the north wind clear across the lake. The ice wasn't even an inch thick and he'd be whizzing across it. If they stopped, they'd break clear through, but they never stopped. He was a great man, my father."

"Do you have any proof of his riding the deer?" Questioned Susan, after taking a long sip of her rum and coke.

"Yeah, I do. My dad kept Yellowhair's stopwatch and never reset it."

"Where is it."

"I've got it somewhere back at the house. Do you want me to bring it in?"

Charlie interjected. "It's true Sue, I've heard some of Diz's father's friends, some of the old crew, tell me personally that Eddy did shit like this all the time. He was one crazy Indian, of that much I'm sure. I've even seen the stop watch, Sue."

David Larson stayed out of the conversation, just as he did most conversations. He just sat there on the corner of the bar looking like a ghost. David was thin to the edge of gaunt. He was in his early sixties or late fifties, but no one knew his age for certain. He drank wine. White wine and lots of it. Dena knew a little bit about him and shared it with other customers when David wasn't around.

Five years ago his wife had died of a brain tumor and David took it hard. He retreated into himself and started drinking. He sometimes got so drunk he simply put his head down on the bar and fell asleep.

Dena felt sorry for him. It was like watching a person dissipate in front of you.

David kept getting thinner, greyer and quieter by the week. He was in some kind of personal disappearing act wherein one day, while sitting at the bar, he would simply vanish, leaving nothing but a half-empty glass of wine. Diz would finish his wine and wish David well, wherever he had dissolved to.

"You still trying for the Monte Carlo, Charlie?" Asked Mark Knutson in an effort to change the topic of the conversation.

"You damn right I am."

"You still after that dancer, you know, the one who works at Sugar Daddies—ahhh, what's her name?"

"Her name's Crystal, Crystal Lovelock, but she's not been dancing much lately."

Sad but true. After the nun debacle, the club's owner, Jimmy Cortese, had taken Crystal off the regular rotation. Crystal still danced on Monday and Tuesday nights, the slowest nights at the club, or sometimes filled in when one of the other dancers got sick or was having her period but Crystal, like all aging strippers, was slowly, methodically being put out to pasture.

"Why's that?"

"She did this nun thing and it kind of bombed."

"Ya mean she did a stripper act as a nun? Man, I would have loved to seen that one. I used to go the Catholic school for a while. I'd love to see it, Charlie. Is she still doing it?"

"No, she almost got fired over it. It was tacky. She wore this dominatrix outfit under her habit but it was just too strange. I think it made some of the regulars feel kind of guilty or something."

"Ah shit. It sounds good to me," concluded Knutson.

Everyone kept silent for a while, glancing up at the hockey game on the TV on occasion while nursing their respective drinks. The cocktail waitress came up to her station, ordered, waited for blenders to finish blending, bottled beers to be cracked open or mixes to be poured then ran back with her orders without saying anything. Money changed hands. Tips were typically meager.

The casino was firing on all cylinders, making money hand over fist and giving the lonely inhabitants of northern Minnesota a few hours of diversion from the bitter cold that dominated the landscape just beyond the front door.

"You going to play the nickel slots tonight, Diz?"

"I can't Charlie. I'm sticking with the two cent slots until I win some cash back. I ain't had a losing streak like this in years, Charlie. I can't seem to break it."

It was true. Diz was caught up in a very bad losing streak. Between the drinking binges with his cousins and this extended run of bad luck at the Black Bear, Diz was close to flat broke. He was down to a hundred and eighty bucks and still had three weeks of December in front of him. Come January first he would get his disbursement again but he was falling so far behind with the rent, the electricity, heating fuel and groceries that almost all of that money was spent before he ever got his hands on it. Diz was slipping.

"I need a change of pace, Charlie. I need to break out of this treadmill I'm caught in. I've got to go somewhere, do something. Hell, I don't know what it is, but I've got to move on. I got the itch real bad, Charlie. It's killing me."

"Help me win the Monte Carlo, Diz, and I'll take us somewhere."

"Where?"

"I don't know, you pick the spot. There's got to be someplace nearby you want to see."

"I'll think about it. But I ain't got no five spots to drop in that hungry Big Bertha."

"I'll front you the money Diz, you just pull the handle for me. I've played it so much I think I'm jinxed at this point. Maybe you can break the spell."

"Fine."

Charlie and Diz finished their drinks, said goodbye to the others still leaning on the bar and walked off into the flourescent oblivion of the casino floor. Midnight came and went as the tiny Jefferson cameos slid down the throats of a hundred hungry slot machines. Diz kept losing just as Charlie was winning. David Larson sat at the same corner of the bar all night. No one but Dena noticed him.

Sue spent every penny she had brought with her, then tried to borrow some money from Charlie around one in the morning. Charlie told her to go home to her two unwatched kids. She did, though reluctantly.

By three a.m. Charlie was exhausted. Crystal wasn't dancing tonight so there was no reason to go to Sugar Daddies. Charlie went home, laid his head on the yellowed pillow cover and fell asleep. He dreamt of his wife and kids back in Duluth, only his wife wasn't his wife. She was Crystal. He was happy in his dream, unlike the world he was living in.

*****

"How is it out there?"

"Dead, Crystal. I counted three, maybe four guys in the whole goddamned bar. It's Monday night girl, what the hell do you expect?"

"Shit."

"When are you up?"

"I'm up after Heather. She's out there dancing now."

"Good luck, I'm done. I ain't hauling my ass out there to try to do lap dances with any of those losers. They look like they ain't got a pot to piss in."

"I hate Mondays, Vicky. I'm getting sick and tired of this bullshit."

"Me too, Crystal. Maybe I'll put my application in at the paper mill or something. Once Jimmy takes you off weekends, you can't make shit dancing."

"You're telling me."

They were in the dressing room, though most of the girls called it the undressing room. Sugar Daddies was empty, as it was most Monday nights at ten-thirty. There were in fact five guys in the entire place, Vicky hadn't noticed the old man in the corner wearing farmer's jeans and a dark wool coat. He was the kind who went to strip clubs and always sat off in a corner. Secretive with a twist of perverse. The kind of customers all the girls steered clear of.

It was mid-December, a notoriously slow time for strip clubs. Once Christmas was over, during the week between Christmas and New Years, business picked up. But the past two weeks had been especially slow. Reluctant husbands were being dragged to shopping malls, money was tight and, aside from the weekends, Sugar Daddies was a topless ghost town with a good beat and brass pole in the middle.

Vicky had made eighteen dollars since the doors opened at five. Crystal had fourteen dollars and three quarters, which fell out of her g-string the minute she stood up. The guy who slid the quarters in had found them in his pants pocket, left over from his weekend outing of the Black Bear Casino. Coins and strippers never mix.

Crystal Lovelock was slowly, insidiously, going broke. Once pulled from the regular weekend line up it was only a matter of time before she would have to stop dancing altogether. That's what the owner wanted.

For him, Monday and Tuesdays nights existed for two reasons. First, they were great for training fresh, young dancers on how to strip, how to work a crowd or put their own special pelvic shine on the brass pole. On the other side of that same equation, Monday and Tuesday nights offered the ideal venue for putting the older girls, or the dancers who weren't cutting it, quietly out to pasture. It was Jimmy's way of easing them off the payroll and out of his club. Jimmy knew damn well a dancer couldn't make a living at Sugar Daddies without having either a Friday or Saturday night to disrobe. There just wasn't enough business out there.

So Crystal and Vicky were going broke. Vicky had already crossed the line to pay the rent a half dozen times in the last two months. For Vicky, who was a tight 29, it wasn't a question of age, but the fact that she couldn't dance. When Jimmy watched her work the pole from the back of the club it appeared at times like she was having some kind of epileptic seizure. It seemed as if she was only hanging on to keep herself from falling to the floor. When Vicky actually got down on the dance floor, her sexy convulsions were so awkward that Jimmy thought he should put a spoon in Vicky's mouth to stop her from swallowing her tongue. The only reason Jimmy had kept her on so long is that Vicky Vice, her full stage name, was a good-looking redhead, and redheads were hard to find. He just wished Miss Vice knew what rhythm was.

Unlike Vicky, Crystal resisted turning tricks to supplement her income. She hated resorting to the world's oldest profession but when the rent came due and she was lacking sufficient funds she always found herself asking the same age-old question, "What's a girl to do?"

A month ago there was that good-looking kid from Hinckley who had become a regular on Tuesday nights. She did a couple of lap dances for him and near the end of one of them he asked her if she ever worked any overtime. Hell, this kid couldn't have been more than 23, with a well-trimmed beard, nice clothes and a lean, muscular body that would have turned the head of any dancer. Crystal would have probably done him for free.

When she found out later he was willing to go fifty for oral and a hundred for the works, Crystal decided it might be OK to relax her rules for this handsome hunk of a farmer boy. She had taken other propositions in the past, but far fewer than some of the other dancers. Crystal had a sense of pride, though it was currently lost in a shoe box full of past-dues.

Needless to say, Crystal proved herself quite capable and soon enough, the Hinckley kid was introducing her to another good-looking friend of his and then it was $150 for a three way, etc. etc. etc. By month's end, it started to get kinky. Turns out the two boys had a thing going as well, which sometimes gave Crystal time for a welcome cigarette break. She just couldn't watch them go at it, even when they offered to pay her extra. A week after the homosexual thing went down the Hinckley boys mentioned bringing in another girl, and possibly another guy next Tuesday. They also talked about bringing in a video camera.

That's when Crystal opted out of the ménage à trois, quatre, cinq, whatever. She didn't want one of her two brothers finding their sister on some Internet sight with a bunch of locals having a down home orgy in a rent-by-the hour motel. Besides, Crystal had already made the rent, with some cash to spare. The handsome, bi-sexual Hinckley boys had little trouble finding a replacement.

Crystal had never imagined herself as an exotic dancer when she was growing up. Going to Esko High, a cheerleader, a good student and very popular, Crystal wasn't even Crystal then. She was Lois Carlson—a sweet, attractive teenager who lived in a standard-issue double-wide mobile home parked on eight acres of poplar woods and swamp a half-mile north of old Highway 61.

Her mother and father had divorced when Lois was nine. Her father had more or less abandoned the family after the divorce and, in typical fashion, Lois had managed to blame herself for his leaving. She loved her dad dearly and never understood why. He moved to Minneapolis where he found a new wife, a new life, and never looked back. Her mom, who had a drinking problem, married her husband's brother a year after the divorce. Lois's uncle now became her step-dad. His name was Leonard Carlson.

A few years later he turned out to have more of an interest in Lois than he had in his brother's former wife so that marriage didn't last. Coming home drunk after work one night he made some very unwanted moves on Lois which, once Lois's older brother found out, almost cost Leonard his life. Lois's mother, Virginia, upped her alcohol intake and divorced a second Carlson boy inside of four years.

Their double-wide was a typical northern Minnesota subsistence homestead. Lois had two brothers, one three years older than she, and another five years her junior. The youngest still lived with her mom in the trailer while the other had moved to Florida six years ago. None of them stayed in touch. The trailer was surrounded by a half-dozen non-functioning vehicles, a bathtub once filled with lovely flowers but presently filled with weeds, a tipped over birdbath, assorted hoses, old mattresses—in short, all the trappings of Scandinavian white trash.

Crystal's mother knew her daughter was an exotic dancer. She didn't approve but realized there was nothing she could do. It was, as it often is, a long and tedious fall from cheerleader to stripper. It started when, after Lois got out of Esko High School, she decided to put off going to vo-tech for a few years to get some "real life experience."

Lois, *aka* Crystal Lovelock, got her "real life experience" in spades. She started working at an office supply store in Cloquet. Then, like many a young semi-rural girl in her early twenties, found out what the term "partying" meant. She and her co-workers started "partying" all over Cloquet, Duluth and eventually ended up in Superior, Wisconsin. Those years, Superior was known as Soup Town, or party central. At twenty-three, Lois Carlson had her very own well-defined drinking problem. Sliding effortlessly down the path of least resistance she soon found her way to the biker bars. That's where she met Billy Agnew.

Billy, who was fourteen years older than she, reminded her of her father and the scene was set. For the next decade Lois and Billy were an off-again, on-again item. Billy proposed to Lois three separate times over that lost decade and Lois said yes to each proposal. Inevitably, somewhere between the proposals and the wedding, they would get a little too drunk on some Saturday night, fight like street cats until dawn and call the quote—unquote—"motherfucking wedding" off. To support herself, Lois worked odd jobs, things like waitressing, gas station attendant and grocery clerk. Easy jobs to get, and even easier to quit.

At 27, Lois became pregnant but lost Billy's baby to an early miscarriage. Their relationship ended the night Billy Agnew lost control of his Harley coming off the Richard Bong Memorial Bridge heading back to their low-rent duplex in Gary, New Duluth. He was going over a hundred miles and hour when his bike slammed into a guard rail. His blood alcohol level was the same as 3.2 beer. It was a horrific accident. There was no saving him.

After the accident Lois fell into a clinical depression. She started drinking heavily and more or less boarded herself into their dumpy apartment until she was evicted. She moved back to Esko for a while to live with her mother and younger brother. That welcome mat wore thin within a month.

That's when Lois read an ad in the Cloquet Pine Journal that the Sugar Daddies, a soon to be opened strip club, was looking for exotic dancers—no prior experience needed. Lois needed a job, and not having had any kids, she still looked good at thirty-two.

Jimmy's predecessor, Peter Gunderson, hired her on the spot. Within months, Lois Carlson, now formally known as Crystal Lovelock, was raking in the money. She bought a new car and a set of new tits within the first six months of dancing and found herself as happy as she had ever been. She loved how the men loved to watch her, especially the older men.

Five years ago, realizing her dream of being a mom some day were over, she decided to eliminate any risk of pregnancies during some of her overtime work and decided to have her tubes tied. She cried the day she drove into Duluth to the Miller Dwan Medical Center to have the procedure done. Despite the biker lifestyle, her years of partying and her troubled past Lois Carlson had always held out a ray of hope that one day she might have a child of her own. That Thursday afternoon closed the door on that dream. In a way, it saddened her even more than Billy's untimely death.

So, it was down to this for the soon to be 39 year-old exotic dancer. Monday and Tuesday nights with an occasional weekend subbing for one of the younger, prettier girls. That, and doing various Johns now and then to make the rent. Life sucked, thought Lois to herself. Vicky concurred. Sucked big time.

Chain of Fools

Chapter 6: The Divorce

Can you blame me? Can you blame my father? Hell, can you blame Maggie or Paul for that matter. Or Paul's father, whoever the hell he was. And Paul's fathers' father before him. It just goes back, further and further into time, weaving through the generations like some bad thread tying all of us together.

Like we're entangled in this drawer together—the junk drawer of humanity. A place where you find those leaky AAA batteries, incest and mismatched Tupperware covers. A drawer full of old notepads, pens that don't write and extramarital affairs. Then there's the string. Useless yellowed string that ensnares every piece of crap in the drawer like it was all hopelessly caught in some kind of random gill net—we'll call it the 'gill net of fate.'

Damn, I like that term, the 'gill net of fate.' That's why you can't really blame me for nursing this vodka and coke sitting beside me any more than you can blame Maggie for catching fire or my father for ruining his life with booze. We're all victims here. We're the dying fish struggling in this mile-wide gill net. From the day we were thrown into this shithole, we never stood a chance. That's why we drink, smoke cigs and pot, pop pills, screw, jack off and don't give a damn about the outcome. We're slowly drowning, each and every one of us, in this screwed up gill net of it all.

Maggie Stupidnski filed for divorce in May of 1926. She became the plaintiff, Paul the defendant. Paul had walked out of Maggie's life on Oct. 1ˢᵗ, 1924, and never looked back. Paul had deserted his wife and all his children. Maggie contended it was all Paul's fault. Paul blamed Maggie. They were both right.

It started early, their troubles with each other, as early as their troubles with the law. In May of 1915, amidst the early push toward nationwide prohibition, Carleton County voted itself a "dry county." Maggie, having learned the nuances of turning a sack of potatoes into alcohol from her parents, suddenly found her distilling talents in high demand. On a small rented homestead outside the town of Kettle River, Paul, Maggie, John and young Joseph took to peeling spuds while the infant Andrew looked on. Spuds were cheap. The clear 180 proof liquid coming out the other end of the still wasn't cheap at all. For Paul and Maggie it must have felt like they had discovered the sorcerer's stone— the beautiful alchemy of a country still in a dry county—it was as though they were fermenting money.

Following the vote that year, Carleton County closed every bar, saloon, tavern and local pub on November 27ᵗʰ, 1915. Maggie and Paul were absolutely thrilled.

Two months later, on Jan. 16ᵗʰ, 1916, Maggie, Paul, Mr. Ikons and Anton Marhifski were busted by two undercover detectives brought in from Duluth. The raid took place at Marhifski's general store in Kettle River. The sting produced "considerable amounts of liquor at the general store and in the Stupidnski's home." The largest stash was found in a secret compartment in the general store under the stairway going to the upstairs apartments, which were common above most commercial establishments back then.

Paul received the first 90-day sentence, which was soon to become a long string of 90 day sentences. According to the newspaper accounts, the judge fined Marhifski some $220.95 for his transgressions. In 1916, two-hundred and twenty dollars was a hell of a lot of money.

Paul, on the other hand, who had some earlier run-ins with the law, was not allowed to buy his way out of the bust. Instead, the judge ordered him to the work farm. Maggie, with three kids to look after, got a suspended sentence and was sent home. It must have been hard on her, going back to a farm where the authorities had just absconded with her cache of moonshine. Maggie was quick to realize that, despite the lost liquor, it was better than going to jail. Besides, she reasoned, the still itself was safe and sound, tucked away out on the back forty and Maggie'd be back in operation before Paul was sprung.

An accomplice, a Mr. Beach, was also apprehended in the sting. His hotel, adjacent to the General Store, was found to harbor a variety of gaming devices in the back room. Though none were named in the official arrests, I have to speculate that there were probably ladies for hire working the hotel rooms upstairs as well. It was like a one stop shopping mall for the hoodlums, gamblers and drunkards of Kettle River, Minnesota, circa 1916.

Little Scarface Joe, who was barely three at the time, was getting some early show and tell from his handcuffed parents that would leave a lasting impression on the boy. He must have loved peeling potatoes and watching mom stomp down the mash while Paul did his stretch in the County work farm.

Shortly after Paul was set free in May of 1916, they both high-tailed it out of Carleton County to Duluth. Besides, St. Louis County was anything but dry, so for the next few years running, the couple returned to as close to normal as they would ever get. Paul went back into the north woods to chop down trees while Maggie raised the kids and enjoyed her legal inebriations.

It didn't last. St. Louis County, along with every other county in the U.S., went dry on January 16th, 1920, the start of national temperance. Opportunity once again came a knockin' and in March of 21, a little more than a year after prohibition started, Maggie was arrested for running a Blind Pig. She and two accomplices, Lazara Palma and Albert Hochevar. All three were busted in a raid on Maggie's home on March 11th, 1921. Palma and Hochevar were thrown in for the standard 90 days while Maggie, who had grown accustomed to playing the helpless, misguided woman with a brood of six, was given a suspended sentence. Paul was working up near Cotton, Minnesota, at the time, wiping out virgin stands of Norway pine and screwing the local country girls.

For the next few years, the fun continued. In January of '22 Maggie was arrested for Disorderly Conduct. In April of '23 Paul was arrested for unlawfully having intoxicating liquor in his possession. In May of '24 Paul was sent to the St. Louis County Work Farm for keeping a Blind Pig. Maggie, as usual, was given another hardship-inspired suspended sentence. She must have been lonely that year because sometime during Paul's three month stay in the work farm,

Maggie found herself inexplicably pregnant. Paul, breaking rock and sobering up at the work farm, was taken aback by his wife's miraculous conception when he finally returned home in August of 1924.

There were other arrests, raids and encounters during the early, roaring '20s, but not all of them made it to the police blotter or the local paper. Maggie herself, with the judge's sympathies finally wearing thin, did a stretch in the St. Louis County Work Farm in '23.

They had other issues running concurrently with their bootleg operations. Scarface Joe, their youngest, was in and out of Redwing during this same time period. John, Maggie's illegitimate child, was terminally stuck in the fourth grade. He was fifteen at the time, which must have made for some awkward moments—towering over the other kids like an NBA basketball player in a group of pygmies. Andrew, their second son born shortly after Joe, was working on his own rap sheet while Stanley, my father, was learning to walk between empty bottles of bootleg liquor strewn about the floor. Add to this scenario a little girl whose paternity was in serious question, and there you have it, the Stupidnski's circa 1925. Norman Rockwell be damned.

When Paul was released from the Work Farm in July of 24, he soon discovered that Maggie was with child. It was a little unsettling for him, to put it mildly. Paul wanted to kill the son-of-a-bitch who had knocked up his bride but Maggie, acting wisely, refused to tell Paul who the father was. Just before Irene was born, Paul stormed out of the house for good.

Initially, Maggie was dead certain Paul would come back. She was convinced Paul would miss his adorable little juvenile delinquents, her wicked moonshine, the screaming kids, several of whom weren't even his, but most of all, his weekend wife beatings. Alas, Maggie was wrong—Paul never came back, not even to smack her a good one for the road.

Finally, after two years with her husband in absentia, Maggie filed for divorce. The last she heard was that her husband was somewhere near International Falls, logging and drinking, or drinking and logging depending on which day it was. The court sent Paul's divorce papers up to the Sheriff of Koochiching County to serve him in the spring of 26, but after months of wandering around the backwoods of that black fly-infested wilderness, Paul was never found and Maggie decided to proceed without him.

On the 1st day of September, 1926, the divorce went forward without the defendant in the courtroom. Hell, Paul didn't even know his wife was divorcing him. True to character, Maggie had a laundry list of reasons for wanting out of what was left of their tattered marriage.

My personal favorite, and I can only guess that the judge agreed with me on this pick, was Paul's cruel and unusual punishment. It was a well-known fact that Paul beat Maggie, and did so on a regular basis. The welfare agents had found her bloodied up several times and the two of them fought like rabid dogs when they got liquored up. Maggie added that the defendant had, "on numerous occasions, assaulted plaintiff with force and violence and threatened to kill plaintiff."

Maggie went on to add that Paul used vile and abusive language towards plaintiff in the presence of outsiders and children causing her great grief, mental suffering and humiliation. Maggie also brought up the infamous venereal disease incident of 1914. She went on to say that because of Paul's vicious and vulgar habits and the general lowlife, scum-sucking moral character of the defendant, she alone should have custody of the children. That, and Paul should be forced to cough up $150 a month in child support.

Paul was not there to defend himself, so the judge threw the book at him. The judge, behind his chamber doors, must have been in stitches. There is the age-old adage, "The pot calling the kettle black," that comes to mind, only in this case it bordered on the absurd. The judge had to be familiar with Maggie's repeated arrests, rumors of prostitution, her Blind Pigs, and her own low moral character. To take one good look at this derelict, disgusting one-eyed bootlegger and realize that she was about to gain custody of these poor kids because her equally derelict husband couldn't even show to defend himself must have sent shivers down the judges spine. This was a lose-lose ruling if there ever was one.

But lacking any defense or say in the matter, Paul lost. The judge granted Maggie her divorce, the custody of the kids, but not the $150 a month Maggie was looking for. Instead the judge cut that sum down to $50 The strange thing was that the judge, either consciously or unconsciously, forget to add the words, "a month" behind the $50 stipend in the final divorce order. Paul, who resurfaced in 1928, quickly paid Maggie her $50 as a one-time disposal fee and wiped his hands of the whole matter. Maggie was livid.

By this time Maggie was shacked up with her new boyfriend, Ted Ring, whom we will get to later, but it didn't take her long to head back into court to get the words, "a month" reinstated into the divorce decree. Since Paul had no other assets, it was essential that Maggie get that money. She had built it into her bootlegging business plan.

Paul, now pissed off and finally given an opportunity to defend himself, decided to counter-attack. He dragged in a character assassination witness by the name of Miss Gertrude Stelten, who went by the nickname, Gerty. She signed a sworn affidavit on May 6th, 1929, stating that the plaintiff, One-Eyed Maggie, was currently living with Ted Ring and was a woman of no moral character, which I believe is a step below low moral character, who had repeatedly, to Gerty's knowledge violated the prohibition laws, slept around for legal tender and other considerations and, as if the other accusations weren't enough, added that five-year-old Irene is without question, "NOT" the child of the defendant.

Paul entered in his own affidavit and it followed the same low-road as did Gerty's slanderous testimony. Paul offered up some of his own extra-black dirt to throw Maggie's way. He must have relished this opportunity to finally get even.

Paul started by declaring that there was no way in hell he could pay $50 a month because he only made $70 a month while working at Clyde Iron Works. He did offer to pay a modest amount for the support of one child, my father—little Stanley, and that was it. In his lengthy deposition Paul swore that Irene was not his child since, at the time of her conception, he was breaking rock at the County Work Farm.

But wait, there's more: Paul wanted to set the judge straight on the whole enchilada. He went on to add that John Mishap wasn't his kid, so Paul didn't owe Maggie a dime for that piece of work. Beside that, John Mishap had finally dropped out of his marathon stretch in the fourth grade, turned 18, and split. Little Scarface Joe was dead, having died in Redwing in '28. Andrew, who was 15, had left Maggie's hell hole to work at a relative's farm in Poplar, Wisconsin. Elisabeth, 12, had been removed from the home by the Minnesota Child Welfare Department and was presently residing at the Home of the Good Shepard in St. Paul, and Edward, only 11, had finally made it to the State School for the deaf and dumb in Fairbault.

Paul ended his affidavit with a familiar theme—he added that Maggie had recently been arrested no less than five times for violations of the liquor laws and that, at present, she was running a Blind Pig out of her rented dump on Michigan Avenue. The judge probably bought his own bootleg whiskey from Maggie. Her bootlegging operations were common knowledge at this point.

It didn't help Maggie's case any in that she had just been arrested on Oct. 15th, 1928 for running the very Blind Pig Paul was referring to. Maggie, with Stauch and Irene still at home, once again received a reprimand and a suspended sentence. God, Maggie loved her kids if for no other reason than they were time and time again her get out of jail free card.

The judge, with the wisdom of Solomon, probably should have had both of the remaining kids sawed in half and divided equally between these two lunatics, now found himself in a real quandary. In a way, he knew his ruling wouldn't matter. If he found against Paul, which he did, he knew that Paul would be in contempt of court within a month for not paying whatever child support the judge ordered him to pay; while, should he find against Maggie, Paul and his newfound slut Gerty could theoretically end up with the kids. The thought of which turned the judge's stomach.

He sided with Maggie and ordered Paul to pay $25 a month for the solitary support of Stanley Stupidnski. Maggie went ballistic. She leapt up and made a bee-line toward Paul and his strumpet, trying to tear his goddamned eyes out. The bailiffs restrained her from doing so but it made for some great low-brow courtroom drama. Jerry Springer is old news when it comes to my family.

The judge was right, because beyond the one-time $50 pittance, Paul never paid Maggie "a cocksucking dime." Paul spent another 90 days in the Work Farm for contempt of court, but after his time was served the entire system gave up on him. Over the decades Paul had gotten used to the Work Farm and knew all the guards, any number of inmates and the warden on a first name basis. Once back out, everyone, including the judge who ordered the child support, knew Paul wouldn't pay, so everyone settled for an action commonly referred to in legal jargon as "why bother."

Aside from the solitary $50 bill, Maggie Stupidnski would never see a penny in child support from her deadbeat husband. A few years later, in 1932, the State of Minnesota would remove the last two children from Maggie's cesspool so, in a way, it hardly mattered. That more or less sums up the roaring '20s for the Stupidnski family. Aren't gill nets wonderful?

The Riverside Bar

"Sand Creek, Charlie, remember the Sand Creek Massacre. How could they have done that to us? Hundreds of innocent women and children, old men, young boys, dead for no reason. How about the Dakota Wars right here in Minnesota, or the Souix Wars, the Black Hills War, both fought over your precious gold. What about Wounded Knee, Charlie, who's going to explain what happened at Wounded Knee. It's not fair, it's never been fair!"

Diz was slurring his words, his voice growing louder and louder at the Riverside Bar. Happy Hour was rapidly sliding into unhappy hour. Diz had arrived at the Riverside an hour before Charlie, giving himself a four beer head start in their long race to nowhere. So now he was at it again, on one of his Indian vs. White Man tirades, foaming at the mouth with five-hundred years of rage.

"Little Big Horn. That's the only battle that matters. Crazy Horse, White Bull, Black Elk, all of them unafraid of the white man's Gatling guns. Charging the cavalry, killing that bastard Custer and his men. Serves them right, dying to the last man.

"Little Big Horn, the Pine Ridge uprising when Clearwater and Lamont were gunned down by the FBI, that's what it's all about, Charlie, that's our fight to the bitter end."

"I know, Diz. I know."

Diz, completely intoxicated at this point, was rambling. Charlie couldn't even remember how they had gotten on the subject of Native Americans but regretted the fact that they had. When Diz went down that path it was all but impossible to get him back out.

"It's that Manifest Destiny crap that kills me, Charlie. Where did you people come up with this idea that you are somehow better than us. We don't poison our environment, we don't cut down the forests to the last tree standing, we didn't pave half the damn continent, we didn't bring the buffalo to the brink of extinction or kill off the passenger pigeons. You guys did. You white guys did.

"We lived with nature, Chuck. We hunted the buffalo, deer and elk, harvested the wild rice in the fall and lived off the land. We are the true stewards of the land, you are the race hellbent on conquering it all, having your self-proclaimed dominion over nature.

"Manifest Destiny was just your sorry ass excuse to kill us savages. It was genocide, cloaked in some pseudo-religious bullshit. If you were the chosen people, then we were the unchosen. We were the ones trying to keep our babies warm in blankets smeared over smallpox sores. We were the ones who suffered and died."

Charlie knew there was no stopping Diz at this point. The bartender was trying to be polite about it but you could see Diz's rampage was getting to him. There were two truckers sitting across the bar who were clearly annoyed by Diz's drunken soliloquy. It would only be a matter of time before Diz said something over the edge.

There had always been conflict between the Fond du lac Indian Reservation and the surrounding communities. Scanlon and Cloquet had both seen their share of trouble. Bar fights, vandalism on both sides, accusations, mistrust, questionable arrests, typical white man/red man small town animosity that started hundreds of years ago when the land that is Minnesota was first taken from the Dakota Sioux and the Chippewa or Ojibway as they are sometimes called. The broken treaties, the hanging of 38 Dakota warriors in Mankato on Dec. 26th, 1862. A protracted race war without merit or end.

Diz took another long pull from his draft beer and started back in.

"Custer was a bastard. You people glorify that butcher in those famous paintings of his valiant soldiers encircled by warriors, looking like some goddamned hero. He got what was coming to him. I just wish Crazy Horse and Sitting Bull would have killed all of them, especially Ulysses Grant, the bastard president who hated us."

One of the two biker-types on the other side of the bar finally broke. He had heard enough.

"Shut your goddamn mouth, Injun. Don't you go insulting our Presidents like that, Grant won the civil war for us and helped to free the slaves. If you don't shut your mouth I'll shut it for you."

Randy, the bartender, immediately sensed trouble. Diz had been drinking for hours and Stupidnski and Nelson were no match against these two pulp workers.

"It's a free country, asshole, and I can say what I want," goaded Diz back to them.

"Not when you're talking about Presidents. That's treason."

It wasn't treason, but the happy hour crowd at the Riverside Bar weren't exactly fine-tuned in constitutional law.

"FUCK YOU!" Shouted Diz across the bar.

The two pulp truckers got up and started walking around the bar. Randy got out a whistle he kept stashed behind the bar and let go with it. The piercing noise didn't even phase the truckers, who kept walking straight toward Diz and Stupidnski.

"He's drunk, you guys, leave him alone." Argued Charlie just as the first guy drew his right arm back to smack Diz in the head.

The bouncer, Carl, had heard the whistle loud and clear and was running toward the showdown. He was seconds too late.

The punch landed right on Diz's right side. Diz, in his stupor, had only half-heartedly attempted to block the fist, fell off his bar stool with a crashing thud. The trucker started to position himself for a kick to Diz's body when Carl arrived.

"Don't even think about it," commanded Carl, standing right behind the trucker in a Kung Fu-like fighting stance.

"Kiss my ass," responded the trucker as he let go a vicious kick to Diz's abdomen.

Knowing these two might start to beat the living shit out of Diz, Carl did what bouncers are hired to do, he slammed his fist into the back of the first truckers head so hard that he landed on the floor beside Diz. His friend took a powerful swing at Carl, but, anticipating it, Carl ducked.

When he rose back up Carl landed three or four punches before the other guy knew what had happened. Randy, who seconds before was behind the bar, was now standing behind Carl with a baseball bat. Stupidnski stayed out of it. Overweight and totally out of shape, the best he could offer was to sit on someone, and only if that someone were already knocked unconscious.

With the kick to his stomach, and his belly filled with beer, Diz started throwing up. Some of his barf was getting on the arm of the trucker who was lying on the floor right beside him. The trucker had landed on his face and his nose was bleeding from the impact.

"Now get the hell out of here. All of you!" said Carl to the four of them. He reached down and took the hand of the pulp wood trucker and helped him up. From the look in the truckers eyes you could see he wanted a piece of the bouncer something awful but Randy's baseball bat informed him that it wasn't a very good idea.

"You guys go first, and I'm going to make damn sure you pull away," said Carl sternly to the two truckers.

Carl and Randy left Diz to his puke and escorted the other two toward the door. Stupidnski got down on his hands and knees and crawled over toward his injured friend.

"You OK, Diz?"

"He kicked me hard, Charlie." Responded Diz in a sullen, broken whisper.

"You wanna get up?"

"No. Let me lay here a while."

By this time Randy and Carl were outside the bar watching the two guys climb into their eighteen wheeler and pull out onto the highway. They wanted to make sure they were gone before throwing Charlie and Diz out. It was dark outside, so they waited until they couldn't see the trucks tail lights any longer before heading back inside.

When they came back in, everyone else in the bar was standing around Diz, who was still lying on the floor beside his toppled barstool in a fetal position. The punch had split open his right cheek and between that, the puke and the truckers nose bleed, the floor looked like hell.

Upon returning, Carl crouched down and asked Diz how he was doing. Diz told him to just give him a couple of more minutes then he would leave. "Diz didn't start the fight," he added.

"I know, Diz. But sometimes you get a little carried away. You should learn to keep yer mouth shut, ya know."

"Yeah."

Charlie went to pay the tab and Randy refused to take his money. Randy felt bad about the whole affair. He'd heard Diz go on and on about the plight of the American Indian a dozen times in the past but it had never come to blows. The last round was on the Riverside. Randy pretty much agreed with most of what Diz said and felt the Indians had received the short end of the stick since the white man arrived in America.

Ten minutes later Diz was helped up by Charlie and Carl. He looked like shit. Puke and blood covered his light brown hoodie and he was still drunk. Charlie offered to drive him home and clean him up.

"Would it be OK to leave Diz's Gremlin parked outside tonight?" Charlie asked.

"Don't worry, Charlie. There's not a person on earth who's going to hot wire that piece of shit."

"OK. We'll come back and pick it up tomorrow."

"Fine."

Nothing more was said. The truckers were no where to be found outside as Charlie and Carl helped Diz into the passenger seat of Charlie's Pinto. After making sure it started, Carl went back into the club to help Randy clean up the floor. Stupidnski started driving toward Diz's filthy mobile home.

"Manifest Destiny." Mumbled Charlie to himself as he sped toward the reservation. "Manifest fucking Destiny."

*****

Winter descended on Northern Minnesota with a white vengeance. No one was happy. Diz kept losing while Charlie kept throwing money at the Monte Carlo. All to no avail, Crystal was falling further behind on her rent and Vicky didn't get the paper mill job, finally settling for waiting tables at a local café. It was snowy, dark and cold most of the time and chronic depression sniffed under the doorjamb of every motel room, apartment and saloon in northern Minnesota like a starving wolf. Spring, by all appearances, was permanently canceled.

At least Charlie was making some progress on his memoir, *Chain of Fools.* Diz had given up at trying to find an angle to have his cameo in the book, and seldom mentioned it any more. Charlie had rearranged his schedule to be sure to visit Sugar Daddies every Tuesday night to watch Crystal dance. To help her out he had become a regular supporter of her lap dances. Despite not being able to win the car and with it, somehow come to the rescue of this fading flower, Charlie had been on a six month winning streak.

His nickel pile, even after throwing 500 of them toward winning on the Monte Carlo every few days into the insatiable mouth of the Big Bertha, kept growing larger. He now had 35,040 tiny bas reliefs of Thomas

Jefferson in working capital. In layman's terms, it was $1,752. His rent at the Golden Gate was paid in advance, and even though his Pinto refused to start in the sub-zero temperatures, it had a full tank of gas.

There was some bad news. The north wind seems to carry bad news as easily as it did the arctic freeze that had settled over the land. Dismount Moose Nelson was having health trouble.

After weeks of having trouble sleeping, trouble to the point where night had become day and visa versa, Diz had broken down and gone to the tribal health clinic. Charlie, noting that Diz's eyes were looking glassed over and off-color, had encouraged Diz to have himself checked out. Diz was sure it was nothing more than a bad case of nerves. Diz hated winter and this year, combined with his extended losing streak, he was especially depressed. He drank when he was depressed. Technically, Diz drank when he wasn't depressed as well.

The doctor took one look at Diz's tainted eyeballs and knew immediately what his problem was. Diz had liver problems. After thirty years of professional drinking, this diagnosis didn't come as a shock to anyone living on the reservation. Cirrhosis of the liver was a community ailment in Fond du lac, just as it was in hundreds of other Indian reservations across America. As common as acne, though considerably deadlier.

After the test results came back, the doctor told Diz what he had told about a hundred other Native American patients before him, "You either stop drinking or your liver is going to fail."

"What the hell do you know about my liver, anyway," was Diz's terse reply. Whereupon Diz took his test results, threw them in the trash can in the lobby of the clinic and drove straight to the Rendevous for an afternoon bump.

Given Diz's denial and predisposition to continued drinking the doctor didn't bother entering his case and name onto any liver donor lists. There were thousands of other patients out there whose livers were failing from hepatitis, Wilson's disease and diabetes who had never so much as sipped a glass of dinner wine. They wanted to live and because of that, any one of them would receive a transplant long before they considered stitching a good liver into Diz. Giving a dedicated alcoholic a new liver was not a sound medical procedure. Finding a good liver to transplant was enough of a problem, which made wasting one on an unrepentant alcoholic unthinkable.

This wasn't the first patient the doctor had seen who had

stormed out of the office after receiving this same diagnosis, nor would it be the last. In a gesture not unlike Diz tossing his test results in the trash, the doctor simply had the staff place Diz's file in a drawer filled with similar cases. That file, though neatly arranged by last name and tagged with attractive color coordinated diagnoses, was, in essence, the garbage can file. These patients would not get better. For them, the prognosis was always the same. It was anybody's guess how long those patients might hang on—days, months or possibly years; recovery was not going to happen. Ever.

Diz got falling down drunk at the Rendevous that same afternoon, then proceeded to get violently ill. He did in fact cut back on his drinking for a spell which helped a bit. He didn't want to tell Charlie about his condition but, one afternoon at the buffet, Charlie started to talk about his own health problems, mostly his weight problem, and one thing led to another.

"Diz, I'm getting kind of worried about my weight," began Charlie as they both sat down at a booth, their trays filled to overflowing with high-fat, high sugar industrial food.

"Oh, yeah."

"I asked Mohammed at the motel to loan me his scale for a while because I've been really short of breath lately."

"And."

"I've gained ten pounds this winter, Diz. It's a bitch not being able to get out and walk some of this weight off."

"Maybe you could go to a gym or something," suggested Diz as he wolfed down a half-a-pound of Texas-style french fries.

"I'd look stupid as shit going to a gym."

"Yeah, you would."

"I've just got to cut back. Maybe I should eat more cottage cheese. That and grapefruit."

"That's a good idea, Chuck."

"How did it go with you last week at the doctor's office? Didn't you have an appointment to see a doctor last week?"

"Yeah."

"And?"

"The doc thinks my liver's screwed up. He says I have to stop drinking."

"I told you guzzling all those leftover drinks would land you in the goddamned hospital someday, Diz. Who knows what kind of germs and shit are in those drinks."

"It's not the germs that's doing it, Charlie, it's the booze itself. He says I have to stop drinking."

"You're shitting me, right?"

"No. And the Doc says that until I swear I'll stop drinking, he won't put me on any transplant lists either."

"Well, are you going to stop?"

"Hell no."

"What did the doc say will happen if you don't stop drinking?"

"My liver will fail."

"That sucks."

"Yeah. It sucks."

Charlie dove into his fried chicken and didn't bother questioning Diz any more about his long term prognosis. He knew better. Diz wouldn't give up drinking and it would simply be a matter of when, not if. That's how it was with Diz and there was nothing Charlie, the doctor, or anyone could do about it.

"Are you going to have any dessert?"

"Yeah, I thought I'd try some of that upside down peach cobbler shit they make."

"Hey Chuck, I have a favor to ask of you."

"What is it."

"If I drop dead before you're finished with your book, can you squeeze me in it somehow?"

"You're not going to drop dead, Diz. You're just going to have to cut back on your drinking."

"Yeah. I'll try to cut back some I guess."

Charlie looked across the booth at Diz, who eyes still held a yellowish tint, and concluded Diz wouldn't cut back on his drinking. Knowing that, he added, "OK, Diz. If you drop dead before I finish *Chain of Fools*, I'll give you a cameo of some kind."

"Thanks, Charlie. I always knew you were my best friend."

*****

"Is he out there?"

"Yeah, he's sitting where he usually sits."

"Ah, shit."

"Don't complain, Crystal. This guy's really got a thing for you and let's face it, without his lap dance money you'd have to resort to the other stuff. You're not exactly wild about the other stuff, are you?"

"No, I don't much care for the other stuff."

"Then get out there and make some cash, girl."

Crystal was hoping the fat guy wouldn't show up tonight. She knew his name was Charlie but she kept calling him John, hoping it would make him go away. She knew he was different from the other guys. It bothered her in a way, the difference. It would have been easier if he was just in it for the pleasures of her lap dance, but it was clear to everyone he wasn't. There was something else, something that bothered her about him.

Last week he bought four lap dances from her and it was weird, reflected Crystal. Normally, a dancer can pretty much tell if the guy whose lap you are working on has a woody or not. It's impossible not to notice if you stop and think about it. That's the whole point of lap dancing. The high school term is probably far closer to the truth than is lap dancing, and that age-old term is dry humping.

Most of the time the guy never takes it all the way to orgasm. Most of the time being the operative phrase. There had been many an night when Crystal felt some John's penis pulsing recklessly beneath her g-stringed ass half way through a song. Hell, Crystal could remember a couple of times when the guy came within thirty seconds of her grinding, skillful motions. The "squirters," as the girls referred to them, always tipped well but were gross-outs. Most of the guys took their problem, so to speak, back home or out to their car with them. Once out of the club, they could solve their problem any way they felt like it as far as the dancers were concerned.

Exotic dancers were there to create the problem—to tease, provoke, cajole, arouse, tantalize, captivate, beguile, in essence do whatever it takes to make the customers want you. Make them undress you with their eyes, despite the fact you are already naked. Make them want you, not for who you are, but what you were—the woman they will never have. The woman who could screw you in half if she felt like it.

Once their work was done, most of the dancers didn't give a damn about what happened to the teased up bull. If the guy went home and banged his two-hundred-and-thirty-pound, four kids later, half-asleep bride, that was his prerogative. If he went to the can, back out to his car, kept drinking until his erection fell down drunk or tried to get one of the girls to work overtime, these were not their issues. The dancers created the problem, which was work enough. They were there to dance and take your cash; the rest was irrelevant.

But this fat guy, pondered Crystal, this guy named Charlie, didn't even seem to have a boner during any of her lap dances. Well, he did have something going on during her last lap dance, but it wasn't much. It just seemed like he was doing it for other reasons, almost like he actually cared about her, and that bothered Crystal. Pushing 39, her career on a steady decline, it seemed very strange that anyone, even her mother for godsake, cared about her.

"Are you going out there or not? If you ain't going to take his money, sugar, I sure as hell will."

"I'll go, just give me a minute."

Crystal took a long, studied look in the undressing room mirror. Her soft blue eyes were a little bloodshot, but not bad. It was from all the smoke, she realized. She looked at her hair, falling down past her shoulders, and realized she needed to do her roots soon. She would have to dye her own hair at home, given her cash flow issues. God, that part of being broke killed her. Her complexion was good and her lips, painted a deep red, were inviting.

Crystal knew she was gaining weight. Not much, but dancers have a much finer measure of their weight than most women. A hundred hungry eyes a night might pour over every curve, every angle of their bodies and those eyes demanded perfection. Crystal raised her arms high up over her head and noted the sag. Vicky called them Wal-Mart arms, those little folds of flab that start to hang down as you age. With her arms back down, they vanished. But when you worked the pole, your arms were above your head half the time, and however subtle, Crystal knew a similar version of her arms could be found anywhere in America rolling a shopping cart down aisle seven.

She stood up, took the hand mirror and turned her back to the make up counter and the larger mirror above it. Without drawing attention to herself she took a quick glance at her ass and upper thighs. It was there. She knew it was there. Jimmy Cortese was the first to see it there. For a dancer, it marked the beginning of the end—cellulite. The very first, faintest signs of it started about four years ago, but now...Crystal didn't keep the hand mirror in place for long. In her eyes it wasn't just dimpling, it was as if the back of her thighs resembled the surface of the moon. Deep, orange-peel like craters pocketing the top half of her once seamless thighs. For a dancer, cellulite wasn't unattractive, it was a death sentence. Cellulite equals Monday and Tuesday nights. Cellulite equals filling out job applications, working overtime at some motel, waitressing, secretarial work, housecleaning or, Crystal dreaded the very thought of it, finding a man.

"Hello, is anyone home?"

Amber interrupted Crystal's moment of self-flagellation, bringing her back to 9:54 on a Tuesday night with eleven men in the club, including staff, four dancers, including herself and an overweight, half-drunk John waiting for his girl to come out and perform an erotic dance on his enormous lap. It was like getting a bucket of ice water dumped on you while standing outside in Minnesota mid-February. Crystal wanted to cry.

"I'm going, damn it, Amber. I'm going."

Crystal walked toward the floor exit door, placed opposite the beaded dance floor entrance. The door led out onto the customer floor and that floor meant cash. Jimmy Cortese paid the girls $3.72 an hour, the same wage a waitress makes. The rest was up to them. If they could convince a hundred Johns to slide a thousand dollar bills into their g-strings on any given night, that was their job. No benefits, no retirement, their past, their present and their entire future rested on the shoulders of a four letter word: cash.

Crystal strolled around the floor for a few minutes, steering clear of the old guy in the dark corner, and asked a couple of patrons if they might be interested in a personal dance. All of them were interested but none of them willing to cough up the $20. prerequisite. After exhausting all other options, in catlike fashion, she made her way toward Stupidnski.

"Hi, John, could I interest you in a private dance?"

Charlie didn't respond. He hated it when Crystal called him John, not that she had ever called him by his real name.

He reached down into his wallet, recently restocked with paper nickels, and pulled out a twenty, slipping it neatly into her g-string. Crystal awkwardly spread her legs, far wider than usual, and slipped down on his lap. She was wearing a thin, see through blouse with nothing beneath it. Her breasts, cosmetically altered to the point where they wouldn't sag at her own funeral if she lived to a hundred and seven, were still her finest attribute. They were now within an eyelash of Charlie's gaping mouth.

Crystal went to work. She undulated, squirmed, squeezed and rhythmically slid in every direction including several compass headings that have yet to be discovered. Charlie, who normally didn't get worked up out of respect for Crystal, found himself unable to abstain from such biological behavior this time around.

Within a minute, like ten thousand Johns before him, he had a problem. Crystal, as she worked her ass on him, was glad. At least he was normal, she said to herself. As normal as lap dancing is. This holier than thou shit he was sticking with was getting to her. If I'm a goddamned stripper and an experienced one, she thought to herself, at least have the dignity to get a woody once I jump on your lap, you asshole.

"Oh, that's nice."

He speaks, she thought. Usually this fat guy hardly said a word.

"Do you like it?"

"Very much."

"Do you want me to stick around through the next song?"

"Yes."

Charlie knew the rules. He reached into his back pocket to get out his wallet. Crystal, in a rare moment that even she couldn't quite grasp, said, "No, you don't need to do that Charlie, this one's on me."

At that moment, after dozens of lap dances, months of voyeurism and countless nights of longing, Charlie Stupidnski instantly died and went to heaven. Crystal had finally said his name.

Chain of Fools

Chapter 7: Ted Ring's Death

On October 24th, 1929, the New York Stock Exchange crashed. The roaring twenties were over. Maggie Stupidnski paid no attention whatsoever to Black Thursday, or the following Tuesday, Oct. 29th when the market plummeted more than fourteen-billion dollars in value. Maggie, and her new boyfriend, Ted Ring, didn't have a dime in the stock market. All of their working capital was tied up in their bootlegging and gambling operations.

In the topsy turvy world of speakeasies, all night poker games and whores, bad times = good times. The great depression, so long as prohibition was still in place, became the great elation for these two small town outlaws. What could possibly be better for liquor sales than semi-suicidal stock brokers, bankers whose banks were on holiday and merchants unable to move merchandise. If ever there was a moment in history when the upper class, the monied class of Duluth, Minnesota, needed a good, stiff drink, this was it. Mrs. Stupidnski and her Norwegian boyfriend soon found themselves in Blind Pig heaven.

Beyond the problems of the upper-crust, when you throw in the soup lines, unemployed workers, union strife, political turmoil and the fact that nowhere else on the planet able to serve a cold beer aside from

Maggie's joint, it becomes bootlegger's nirvana. What was devastating for the nation was a absolute boon for Ted and Maggie Enterprises, and they had a ball.

By the autumn of '29 Paul Stupidnski, along with any hope of receiving child support, had been written off by little Ms. One-eye. The court-ordered $25. a month child support payments had never once arrived via the local post, nor did Maggie ever seriously think they would.

"To hell with him." Maggie told Ted as they gassed up the car for another liquor run to East St. Paul. "I don't need his goddamned money anyway."

It was true. Maggie didn't need his money. With most of her children either taken from her or dead, all she had left in her wayward nest were my father and his half-sister, Irene. Since nine year old Stanley, who either had to grow up fast or starve, was old enough to cook and care for little Irene, Maggie found herself, at 37, free to devote all of her time and energy to her thriving illegal businesses.

"Fuck the children," said Maggie to her big Norwegian boyfriend as they drove off. Life was good.

One of the handful of stories that made it through the filter of my familial screening system was that my grandmother and Ted Ring, a big Scandinavian Maggie had met at her living room speakeasy, were actually in love. The story has it they were hoping to get married as soon as they could get some time off from their demanding moonshine business. Plans were to throw a huge wedding, losers come all.

Maggie, who was used to being bloodied up by her significant other, found Ted to be a refreshing change. In keeping with Maggie's inverted standards, Ted Ring was no angel. On April 9th, 1927, about the same time he was courting Maggie, Ted was arrested by the Duluth police department for disorderly conduct. Ted loved a good fist fight and apparently got into it with a rival Swede down in the Bowery near 6th Avenue West. He spent the night in jail, as did the Swede, but neither were sent to the Work Farm. They were fined $25 each and set free the next morning, both a bit black and blue but none the worse for wear.

Like Paul Stupidnski and so many others in that era, Ted Ring was born in the old country, having immigrated with his parents around the turn of the century from Norway. His father's name was Thorgrin Ring while his mother's maiden name was Corvis Olson. There were, and still are, more Swedes and Norwegians in Duluth than people, so Ted and his family fit right in. He had two brothers, Michael Ring and

Steven Ring. All of them lived in the blue-collar, west end of town.

Ring was not their original surname. Like so many other immigrant names, it was abbreviated by the clerks at Ellis Island within hours of the family disembarking from their human freighter. No doubt the original name was something like Ringsrude or Ringenthal or a thousand variations thereof. Ring was easier to pronounce, decided the immigration officer looking over Thorgrin's paperwork. By the time their entry visa was approved, 100 generations of ethnic heritage were reduced to a four letter word.

"By the way, Ring's your new last name, Thorg, and welcome to America," said the overly efficient immigration officer. "Next," he added, looking to eviscerate someone else's birthright.

By 1930 Ted Ring was shacking up full time with Maggie. On April 29th of that year, he shows up on the Fifteenth Census of the United States of America along with every other wayward soul living at Maggie's run-down apartment. On that particular day John Mishap, Maggie's oldest illegitimate child, happened to be back at home for a spell. John's now a spry, semi-retarded twenty year old who had been unemployed for the past 3 months. He put his occupation down as a common laborer—the kind of high-skilled occupation a 4th grade education will command. Very, very common laborer might have defined his skills more accurately.

In that census Maggie put herself down as the head of the household even though she had no legal income. She put her occupation down as none, not even housekeeping. Stanley and Irene were both still living in the house, ten and six years old respectively. Maggie had not one, but two boarders—the aforementioned Ted Ring and Mr. George Bazon, who would bunk at Maggie's joint for the next 17 years, until the fire of 1947 finally shagged him out.

Both Ted and George were working. Ted was still keeping a job at the Portland Cement Plant out in New Duluth while George was working down at the coal docks unloading lake freighters which, back then, were bringing in heating coal from the mines of West Virginia. They were both lucky to have jobs as the depression was slowly, insidiously, making most of America's workers gainfully unemployed.

Ted Ring was a drunk. If this news comes as a shock you are reading the wrong book. It should go without saying that unless stated otherwise in this screwed up family of mine, always assume the person I'm writing about has an alcohol problem. For Ted, one of the fringe benefits of living with the bootleg queen of West Duluth was free liquor.

"Sell a Pint, Drink a Pint," became their company's maxim.

The fact remains that Ted and Maggie were making money and lots of it. For once in her life, Maggie was never behind in the rent and, in the summer of 1930, just as the depression worsened, Ted bought a brand new Model 30-U, four-door Plymouth sedan. He paid for the car in cash. Plymouths cost more than six-hundred dollars in 1930, which was a small fortune during the height of the great depression.

The sedan was a real beauty and soon became the talk of Helm Street. The roof and fenders were jet black, while the body and hood were a deep maroon. At that time the four door Plymouths all came with the back doors opening forward, a style that eventually became known as suicide doors. They were aptly named, because opening them when you were roaring down the highway was suicidal. The car had a new, powerful 48-horsepower engine and could readily hit 70 miles an hour.

If it looked like a gangster car, it's because it was. The Duluth police had no doubts as to where Ted and Maggie's newfound wealth was coming from but, since half the force were buying their bootleg liquor from Maggie and Ted, they went easy on the couple for the next few years.

The couple needed a fast car to make booze runs back and forth from St. Paul, where they were buying their whisky, vodka and beer. The Carleton County Sheriff's Department had effectively busted up most of the "back 40" stills so the only way to get product was to become a rum runner, making the 160 mile run between St. Paul and Duluth as often as needed to keep their speakeasy well stocked.

It was on just such a run, on the morning of September 14th, 1930, when it all happened. They had left Duluth for the Twin Cities on one of their Sunday liquor runs around nine in the morning. Ted was driving. Naturally then, Ted was also drinking.

Back in the 1930s there were no open container laws, no breathalysers and no radar detectors. Unless you were falling down drunk you were considered more or less sober. When Ted cracked open his flask and started passing it around as they barreled down Highway 61 no one thought anything of it. It was just another lovely, stinking drunk, bootlegging run on a rainy Sunday morning in the fall. Nothing out of the usual.

The accident happened south of Hinckley, Minnesota. Hinckley back then was little more than a one street country town with a hotel, a bank, a gas station and a general store. Located half way between

Duluth and St. Paul, Ted had just pulled into Hinckley to gas up the new Plymouth and take a piss.

All totaled there were eight people in the car when the accident happened. Ted was driving with Maggie beside him. Next to Maggie was Frank Cich, an old friend of the family. The back seat held five more people, John Mishap and his friend Adrian, Stanley and Irene and Martha Cheski, who was engaged to Frank at the time. I have no idea where in hell they were going to put the liquor they were driving to St. Paul to purchase but they probably had a place to stash it. They might have had a car top carrier, or a secret compartment installed. They always brought the children for cover knowing the local sheriffs along the way were unlikely to search for whiskey when there were kids on board. Little did they know.

After filling her up, Ted drove back out on Highway 61 and floored it. About three miles south of town the highway takes a fairly quick turn to the west as the road goes up and over a railroad line running the same north to south direction. The overpass, along with the train tracks, are still there, though Highway 61 has been replaced by Interstate I-35 West.

Back then it was a standard viaduct—creaky, wooden and built out of creosote-soaked timbers. The decking was wood. It was raining that morning and as Ted, by this time loaded, came speeding down the other side of the overpass, he stepped on his brakes to check his speed just before the road curved south again. A big mistake.

On the wet wooden planking of the viaduct the Plymouth skidded out of control. When the brand new car found itself on pavement again it was going sideways. The tires caught hold of the asphalt and, with the weight of the eight people on board, it started rolling. Before it came to a stop in a ditch beside the road, the Plymouth had rolled over three times. It came to its final resting spot upside down, its roof crushed flat.

Why no one was physically thrown from the car was never explained, but somehow all eight passengers somehow managed to stay inside. There were no seatbelts in the 1930s so it must have been complete mayhem inside that automobile as it tumbled off the road.

Within minutes, some good Samaritans had pulled over and were helping to yank the injured kids and the rest of them from the wreckage. Maggie was hurt. She had a large cut on her back and any number of internal injuries. She remained in serious condition for a week.

Frank Cich got off light, crawling out of the car with only a fractured shoulder bone. Martha Cheski was miraculously uninjured and the four kids, despite numerous cuts and bruises, were essentially OK. Ted Ring wasn't.

Ted had broken his neck in the rollover. He was still alive when they pulled him from the hissing car but it was clear that his injuries were severe. They speculated Ted might have clung on to the steering wheel when they rolled, with his neck somehow managing to get between the wheel and the collapsed roof of the car.

One of the people who had stopped to help, loaded the unconscious driver into their car and drove him back to the Hinckley Hotel. Once there a local doctor, Dr. Stephans, was called in to care for them until the injured could be brought by ambulance back to Saint Mary's Hospital in Duluth.

Ted didn't make it, passing away around 4:00 p.m. that afternoon from a broken neck. Maggie, fighting for her life with internal injuries, didn't learn about Ted's death for several more days. She was placed into an ambulance and rushed back to Duluth that same day. Frank Cich was treated and released by Dr. Stephens. The rest of the survivors were ferried by the police back to Helm Street and Maggie's squalid apartment.

The car was demolished. According to the police reports the Plymouth's odometer read 4,000 miles. The Blind Pig operation was shut down for the next month while Maggie recovered. Ted was buried the following week in Duluth with Maggie still in the hospital and unable to attend her lover's funeral.

Maggie eventually recovered from her injuries but never from her broken heart. They tell me that once Ted was killed, Maggie descended into a depression she would never come out of. Their fairy tale world of rum running, big spending and gambling came abruptly to a end that Sunday in September. The new car was towed to a junk yard, Ted Ring was dead and all Maggie had left in the world were Stanley, Irene and George Bazon. Since she didn't give a damn about any of them life got very, very rough down on Michigan Avenue, especially for the kids.

The Black Bear Casino Lounge

"Where the hell have you been this last week?"

"Oh shit, Charlie, you know how it is. My cousins came over last Monday and, well, one thing led to another."

Charlie knew how it was.

"I've got some great news, Diz."

"You won the Monte Carlo?"

"Hell no. No one's won the damn Monte Carlo. They must be making a fortune on that car. At this rate, I don't know if anyone will ever win the Monte Carlo.

"The great news is that Crystal actually said my name, my real name."

"She didn't call you John?"

"No, she called me Charlie and she gave me a free lap dance to boot."

"Haven't you been buying like, three, four lap dances a night from her anyway, Charlie?"

"Yeah, but this free one was the best."

"Yeah?" Diz interest was piqued.

"She worked it so hard, Diz, it was like I found myself in heaven. I felt like I wanted to let loose so bad."

"And you didn't?"

"That's sick, Diz. Hell no I didn't."

"You should have, Charlie. You haven't been laid in God only knows how long and you blew your one big chance, you big, goofy son-of-a-bitch."

"You're such an asshole, Diz."

"Yeah, I am." Diz leaned back over his drink and kept quiet for a minute.

"Hey, Dena, could you bring us another round."

"Sure, Charlie. Same thing?"

"Yeah, two brandy seven's. The cheapest shit ya got."

"Coming right up."

As Dena set about the business of putting two fresh ones together, Charlie, almost reluctantly, asked what Diz and his cousins had been up to, though he knew it was going to be just another version of the same old week-long drunk.

"So what's new with your cousins?" Asked Charlie, though it was hardly new.

"They brought over some homemade moonshine on Monday. They bought this wicked shit from some old farmhouse outside of Kettle River. I'm pretty sure, judging from the taste of it, the shit doubles as paint remover."

"My grandmother, One-Eyed Maggie used to run a still down in Kettle River."

"No kidden'."

"God, I wonder if it's from Maggie's old still. Wouldn't that be totally crazy."

"It'd be cool. Maybe now you can somehow work me into the book."

"Don't start that shit again, Diz. You're not getting into my book. I don't care where the hell your cousins bought their hooch. I thought the doctor told you to stop drinking."

"I did, for almost a month. Then my liver must have recuperated because I didn't get sick at all this time. Do you want to hear what happened next, or what?"

Dena arrived with the fresh drinks. Diz and Charlie, as if synchronized, both lifted the old ones up to squeeze out the last few drops of the watered down brandy before sliding them over to Dena. As they did this, in a ritual that could well have been choreographed, Dena slid the fresh ones to where the old ones had sat and waited for the two drunks to hand her their empties. It was, in fact, a dance. The dance of drunks.

"Sure, tell me what happened."

"You remember those blue pills we got from Falling Bobby Bear's sister's friend, the ones that made me and George Coyote sick as dogs."

"Yeah."

"Well, turns out Rita, Rita Deer Cloud is her name by the way, felt real bad about us throwing up and all and got us some new pills to sort of make up for it."

Oh God, thought Charlie to himself, this is going to be another whopper. Diz went on.

"These were white and like, four time bigger than those tiny blue ones. Rita told Falling Bobby's sister to be sure to tell us not to take more than two and that we would be in for one hell of a good time if we did.

"So all three of us took two each, even though Bobby Bear's sister, Ashanti had given him twenty of 'em. At first nothing happened. We were already so drunk we thought maybe the booze might have canceled out the effect, ya' know, neutralized the pills somehow.

"Then about an hour after eating them all three of us started to get woodies. Like it was really weird. We weren't even telling dirty stories, or watching a porn video or anything when out of nowhere all three of us had these hard-ons that would not go away."

"Oh shit, you guys took Viagra, or some shit like that, didn't you," said Charlie.

"It must have been something like that because two hours later we still had these boners and absolutely nowhere to go with them. So that's when I suggested we go find Bobby Bear's sister and her friend to see if they couldn't somehow help us out with our problem.

"We drove around the Rez for an hour looking for them in the Gremlin. Let me tell you, Charlie, it's a bitch to drive around with a hard-on. The damn thing keeps wanting to hit the steering wheel and it hurts like hell every time you go to push down the clutch and..."

"Please, Diz, spare me the details."

"OK, so we finally find Ashanti and Rita. They were with another friend of theirs, Susan Two Spirit, sitting a house for Ashanti's parents, who had gone to the Bad River Rez in Wisconsin to visit some friends. When we walked in her parents place it smelled like the Feds were burning fields of marijuana or something right in the living room. Those three girls were high as a goddamned kite.

"So I walked up to Rita, the girl who got us the pills, and said, 'your pills here got us a big problem and I think you should help solve the problem.'

"So Rita just starts giggling, you know, how pot heads start giggling, and looks down at my jeans and pretty soon all three girls are laughing and pointing at us guys and we start laughing too because it's really pretty funny."

"So what happened?"

"Well, Rita felt kind of bad and said that if we sat down and smoked some pot with them it would probably make our boners go away."

"Did it?"

"Fuck no, but Falling Bobby Bear started giving the girls some of his Kettle River moonshine and we all started smoking this really wicked homegrown shit that Susan Two Spirits grew last summer and well, ya' know, stuff started happening.

"It was around midnight by then and, even though none of them is anything to write home about, ya' know real pretty or anything, they came up with their own plan to take care of our problem. By this time they were all pretty much smashed on the moonshine and we were all sort of crunched together on the couch and well, things started getting personal."

Diz took a drink from his brandy seven, to wet his whistle, and continued.

"Rita asked if I wanted to go upstairs into one of the bedrooms and hell, with a stiffy still as hard as a rock the idea sounded great to me. Bobby Bear took off with the other girl and George Coyote wound up with Bobby Bear's sister and by morning all of us had pretty much worn the skin off our problems, if you know what I mean."

"I think I know what you mean."

"I'll tell you, Charlie. You ever get a chance to sleep with Crystal you be sure to take two of these."

Diz reached into his pocket and handed Diz two white pills. He winked at Charlie and added,
"These will do you right, Charlie."

The two men soon finished their drinks, squared up with Dena and went out on the floor. Charlie kept reaching into his right pocket, his fingers taking hold of the pills, rolling them round and round like some Chinese meditation balls. He kept thinking of Crystal as he did so. He thought of her last lap dance and these pills. He thought of how it could all somehow, somewhere, someday come together.

As he left the casino that night, once again flush from his prolonged lucky streak, he dropped a $50 on the Big Bertha. He didn't win. But he knew, deep inside, that was going to change.

*****

A few days later, on the evening on March 1st, ironically the same day One-Eyed Maggie was born, Charlie Stupidnski won the Monte Carlo. Well, not exactly.

Technically the winner was Diz, but Diz was using Charlie's money, which gets a bit confusing. It happened late, a time when things like this tend to occur. It happened at the very tail end of a Saturday night, which, technically, was early Sunday morning. Both men were drunk. Not quite stupid, fall down drunk, but stumbling, dumb-as-bricks drunk.

Diz had been losing money all night, starting out with the dollar machines and descending all the way down to the penny slots. It was the first of the month so Diz was momentarily flush with his tribal allotment check. By midnight Diz was no longer flush.

Charlie, on the other hand, was having a great night. He was up $72, or, as he liked to figure it, 1,440 metallic portraits of Mr. Monticello himself. As well as Stupidnski had been doing on the slot machine floor these past few months, he was still suffering at the hands of the Big Bertha.

Diz and Charlie had arranged to meet back at the Black Bear's bar around 2:00 a.m., give or take a half hour. Charlie arrived first, with Diz still out there trying to squeeze some extra pennies out of the first hot slot he had found all night.

Dena was working. God, thought Charlie, Dena's always working. Dena fixed Charlie a nightcap while he watched a west coast hockey game that was still underway on the flat screen TV above the bar. Some kind of game was always being played on that TV, reflected Charlie, even if they had to resort to Japanese baseball games at 5:00 a.m. While he was watching the hockey game, not caring who the hell won or lost, the concept first came to him.

Since he kept winning money but losing the car and Diz kept losing money but never trying to win the car...why not switch? Maybe he could spot Diz in return for some kind of favor. This is what Charlie was contemplating, albeit in a virtual whirlpool of alcohol, when Diz showed up.

"Hey, Diz, what's going on?"

"Same old shit, Charlie. I just can't win this year. Or last year. Whatever."

"Get me something to drink, Dena, I'm dying here," said Diz rather loudly.

Seeing that the bar was empty aside from Diz and Charlie, Dena had no trouble hearing Diz's plea for a cocktail. He didn't have to add the dying bit. "What ya havin' tonight, Diz?"

"A black Russian."

"Kind a late to be drinking that kind of drink, don't ya think, Diz."

"Hell no, Dena, I'll be fine. The Kahlúa helps me sleep."

Dena knew better than to argue with a tired drunk sitting down at the bar after a long night of losing. She went about the business of mixing Diz's nightcap, even though she knew Kahlúa was made from distilled coffee. Hardly a sedative, she thought.

"I got a favor to ask, Diz."

"Anything Charlie. Shoot."

"You still got the itch, you know, wanting to break your losing streak and all."

"Damn straight I got the itch, Charlie. I want to do something, especially now, with spring coming round and all."

"If ya' had the money, and a way to get there, where would you want to go?"

"Deadwood, South Dakota." It was a definitive reply.

"What?"

"Yeah, I've heard they got some kick-ass casinos in Deadwood and I've always wanted to see the Black Hills, especially that statue of Crazy Horse."

"What statue of Crazy Horse?"

"You don't know about the great big statue that dead Polish guy is carving?"

"Never heard of it."

"It's like, huge, Charlie. It's like the biggest statue ever. This Polish guy, hell he might be a relative of yours, well, he and this Lakota Chief, I think his name is Bear something...hmmm, I'll think of it when I sober up, well, they started carving this huge mountain in the 1940s. It's a statue of Crazy Horse riding and pointing his arm out to the east."

"Why the east?"

"I don't know, it's probably just the way the mountain was facing."

"OK. Well, do you want to go there this spring?"

"Shit, Charlie, I can't chance a trip like that in my Gremlin. My clutch is going out and hell, I ain't even got the money to fix it at the moment. I don't think your Pinto would make it there either, do you?"

"No, Diz, I'm talking about the Monte Carlo."

Dena had finished the drink a few minutes ago but stood aside for a while listening to these two men converse. She knew all about the Crazy Horse statue. On a road trip to Sturgis, South Dakota with some biker friends a few years ago, they had continued west after the rally to take in the Black Hills. She had gone to the memorial back then and loved it. Dena loved everything about the Black Hills—the casinos, Mount Rushmore, the beauty of the countryside itself.

"Here's your drink, Diz. Ya know, I've been to the Black Hills."

"No shit. When were you there?"

"A few years back. Me and Eddy— you know, that biker guy I broke up with while back—we both went there to visit after going to the bike rally in Sturgis. It was bike week and man, did we party. It's real pretty country, Diz."

Dena slipped the black Russian in front of him as she spoke.

"That'll be $4.50, Diz."

Diz started to reach into his wallet when Charlie unexpectedly flipped a five spot on the bar.

"This one's on me, Dena, and keep the change."

"Thanks," said Dena, as she picked up the five dollar bill and walked back to the cash register.

"Nice ass," mumbled Diz to himself.

"You got that right," mumbled Charlie in agreement. Charlie then dug into his wallet and took out five twenties. He laid them on the bar, one by one, in a kind of poor man's display of being flagrantly wealthy.

Diz, who was broke, was impressed.

"That's a lot of cash, Charlie. It's too goddamned late to drink up that much cash tonight."

"It's not for liquor, Diz, it's for the Big Bertha."

"Ah, shit. It was hoping it was for cocktails."

"No, this is it." Charlie pointed down to the short stack of twenties and continued. "This here represents twenty pulls on that ugly, thieving arm of Big Bertha. If you win it on the first pull, the rest is yours to keep. But no matter which pull you win that Monte Carlo on, I'm taking you to an all expenses paid trip to Deadwood, South Dakota, no questions asked."

"No kiddin?" responded a bewildered Indian.

"Honest Injun," replied Stupidnski sarcastically.

"When would we go?"

"After the snowstorms stop. You know, in the spring. April, May, something like that. I haven't really worked out all the plans because, well, because we haven't won the car yet, have we?"

"No, but I'm going to win it. I just got off a penny machine that was red hot. Look at this shit."

Diz stood up and showed Charlie his jeans. Both pockets were bulging to the tearing point from hundreds upon hundreds of copper pennies. Charlie was impressed.

"How much you figure you got in there, Diz?"

"Eight, maybe nine bucks."

"Shit, you were on a roll. Let's not let ya' cool off too much. Let's get outa' here and take those twenty shots at that black beauty."

"Sounds like a plan, Charlie. I'm with ya."

Charlie and Diz got up from the bar, and started walking off with their drinks in hand.

"Where you guys going?" Asked Dena as she watched them leave.

"Were going to win the car."

"Great, good luck. I'll be there if I hear the sirens go off."

The two men, the drunken Indian and the overweight middle-aged guy headed toward the front door of the casino with a sense of stumbling destiny. Diz couldn't help but think of how great it would be to stand in front of the Crazy Horse statue in the spring, with the flowers blooming and all the other Indians standing beside him, seeing this fabulous monument to his people...etc. etc. all in this dreamy, post-midnight delusional state Diz loved living in.

Charlie approached the Big Bertha and stood there silently for a moment, as if it were some kind of show down. Bertha remained impenetrable, with her four windows proudly displaying another losing combination of one bell, one Lucky 7, and various fruits. Not a single window had the word CAR showing. She had just taken five more dollars from some disgruntled Swede who was presently crawling back into his beat up truck and vanishing into the endless scrub forests and back woods on Northern Minnesota. The Swede, as stubborn as Swedes are, was still thinking he had almost won the Monte Carlo. He hadn't.

Feeling that wonderful, albeit misguided, sense of inebriation and cockiness, Charlie turned and tried to strike up a conversation with the security guard standing beside the car.

"You got the keys handy? 'cause tonight, she's mine."

The guard, looking to be no more than 18, didn't know how to respond. At 2:35 a.m. on a busy Saturday night, this poor kid was exhausted. Technically, along with three other people in upper management and the two remaining Texas Hold'em dealers, he was the only other person not wasted in the entire casino. Dena, the bartender, had started sneaking herself drinks around 9:30 and was numb from the cerebral cortex on down. The guard wanted to be drunk as well, but he was underage and because of it, the staff had been carefully instructed never to serve him. Dena slipped him a beer now and then but that was it.

"They don't allow us to have the keys, 'cause if someone were to start her up inside we could get carbon monoxide in the building, and ya' know that's a killer, fer sure."

"So what happens when we win? When can we pick her up?"

"I don't know. No one's ever won. But I did see a guy get three cars up last week."

"Three?"

"Ya, all he needed was one more and that last bar with the word CAR on it landed just below the strawberry."

Charlie nodded in acknowledgment, as if the guard were giving him some kind of inside information. Charlie thought, hell, the bitch is lining them up. She's getting ready to put all four cars in a row. She's ready.

There was absolutely no truth to what Charlie was thinking. Big Bertha was a mathematical program of random chance that would produce a winning combination when she damn well felt like it. There was nothing lining up. Well, maybe there was.

Diz stood back, wavering in place, and listened to the exchange between Charlie and the boyish-looking security guard. Diz was tired, almost falling asleep on his feet.

Charlie took out his wallet and retrieved one of the five twenties and took one last, longing glance at the Monte Carlo a few yards away. He slid his first twenty into the cash hungry mouth of this giant slot machine and out of sheer habit reached up and put his right hand on its massive arm. Charlie knew it was easier to just push the button to get the four slot wheels spinning but the arm held a certain casino sense of romance for him. He started to yank it down.

"Charlie, what the hell you doing? I thought I was supposed to play for you." Shouted Diz.

Charlie froze. He suddenly remembered. With a newfound sense of pride, Charlie then turned around and looked down at his secret weapon. Dismount Moose Nelson was standing there—dirty jeans, flannel shirt, a face that looked like the surface of a bombed out moon, bloodshot eyes, dark, greasy hair, the works—wobbling. A wobbling secret weapon. A drunken, wobbling, exhausted secret weapon.

"Well then, get your ass up here!" hollered Charlie, already celebrating his win.

"Ya betcha."

Diz walked up the ramp that led to the platform where Big Bertha stood. It wasn't a very high platform, just two feet above the floor of the casino, but enough to get the slots head a little higher than the hundreds of other smaller slot machines that surrounded her. Big Bertha on a pedestal.

Charlie stood aside as Diz stepped up. The guard wondered what the hell was going on but didn't say anything. Just another couple of drunks on a losing streak, he thought to himself.

Diz, who likewise had a dramatic flair, reached for the large metal arm with the big red ball at the end. He didn't waste a second. He pulled the lever. Charlie, the guard and Diz all watched the four spinning wheels gather speed and start their notorious run. Normally, were it not so late, a handful of passer-bys would be standing around the platform watching them play. Big Bertha's windows were so large you could read the various letters and symbols from half way across the casino. People gathered around hoping they would be there when it happened. Be there when the lights went off, the bells starting ringing, and the four fateful windows all displayed the same bold, black three letter word: CAR.

This late in the evening, there was no crowd. Just Diz, Charlie and the young guard who looked ridiculous in the slightly oversized, quasi-policeman outfit he was required to wear.

The first bar stopped. No CAR. Technically it was already over.

"Fuck," said Diz appropriately. The other bars had other crap on them. Only the third bar up displayed the word CAR. Diz pulled a second time.

Same results, different symbols.

A third time. Ditto, but the first bar had CAR on it.

Fouth...etc.

Fifth...whatever.

Sixth...same old, same old.

Seventh...nope.

Eight...sorry.

Ninth...well. The word CAR had already shown up on two of the first eight pulls. So not one of the three guys watching the machine got overly excited when it came up for a third time. When the second bar stopped at CAR tensions noticeably rose. When the third bar hesitated for a second, like it wanted to go on to a cluster of bright red cherries, then fell back to CAR, the three of them all looked at each other like...is this it?

When the fourth bar tumbled slowly past CAR, too slowly to allow for any hope at all, the three let out a sigh as though they had already conceded their loss, but then...unbeknownst to either of them there was a second bar with the word CAR not far behind it and...

It was, for Charlie Stupidnski, the best moment of his entire life. The bells and whistles started going off, the sirens rang and the dredges of humanity who were still sober enough to be standing all ceased feeding their own machines and started walking toward the noisy Big Bertha. Of course at this hour they looked a bit more like zombies than appreciative spectators. They had that stiff, exhausted walk common to the three o'clock crowd. Gambling zombies.

The guard walked over to Diz, reached into his front right pocket, pulled it out and handed a bewildered Diz a gold embossed envelope.

"Congratulations," said the kid as he shook Diz's trembling hand.

Diz took hold of the envelope, still stunned by his unexpected victory, and for one brief instant had a serious moral dilemma. He realized that this was the perfect opportunity to double cross his best friend. For an instant, almost like an unprincipled hiccup, Diz considered keeping the envelope and accepting the car. He had in fact pulled the lever with the guard bearing witness to it, so therefor he and he alone was the rightful owner of the Monte Carlo. In his stupor he worked out the rest of his hastily imagined argument.

You see, he thought, I really don't even know this fat guy, but I'd just asked him if I could borrow some money from him to play the Big Bertha. All Diz owed this guy, this stranger whom he just met, was sixty bucks, period, plus another twenty in interest.

Then, in a flash of righteousness, Diz recalled all the treaties the white man had broken over the centuries with their dealings with the Native Americans and realized he couldn't do it. Diz couldn't make a deal, which is a treaty in a way, then turn around and break it. He might have his problems—unemployed and more or less unemployable, a drunk, a dragee, un-showered, prone to swearing, etc., etc., etc.—but he was not a cheat or a liar.

The ethical hiccup passed.

"It's not my car."

"What? You just won it. I just saw you win it."

"No. It's his car, I was just here to pull the handle for him. He's my best friend."

Diz felt so good in saying that, 'my best friend.' It was like he had found a bridge across a dark river. Diz knew he was doing the right thing.

"It's his money and it's his car."

The crowd, now numbering fourteen, kept applauding, whistling and calling out 'Congratulations,' 'Way to go,' 'Awesome,' and the like, as all of this was taking place. Even Dena, who had closed up the bar upon hearing Big Bertha go off, was standing there, cheering the two of them on. She was stunned but proud of them for finally winning big.

The guard, figuring it really didn't matter to him, took the embossed envelope back from the Indian, turned and handed it to Charlie. Charlie took it, folded it in half, hugged the guard, hugged Diz, started crying, just a little, and slipped the envelope in his pocket next to his two pills of Viagra. He thought of nothing else in this world for the moment but Crystal Lovelock. The Monte Carlo was his. Crystal Lovelock was his. He hadn't felt this good since he turned off his computer, put on his jacket and walked out of his accounting firm years earlier.

Charlie turned to Diz and said, "Diz, we're going to Deadwood!"

"You got that fuckin' right!" responded Diz as they did a high five before the cheering crowd.

Chain of Fools

Chapter 8: Losing the Kids

After Ted Ring died, all bets were off. Maggie fell apart. As hard as she was drinking before the accident, she drank twice as hard afterward. Without Ted and the new Plymouth making the liquor runs to the gangsters in East St. Paul, Maggie struggled with her bootlegging. Maggie never learned to drive, so finding a steady supply of illegal liquor became her major challenge.

Then there were the kids to deal with. Lacking any parental supervision, Stanley started getting into trouble with the law, just as all his brothers before him. Petty theft, stolen bicycles and troubles at the Adams School all weighed in on this boy without parents. Irene, only six years old when Ted was killed, started having emotional problems. Having been traumatized by the fatal accident and horrid conditions at home, Irene started to withdraw into herself. She stopped speaking. Her first grade teachers didn't know how to handle it. They notified the State of Minnesota about Irene's deteriorating condition.

The Minnesota Child Welfare Board became involved. They started monitoring the family more frequently, asking more and more questions. The social workers began wondering what course of action might have to be taken if things didn't start to improve. The self-silenced mute daughter, the up-and-coming juvenile delinquent, the drunken mother, and the squalid living conditions made for a perfect storm of dysfunction, and the storm clouds started pouring soon after Ted Ring died.

Maggie started having trouble with the law. Whereas Ted Ring knew his way around the Duluth Police Department, Maggie Stupidnski didn't. Without Ted there to fend them off with bribes of money and liquor, the cops were all over her. She was arrested in July 1931 for disorderly conduct and was raided and arrested again two months later for running a blind pig.

Both arrests resulted in fines Maggie was barely able to afford but because of the two remaining children her sentence was suspended once again and she was put on probation. In August 1932 she was held in contempt of court for failing to visit her probation officer and she was sentenced to sixty days in the county work farm. A sister watched Stanley and Irene while Maggie did her time. It was the only two months Maggie was sober during that entire decade.

In November 1933 Maggie was arrested again. This time she wasn't caught selling her liquor but drinking it and was arrested for being intoxicated. Hell, Maggie was always intoxicated. Arresting her was only a matter of finding probable cause to enter her place. Once inside Maggie's joint, there was always something available to charge her with: disorderly conduct, selling intoxicating substances, unlawful possession, drunkenness or operating a blind pig. The only charge that was never brought against her was prostitution, but they all knew damn well those rumors were true.

Everyone in town knew Maggie could be bought. When Prohibition was repealed, starting with the 3.2 beer bill in April 1933, Maggie's bootlegging operation had started to fall apart. By December, except in the handful of dry counties that refused to return to the evil ways of John Barleycorn, all the laws pertaining to the federal prohibition of liquor were gone and, with them, her primary source of income.

Out of desperation, Maggie turned to the world's oldest profession. One of my older cousins, who lived in her neighborhood at the time, tells me that most of his high school buddies paid One-Eyed Maggie to end their virginity, although looking at what few aging photographs of her I have, I can't help but wonder why they didn't elect to remain virgins.

Maggie needed the money and as long as the local drunks, Indians, and high school kids were willing to pay cash for her services, it helped to keep the landlord off her back. Hell, chances are the landlord, once or twice, helped to keep Maggie *on* her back.

In April 1934 Maggie was arrested once again, this time for selling intoxicating liquor without a license. The social workers from the Minnesota Child Welfare Board were livid. By this time Stanley was fourteen and Irene ten. Both children were struggling in school and Stanley was quickly acquiring his own rap sheet, though he never managed to match the crimes that sent his oldest brother, Scarface Joe, to Red Wing and his untimely death.

In October 1934, in the depths of the Great Depression, Maggie was arrested for a second time that year, this time for drunkenness. The Welfare Board then decided to remove the last two children from Maggie's home. In 1934, times were very, very tough. It's difficult to imagine how bad it must have been at Maggie's place to remove two children during the worst period of the Great Depression.

Maggie, both despondent and sick and tired of having to raise the two kids, put up scant resistance.

"Take the little bastards," she told the board people who came in November for the two children. "I've fuckin' had it with 'em anyway. They ain't nothin' but trouble."

When Stanley and Irene were loaded into a state vehicle and driven off, Stanley didn't bother to shed a tear. He was sick of scrounging for food every evening, living in a house that was never cleaned, and having to care for his little sister.

Irene, by that time, was a total disaster. She never knew who her real father was. Ted Ring, who had taken her in, was four years dead and gone, and Maggie, her own mother, never gave a rat's ass about her.

Naturally, Irene was a psychological minefield. Barely speaking, unable to handle school, and socially isolated, Irene would never truly recover. They took both children to the Saint James Orphanage in Woodland until child welfare could find them foster homes.

Stanley was lucky. One of Maggie's brothers, noting that Stanley was a strong able-bodied fourteen-year-old, decided to take him in. He lived on a dairy farm in Kettle River. His name was Stefen, though my father always called him Uncle Steve. Stanley had dropped out of school in the eighth grade, so he was free to work full time at the farm, helping to milk the cows, clean the barn, and mend the fences. Uncle Steve didn't drink. For young Stan, life on the farm was far better than had been with his one-eyed mother.

Irene wasn't as lucky. Clinically withdrawn, barely able to carry on a conversation, and crippled with a decade of emotional scarring, no one wanted her. She was too frail and young to be of any real use on Steve's farm; remember, times were hard. Though the welfare board searched high and low for a home for her, Irene remained in the orphanage for five lonely years.

With the kids removed and liquor readily available across most of Minnesota's northern counties, Maggie turned to prostitution. She would screw or suck anyone who came up with five dollars. When she wasn't on her back or giving head she was usually drinking, when she wasn't drinking or whoring she was gambling.

Maggie was busted for drinking in April 1935, in September 1937 for drinking, and in October 1939. With a rap sheet of more than two dozen arrests and scores of warnings and reprimands, Maggie was a cut-rate career criminal: swearing a blue streak, drinking, gambling, chain-smoking and whoring made Maggie Stupidnski a prime candidate for the centerfold of *Bad Parenting Magazine*.

Then war broke out. After Pearl Harbor, the Duluth police had more important things to do than arrest the aging drunk who lived below the tracks on Helm Street. Maggie and her charades faded into the background of bigger issues like Nazi blitzkriegs and the strength of the Japanese navy. Maggie disappeared into the tenement slums of Michigan Avenue and nothing shows up in the public records again until the fire of 1947.

Irene remained in the orphanage until 1939, when she was adopted at fifteen by a Christian couple who lived in the east end of town. Stanley stayed on the farm until the 1940s, when he enlisted in the U.S. Army. The 30s were over. During the next decade Maggie would go up in flames, my father would marry my mother and my personal genealogical nightmare would continue.

The Black Bear Casino

The following Monday morning at ten-thirty, Charlie showed up at the Black Bear Casino with his envelope. He walked into the casino and panicked. The Monte Carlo was gone. It had been replaced with a Chrysler LeBaron convertible. His first thought was that someone had stolen his car on Sunday, when he and Diz had gone on a world-class drunk over in Oliver to celebrate their victory. Then he realized they had probably taken his car off the floor because he'd won it. No one is going to play the Big Bertha for a car that's already spoken for. The Chrysler was cherry red, and had he not won the Monte Carlo, Charlie would have been all over this snappy convertible.

Diz was supposed to come along when he picked up the car but just before Charlie left the motel, Diz had called complaining that he was sick. It was his liver. Maybe his pancreas. Hell, it was his entire body rejecting the chemistry of too much liquor to process in too short of a life.

Stupidnski walked up to the guard watching over the Chrysler and showed him the gold-embossed envelope containing the paperwork with the winning verification. Having the exact same envelope with a different VIN number on it currently tucked in his front pocket, the guard knew what Charlie was looking for.

"Congrats! So you're the winner, huh?"

"Yup."

"She's parked out back, but you have to go up to the office and fill out a bunch of paperwork. You know: title, taxes, stuff like that."

"Yup. Where's the office?"

"Go upstairs, turn right, and you'll find a brown door right next to the bingo hall. Just knock and someone will let you in. It's a nice car you won, you lucky bastard," the guard added.

"That it is," agreed Charlie, as he headed for the stairs.

Within the hour, after paying the Minnesota sales taxes out of his gambling reserve funds and completing all the title work, Charlie was escorted out by one of the Black Bear Casino managers toward the back parking lot. Opening an employees only door, Charlie and the manager found themselves standing outside on a gorgeous Monday in early March, at high noon, staring at the Monte Carlo, parked twenty feet away. The slick black finish, gleaming beside a huge white mountain of snow that had been plowed into this far corner of the casino's parking lot, shone even brighter than it had under the lights of the casino.

"Here's your keys. Remember, you need to call your insurance agent right away and put the car on your policy."

"Will do," Charlie replied in the most authoritative voice he could command.

Not surprisingly, Charlie didn't have an insurance agent. His Pinto wasn't worth insuring, and he hadn't even thought about insuring the Monte Carlo. Hell, Charlie calculated, I've put less than $1,000 in Big Bertha pulls into the car, and insurance is a pain in the ass. Charlie was an accountant once; he knew risk management.

Not wasting a moment, he opened the door and slid behind the wheel. The door was huge in comparison to his Pinto, being a two-door sedan. He slipped in the key and started her up. The engine sounded smooth and amazingly quiet. The muffler had fallen off his Pinto a month ago, so Charlie was used to driving a car that sounded like an amplified Harley.

All the instrument-panel lights lit up and worked. Hell, everything worked, mused Charlie to himself as he looked the plush gray-leather interior over. This is going to take some getting used to, he thought. Especially the new car smell. His Pinto—well, it didn't smell, it reeked. Mostly of cigarette smoke but you could add month-old emergency donuts, spilled whiskey, stale beer, and a pile of unwashed laundry in the trunk to the list. The new car smell annoyed Charlie, but he knew, given his lifestyle and smoking habits, it wouldn't last a week.

He closed the door gently, pushed a button to lower the driver's side window down, hollered, "Thanks for everything, I'm outa here," to the assistant manager, and sped away. On his way out of the parking lot he intentionally drove past his lonely Pinto and winked.

He figured he could pick up the Pinto in the next few days when Diz was feeling better. The kid who worked the night shift at the Erickson gas station wanted to buy it from him. Charlie was asking $275 but they settled on $238.50. It was triple what a junkyard might have given him and it would help offset the state sales tax, which was an unexpected expense.

No one would bother to tow the Pinto away. It had that look that said, "If you tow me, you own me," because no one in their right might would pay a $175 towing bill to retrieve a $250 car. The tow truck operators in Carleton County were familiar with cars like this and avoided them like the plague. They knew damn well no one would ever show up to claim them, and it took ninety days of precious yard storage to clear their titles to the point where the junkyards would crush them, so, to put it in their own words, "There's no way in hell I'm towing that piece of shit," was how it always ended.

The Pinto was economically untowable so Charlie knew he could leave it in the parking lot for years if he had to. Charlie was right.

But his thoughts were elsewhere as he drove up the on ramp onto I-35, pointing north toward the Golden Gate. His thoughts were on Crystal and his plans for tonight. He knew he wanted to get to the club right at five, when there was still enough daylight left for her to see the new car, but he wondered exactly how he was going to lure Crystal outside. He was nervous, excited, scared, and elated at once. In short, Charlie needed a drink.

*****

By four-thirty that same afternoon, Charlie Stupidnski was legally drunk. He had purchased a liter of Petri vodka to celebrate his win and finished off half the bottle within hours, mixing it with ice and Diet Coke. He was trying to get up the nerve to ask Crystal out for a date. With the brand-new Monte Carlo in his corner, he felt that tonight was his best chance. Charlie wasn't crazy, thinking that the car would ultimately get him the girl. The car was slick, new, shiny, and sharp.

Charlie was, conspicuously, the complete set of antonyms to those adjectives.

It was less than three blocks from the Golden Gate to Sugar Daddies, so he calculated that his chances of getting pulled over for driving drunk during that ninety-second trip were nil. When he got behind the wheel and fired her up for a second time that day he actually started to cry. This was the best thing that had happened to him since he walked out on his wife and kids seven years ago. He sensed it was a turning point. Not that he was about to drive back into Duluth and ask for his old job back—he'd drive his new car off the Skyline Parkway before doing that—but because the Monte Carlo made him feel important again. The car gave him a sense of status. He was no longer a fat, lonely alcoholic living on the fringes of society. He was a winning fat, lonely alcoholic living on the fringes of society. Huge difference.

Knowing how drunk he was, Charlie pulled out onto Highway 36 cautiously. He stayed focused and made it over to the club without incident. There were only a half dozen other cars in the parking lot at 5:10 P.M. Most belonged to the staff. Only one car belonged to a paying customer and it was an old Ford pickup. Amid the rusted, dented, and abused automobiles parked beside her, the Monte Carlo stood out like a marquis-cut diamond in a coal mine. Only Jimmy Cortese's Hummer, parked at the edge of an abutting field, could hold a candle to her.

Charlie went inside the smoky cavern that was Sugar Daddies, day or night. He looked over to the dance floor and took note of a new girl working the pole. Mondays, especially early on, were reserved for auditions. Jimmy Cortese was sitting in the front row, watching this young dancer's every move. She had a great body but vied with the pole for rigidity. Try as she might, tight tits and sweet ass notwithstanding, this girl would never be a stripper.

Charlie still didn't know how he was going to deal with Crystal. Luckily, in the end, he didn't need to. He walked up to the bar to order a drink.

"Vodka Seven, Randy."

"Comin' up, Charlie."

By this time, having come to the club nearly every Monday and Tuesday for the past three months, Charlie knew everyone who worked there on a first name basis. Hell, he'd even got to know Jimmy Cortese pretty well, though Jimmy made it a policy to keep his distance from the clientele.

Randy had the drink on the bar within a minute. He slid it over to Charlie and asked, "So are ya drivin' her already?"

"The Monte Carlo?" replied Charlie, taken aback by the fact that Randy had already heard about his win.

"Well, I'm sure as hell not talking about that ratty old Pinto, now, am I."

"Yeah, she's out in the parking lot."

"Cool, man. Would it be OK if I took a look at her?"

"Sure. But how'd you find out I won?"

"Hell, Charlie, everyone in Scanlon knows you won. It's a small town. Hang on a minute."

Randy walked back toward the cash register and got on the intercom phone that Jimmy had installed a few years back. It connected to the undressing room, the DJ's booth, the bouncer stations, and to Jimmy's personal cell phone. When fights broke out or one of the girls was running late, the intercom proved indispensable.

What happened next was nothing short of a miracle. Randy had gotten on the phone to ask the three dancers if they wanted to see Charlie's new car. Two of them were auditioning strippers, and the third girl was Crystal.

Within five minutes, still dressed in their street clothes, all three were at the bar, hanging all over this self-made thousandaire.

"I hear you won the Monte Carlo," said Crystal to Charlie, as she slipped in close.

"Well, Diz pulled the handle, but it was my money. So, yeah, I won it."

Then Crystal answered the question Charlie had dreaded asking since the four wheels had cosmically aligned at 3:12 the previous Sunday morning.

"Want to take me out for a ride in her later?"

Charlie choked. He was completely caught off guard by Crystal's request. Did he want to take her for a ride later? God, *yes*. Oh, my goodness, *yes*. Unbelievable, indescribable, beyond belief *yes*. But for the moment Charlie couldn't speak.

Jimmy, the owner, finally broke the deadlock. Jimmy had grown disenchanted with the unoiled but well-built robot trying to rub her lovely ass up and down the brass pole and walked over to the bar to check out what was happening. He would fire this cardboard wannabe later but he couldn't bear watching her another minute.

"Congrats, you lucky son-of-a-bitch! Let me buy you a drink."

"I haven't even taken a sip of this one yet," replied a dumbfounded Charlie, pointing to his drink.

"Well, then, I'll buy you one when you get back in. If you want to show these girls your new car you'd better hurry, Michelle's up next."

The bartender, who had instigated the whole event, turned to his boss and said, "Can you spot me for a minute, Jimmy, I want to have a look at her too."

"Gotcha, Randy."

Once outside, it took a few seconds for everyone's eyes to adjust to the daylight. It was a beautiful near-perfect March evening. The sky was clear and the setting sun was casting that deep, luminescent yellow light that makes everything it falls upon look glorious.

The Monte Carlo, still wearing the $200 wax job the casino owners had put on her, looked utterly sublime.

"Oh, my God!" exclaimed Crystal when she saw it, "It's gorgeous. Can I sit in it?"

Charlie was in some kind of delusional state at this point. Please, please, let me never wake up, he begged.

He pushed the remote on his key and the car unlocked. The girls scrambled in. From the drivers seat behind the wheel, Crystal smiled up at Charlie, as though she were starring in a hot Chevy commercial.

"How do I look?"

Once again, Charlie found himself unexpectedly silent. How did Crystal look in his new Monte Carlo with the perfect afternoon sunlight falling on the parking lot and two really hot young dancers, one in the passenger seat and one sprawled across the backseat, and Charlie, still drunk, with Jimmy, the owner, waiting to buy him a round back in the club? Hell, thought Charlie, if I die right now it's too good to be true. He finally spoke.

"You look great."

"So do we have a date later?"

Charlie froze just an instant, then answered her. "You betcha, Crystal."

Dreams can come true.

*****

The club was slow, as it generally was on Monday, so Randy was probably going to let the girls leave early. Around eight, after finishing off four complimentary drinks from various staff members, including Crystal, Charlie realized he had to eat something. Crystal had just finished her second dance of the night, focusing her attention solely on the man with the Monte Carlo, and Charlie figured it was the perfect time to grab some kind of dinner.

For a moment he thought about walking across the street to the Erickson station and wolfing down a half dozen of their lukewarm hot dogs, but when he got out to the parking lot, he felt he just had to take the car for another spin. He was, at this point, three times over the legal limit. Had Charlie been forced to take a Breathalyzer test he might have busted the machine, but on the other hand he was too drunk to give a damn.

He slid behind the wheel and fired her up. This was the first time he had ever seen the dashboard instruments lit up at night. It was awesome. He pulled out of the parking lot and pointed the Monte Carlo south. A little over four miles away lay the only eating establishment on the planet that could appease his ravishing hunger, the all-you-can-eat buffet at the Black Bear Casino. Besides, he thought, as the car hit seventy-five, Mondays were the seafood buffet, his all-time favorite.

After completely destroying their deep-fried shrimp reserves, ravishing the salad bar, not once but twice, and devouring approximately 43 percent of the buffet's walnut encrusted walleye fillets, Charlie hit the john for a massive download, played twenty minutes' worth of nickel slots to help digest his food, walked right past the Big Bertha, and drove back to Sugar Daddies. He was stuffed. He had just eaten close to six pounds of food, impressive but nowhere near the nine-plus-pounds world record currently held by some skinny harmless-looking kid from Japan.

By the time Charlie got back inside the eternal midnight that was Sugar Daddies it was ten o'clock. There were four customers in the entire joint, plus the staff. Jimmy Cortese had left an hour ago, after telling the girl who danced like an arthritic Al Gore that she needn't come back. The second dancer, Michelle, was hired starting Friday, and the third was on the cusp. In hopes of coming to a decision about whether or not he would hire her, an incredibly hot redhead who had possibilities but needed to further hone her skills. Jimmy had decided to take her back to his place for a few drinks and conduct a more intimate interview. At the same moment Charlie was pulling into the parking lot of Sugar

Daddies, Jimmy Cortese was humping the redhead on his living room couch. Her interview was going well.

Jimmy had told Randy, as he often did, that if things didn't pick up any to shut the club down around ten-thirty. Unless there was a holiday or a special event in Cloquet, a logging convention or a hockey game, Sugar Daddies generally closed down early on Mondays and Tuesdays. Crystal had one last dance left, and she was hoping Charlie would be out there. She had seen he was missing on her last two outings.

When Crystal came out for her last dance, Charlie was in his favorite seat, more or less sober after eating his fill at the buffet and anxiously awaiting his first real date in four years. He did go out with one of the secretaries for the first year after leaving his firm but nothing came of it. She was so proud of him for not putting up with the "establishment bullshit" and for walking out that she called him two weeks after he quit and asked him out.

They dated off and on for about a year until Charlie ran out of money: then she broke it off and started seeing a used car salesman. Charlie soon faded into low rent apartments and part-time work on Quick Books for a couple of partnerships who couldn't afford big accounting firms. He worked on a cash-only basis, doing everything he could to avoid paying either alimony or child support.

Over the next two years Charlie had solidified his status as a fully evolved alcoholic and one by one, lost all his marginal accounts. At about the same time he started taking up chronic gambling at the Fond du Luth Casino on Superior Street in downtown Duluth. His background in accounting helped him understand the statistical nature of slot machines. Charlie seemed to have a sixth sense when it came to which machine was ready to cough up some nickels and which machine was best left alone.

Charlie never played the quarter, dollar, or five-dollar slots because these were all programmed to enrich the casino, not the customer. The nickel slots and—even more so—the penny slots were geared toward paying off. Once the gambler felt confident enough, his pockets overflowing with hundreds of copper profiles of President Lincoln or scores of alloyed coins displaying cameos of President Jefferson, the casino naturally assumed that he or she would step up to the higher-paying machines. It was at those higher costing machines where all the outflowing pennies and nickels would quickly reverse direction and start heading back into the casino's coffers. Ninety-nine percent of the time, the casino operators were correct in their assumption. The players, emboldened by the petty-cash winning streak, moved up to the hungrier slots and fed all their pocket change back into the system.

Charlie, Diz, and a few dozen others never fell for that. They stuck with the nickel slots and looked at every dollar bill they earned as an assemblage of twenty individual coins or, if times were really awful, a hundred hard-earned pennies. They lived on coinage. They paid the rent in nickels, did their laundry in nickels, cleaned out the buffet stations in nickels, bought gas and toothpaste—hell, they watched strippers take off their clothes for nickels—twenty nickels at a time, converted to what Diz referred to as paper nickels.

Over time, Charlie found he didn't like living in Duluth. The motels were more expensive and the Duluth police department kept dogging him, trying to make him pay his court-ordered child support. He had moved out of town eight months ago to the Golden Gate Motel. He loved his new room. The Cloquet police didn't know him from Adam and that fact alone appealed to him.

When he met Diz late one night at the casino bar, he knew it was the right decision. Diz and he were like two long lost brothers who had somehow found each other in a world filled with strangers. The fact that they both gambled, drank, smoked pot, and lusted after Dena's ass helped them grow to understand and appreciate each other. When Charlie turned Diz on to his recently discovered buffet busting technique, a true lasting friendship was born.

But over time, Charlie grew lonely. That's when he discovered Sugar Daddies. The girls helped alleviate his loneliness, one dollar bill at a time. When he first saw Crystal dancing, he knew she was the one. She was perfect: her dyed blond hair, her blue eyes, her surgically enhanced breasts, everything. Now, as she wrapped her long legs around the brass pole, cellulite notwithstanding, he knew that in half an hour she would be sitting next to him, driving down old Highway 61 to nowhere. Just along for the ride—the ride of life.

*****

By the time Crystal made it out of the undressing room it was almost eleven. With the dancing over, Charlie had left his place along the edge of the empty runway to return to a drink and Randy's company. The two of them made small talk as Charlie finished his cocktail.

He was clearly apprehensive about being alone with Crystal. He had been fumbling around with the two Viagra pills in his pocket, rolling them between his fingers like Chinese medicine balls while deciding whether or not he should take one or, God willing, both of them. One minute he thought, *no*, it's too soon. What if I take them and she says no? The next minute he debated taking just one, so if he did have a problem and she said no it wouldn't be so terrible. A moment later he was convinced tonight was the night and he should swallow them both: armed and dangerous, ready for the sex of a lifetime.

He was still playing with the pills when Crystal walked up to the bar.

"Ready?"

"Sure."

"Do you want to finish your drink?"

"Nah, I'd rather go for a spin."

"Do you mind if I give her a little test drive?"

"No, I don't mind. Where do you want to go?"

"I'm sort of hungry, how 'bout heading down to Duluth to catch a bite at the Truck On Inn? It's open all night and they serve great hash browns."

"Sounds good."

He turned around and laid a ten spot on the bar. "Keep the change, Randy."

He lifted up his vodka Seven and in a well-practiced ritual put the cocktail up to his lips, tipped it back, and finished it off in one long steady pull. It hit the spot, helping to calm his jittery nerves.

"Let's go."

Crystal and Charlie walked out to the car together, saying good-bye to the bouncer as they left. As they approached the car, Charlie hit the remote. The car chirped as the driver's side lock opened. He rushed ahead a bit and opened the door for his date.

"Thank you. You're such a gentleman."

Crystal slid into the driver's seat, surveyed the dashboard and the instrument panel, and inhaled the glorious new car smell. She was a bit disappointed to discover that the car was an automatic and not a stick. Sticks were more exciting.

Charlie walked around the back of the car, pressed the remote a second time, and the passenger-side door lock popped open. He sat down beside her, feeling a little awkward about not being behind the wheel, and handed her the keys.

Crystal put the keys into the ignition, clicked on her seat belt, slammed her door shut and fired her up. Once started, she shoved the pedal down hard and revved her up to the point where Charlie thought they might blow a rod right in the parking lot.

"She sounds great!" Crystal exclaimed, clearly excited by the roar of the engine.

"Maybe you shouldn't rev her up so much. It's a brand new engine and needs some breaking in," cautioned Charlie.

"She'll be fine. They break them in at the factory these days."

Crystal pulled out of the parking lot and headed toward the freeway into town. She hadn't been behind the wheel of a new car in fourteen years. That was when her long dead biker boyfriend had somehow ended up with a stolen Chevy Malibu in a screwed-up drug deal. He totaled the car a month afterward, so she really didn't get to drive it much.

Once Crystal hit the on-ramp, Charlie realized what he was in for. By the time she was merging into an empty freeway lane, Crystal was hitting ninety. Once on the freeway itself, the speedometer quickly pushed 110 miles an hour, and they were screaming toward Duluth. Charlie, who was used to his Pinto and by nature a very cautious driver, turned white as a passing snowbank.

"Wow," exclaimed Crystal, "This bitch handles great!"

Charlie didn't know what to say. He didn't want to reprimand her for fear of ruining the evening. He looked down at the speedometer, and it now read 125 miles per hour. He had never gone this fast in a car in his entire life.

Within minutes they were approaching the top of the long winding hill into Duluth. They had passed a half dozen cars along the way and Charlie was ecstatic that none of them were cop cars. They were doing fifty miles over the speed limit and the ticket would be astronomical. Besides, Charlie had no insurance; he hadn't even had time to register the car yet. If we get pulled over, he decided, it's going to be a royal clusterfuck.

"I think you should slow her down a bit when we hit the hill." Charlie said guardedly.

"Yeah, you might be right."

Crystal immediately lifted her right foot off the accelerator and hit the brakes. Within seconds, amid the sound of screeching tires, the smell of burning rubber, and Charlie's sensation that all his 250 pounds were about to be thrown through the front window of the car, the Monte Carlo was back down to the legal speed limit.

"Holy shit!" Charlie shouted, unable to contain himself.

"Cool way to slow down, huh?"

"Kind of weird, really."

"Yeah, I learned it from my ex-boyfriend. He's dead now, but he was one hell of a driver."

"I'm sorry. How'd he die?"

"Motorcycle accident, right over there—Crystal pointed toward a bridge in the distance—on the Bong Bridge. He was going too fast on his Harley and lost control. No helmet. You know how it is."

"Yeah."

Two minutes later they drove by a highway patrol car with his radar gun out, parked around the corner at the bottom of the hill. Crystal was going only eight miles an hour over the speed limit, and the cop decided to wait for a speedier victim.

"Good call, Charlie."

They took the 27th Avenue West exit and headed toward the Truck On Inn. Crystal was in heaven, driving this brand-new machine around like she owned the world. Charlie was a bit more undecided. She drove like a madwoman, he thought. She's got nice tits, but she drives like a madwoman.

They took a booth and Crystal ordered breakfast. Charlie ordered coffee and a Danish. He was still stuffed from the buffet and would remain stuffed until tomorrow afternoon, when he would reload up on Tuesday's China Night Special. The pork fried rice was his favorite.

They made small talk over dinner. Crystal complained about her Monday and Tuesday night shift, and Charlie listened patiently. He watched her lips move, heard the tones of her voice, and looked into her lovely blue eyes. It didn't matter what she was saying, he was infatuated.

When he picked up the tab, he threw in a nice tip to impress Crystal. He knew he'd get up another $250 for the Pinto in a few days, so for the moment he was wealthy. By one in the morning they were driving back toward Scanlon to pick up Crystal's car.

Crystal, feeling a bit sleepy from consuming a mountain of hash browns, a western omelet, pork links, and a glass of milk, let Charlie drive back. He was glad. Crystal drove as though she were behind the wheel of a roller coaster. One ride with her behind the wheel was enough.

They got back to the parking lot at Sugar Daddies around two. When Charlie turned off the ignition in the parking lot beside Crystal's car, there was an awkward pause. Charlie cleared his throat while Crystal just sat there. Is this guy was going to put a move on me or what?

Charlie broke the silence. "I had a great time, Crystal. Can I see you again sometime?"

"Sure, Charlie. How 'bout tomorrow night?"

"Same time?"

"Yeah, around 11:00 or so. Maybe we could take her down to Hinckley for breakfast at Toby's."

"Sounds great."

Charlie thought, long and hard, about leaning over to kiss her. But he didn't. He knew it wasn't the right time. Oh, God, he wanted to kiss her so badly—and do far, far more than just kiss her. But he didn't.

Crystal, impressed and a bit confused by realizing this guy wasn't going to try to jump her bones on the first date, opened her door, got out of the car, and said, "See you tomorrow then."

"Eleven o'clock, right?"

"Right."

Crystal blew him a kiss, jumped into her car, and drove off.

Charlie started cursing. "What the hell am I doing? I blew it, I blew it, I fucking blew it. Jesus H. Christ, I'm a goddamn idiot!"

Charlie's profane soliloquy continued along those same lines for another few minutes. He reached into his pocket several times to check on the two white pills, making sure he hadn't accidentally taken one or, God forbid, lost one back at the Truck On Inn. Sadly, they were both still there, unscathed but getting smaller from all his nervous fumbling.

He started the Monte Carlo, drove the three blocks to his motel, went inside his dingy motel room, and sat down on the edge of his bed. He wanted to cry.

Tomorrow night, he consoled himself, there's always tomorrow night. He took two long slugs of his half-empty vodka bottle to settle his nerves, stripped down to his underwear, and crawled into bed. He stared at the water stains above him, noting that Australia was on the move. The roof must be leaking again. He fell asleep quickly, dreaming of Crystal's tits.

Chain of Fools

Chapter 9: Stanley

My father, Stanley, or Stauch as he became known, joined the army in 1941. Living away from Maggie at Uncle Steve's farm had changed him. Uncle Steve had straightened Stauch out by teaching him the merits of sobriety and the honest rewards of a hard day's work. The Stanley Stupidnski who enlisted that December, a week after the Japanese attacked Pearl Harbor, was not the same boy who had been removed by the state from his mother's wretched home seven years earlier. Stauch was a twenty-one-year-old young man who wanted to fight America's enemies, the Nazis and the Japs. Little did he realize that his real enemy—his anger, his rage—lay dormant within him, just waiting to launch its own surprise attack.

Stauch drank back then, but nowhere near the level of his mother. He was a social drinker, enjoying a beer or two during his weekends off at boot camp, having an occasional drink when he came back home to his uncle's for a few weeks before shipping out to the Pacific theater. Normal stuff, nothing out of the ordinary.

My parents didn't meet until after the war, after Stanley had finished his four-year tour of the Pacific, fighting in the Philippines and ending up in military intelligence, the world's most notorious oxymoron.

Beatrice LeBlanc, my mother, walked down the aisle with her own freight on board, just as Maggie before her and Paul's mother before either of them. Having illegitimate children runs in our family. My mother, in a noble attempt to set a familial record, actually walked down the aisle with one bastard in tow and the other in the oven, neither child related to Stauch or to each other, except through the obvious womb connection.

My mother's family, though hardly dysfunction free, is far less captivating than the bootlegging prostitute on my father's side. Like any family in America, when you squeeze hard enough, some discolored juices will eventually ooze out. The LeBlanc fluids were just not as blood red as Maggie's, though they had their moments.

Beatrice's mother was a Caron, the same Carons who own and operate one of the most renowned perfume houses in Paris. Clara, my grandmother on my mother's side, was born in Michigan in 1891, one year before Maggie. Her parents, both French, had come to America during the age of immigration, 1870 to 1910. The Caron family, composed of three brothers who traveled together, had left France shortly after the civil war ended in the States. One of the brothers, my great-grandfather, Oliver, was still working in the family perfume business before he elected to join his two siblings and hop a freighter to the new world. Like the millions of other European pilgrims of that time, they all came in search of the great American dream...

"Give me your tired, your poor,
Your huddled masses yearning to breathe free,
The wretched refuse of your teeming shore.
Send these, the homeless, tempest-tossed to me,
I lift my lamp beside the golden door!"

The Caron brothers may have been a bit put off by the "wretched refuse" of Emma Lazarus's famous inscription, but not enough to make them turn around and return to France. Eventually, all three found their way into the expanding heartland of the new nation, and one brother, Oliver, eventually turned up in northern Michigan.

Beatrice's grandmother, a Benoit, hailed from Massachusetts, where they had arrived in the late 1870s pursuing the same elusive dream as Oliver. The couple met and married in Michigan, then worked a homestead in the wilderness of the upper peninsula not far from Sault Saint Marie. Grandma Clara was born there, though she didn't remain in Michigan for long.

Their homestead went well for the first few years. Oliver kept busy building log cabins and pole barns for the steady stream of new arrivals. He cut his own timber to build these homesteads, which helped to make it a profitable enterprise. The profits plummeted, however, soon after he sawed his right arm off in a milling accident. Armless carpenters are never in high demand.

They sold the homestead and moved to the boom town of Crookston, Minnesota, where Oliver did odd jobs while his sons worked on nearby farms and his daughters found employment in local sweatshops sewing women's clothing and making felt hats, using the plentiful beaver pelts from the surrounding north woods. Sometime around 1907, Clara met my grandfather, Albert LeBlanc, in the town of Crookston. Albert had come looking for field work amid the fertile soil of the Red River Valley—the Valley of the Jolly Green Giant, as most of us now call it: ho, ho, ho.

Albert LeBlanc was born in Centerville, Missouri. His mother's maiden name was LaBelle, his father's name LeBlanc. As it turns out, his father's father, my great-great-grandfather, had come to America just after the French Revolution. His family fled to England during the reign of the guillotine, complete with white chalk marks clearly displayed around their (royal) necks. Shortly thereafter they shipped off to French Canada, winding up in Quebec City.

All of them spoke French far more than English. But things were still in flux and Mederic LeBlanc, my great-grandfather on my father's side, eventually arrived in central Missouri during the 1870s, where he met another Frenchwoman, Ms. LaBelle. They fell in love and married. Albert LeBlanc was born on March 3, 1879, in Centerville (a.k.a. nowheresville) Missouri. I have no idea how many brothers and sisters my grandfather Albert had, but judging by their devout Catholic upbringing, we should assume at least a dozen.

Albert and Clara were betrothed in Crookston on April 29, 1909. True to their upbringing, Clara was pregnant within the year. Much to her credit, Clara remains the only person I know of in my entire family who walked down the aisle without carrying an infant in her arms or womb, either the groom's or someone else's. In 1911, the first of thirteen LeBlancs arrived into this world. Except for a few brief months between deliveries, Clara would be pregnant for the next twenty years. They loved to make love and, lacking any kind of birth control, the results of that lovemaking were always the same: more and more little LeBlancs. My mother, Beatrice Anne, was the eigth.

Their first child was a girl, named Florence Julia. Their second was Rose. Third, Beulah, followed by Clarence, Raymond, Lorina, Lloyd, Beatrice, Armeline, Therese, Jeanette, Arnold, Jerome, and finally Arthur, who was born on July 21st, 1930. After Arthur, Clara became pregnant two more times. Both pregnancies ended in stillbirths, the last child, being a little boy, died shortly after their twenty-fifth wedding anniversary in 1934. By then Clara had simply worn out the machinery of childbirth.

Beatrice was born in Crookston, as were most of the LeBlancs. Albert had purchased a pool hall shortly after Prohibition ended. The business was doomed from day one. The Great Depression hit farming communities especially hard, and the town of Crookston was no exception. To try to make a go of it, Albert extended credit to anyone who was breathing. The end result was predictable. The pool hall went bankrupt and, with no other work to be found in Crookston, the family moved to Duluth in the late 1930s, and Albert took a job with the Duluth Mesabi and Iron Range Railroad.

Shortly after World War II began, the iron ore industry in northern Minnesota mushroomed. Tanks, ships, guns, and jeeps require one hell of a lot of metal, and towns like Virginia, Hibbing, and Duluth quickly found themselves thriving. The LeBlancs, with Albert's steady income, bought a house in the West End. Although West Duluth was his normal station, the night he died he was relieving a sick kid who worked over the hill in Proctor. It was in that railroad town where the heavily loaded trains arrived from the iron range before making their dangerous descent down to the ore docks fronting Saint Louis Bay. From there these same lake freighters left for Erie, Pennsylvania, and the steel mills of Pittsburgh.

It was one of those same trains that killed Albert on November 30, 1943, at the height of war production. The accident happened on a foggy evening, common for late fall. Albert was working the railroad yards in Proctor, assembling a trainload for the downhill run and the lake freighters that were waiting below for their precious ore.

Because the over-600 foot drop into Duluth was so steep and precarious, they needed up to five engines when making the descent, not for power but for extra braking. Even at that, more than once the brakes failed on that three-mile-long slope, resulting in half the train and tens of thousands of tons of ore plummeting off the end of the ore docks into the bay. It was Albert's job to reshuffle the cars and engines into these metallic caravans before they left the flat plain of the Proctor yards.

It was an extremely dangerous job, especially for an old man in his sixties. Some of these cars, weighing in at hundreds of tons each, moved via steel on steel, so they were virtually silent. Apparently, at some point during Albert's shift on that dark foggy night, one of the cars hit him. He fell on the tracks and was severely mangled. Before they found Albert, a half-dozen additional cars had run him over as well so it was a closed casket funeral.

The railroad gave Clara $300 as a farewell annuity, hired a younger kid whose body parts were still intact, and walked away. There were no wrongful-death attorneys knocking on Clara's door, nor did Albert have any life insurance. Clara, at fifty-two, found herself with a dead husband, an unpaid mortgage, and six hungry kids to care for. They somehow managed, but it wasn't easy. Clara did an outstanding job keeping her sprawling flock intact. The last I counted I had 64 first cousins and more than 280 second cousins. Statistically speaking, I am related to everyone on earth.

Twenty-three year old Beatrice was devastated by the loss of her father. It wasn't easy being the middle child in a baker's dozen, and with Albert gone it became even harder. She was an attractive, needy young woman who, like so many others, wanted to find love.

Love kept eluding her, but the sex was great. Eventually the sex resulted in, you guessed it, pregnancy. There were no pills and hardly any condoms, and even if they had known of any birth control aside from the ludicrous concept of the rhythm method, birth control was strictly forbidden.

Beatrice soon found herself with child. My half-sister, Anna, was the end result of her first liaison, having been born out of wedlock in 1943. My half-brother, Buddy, came next. Apparently Beatrice was a lot more fun to sleep with than she was to marry. Buddy's father, a local Swede, somehow managed to skip town before Clara got out the shotgun and walked him to the altar.

The tough part of this story is that Beatrice became pregnant while she was still dating Stauch. Her condition was a little awkward to explain to her fiancé, no matter what kind of story she came up with. Knowing that having two illegitimate children by two different fathers in the 1940s might prove a bit disconcerting for the religiously devout LeBlancs, my father stepped up to the plate and offered to take my mother's hand in marriage.

They say she didn't show at the wedding, but no doubt tongues were wagging when Buddy arrived a few months shy of the required nine. Most people, including myself, never knew that Stauch wasn't the actual father, so it wasn't a big deal. Stauch accepted the kid as his own, just as he did Anna and Buddy and there you have it, one happy mixed-pedigree family strolling hand in hand into the 1950s. It's important to understand that there is a difference between accepting these children and loving them. With One-Eyed Maggie as your teacher, loving your prodigy, whether rentals or real, becomes a push. The dysfunction's always there— you just have to squeeze families a bit to get the juices flowing. Like making lemonade out of lemons, hold the sugar. Extra tart.

Happy Hour at the Riverside

"What the hell is wrong with you, Charlie?"

"I'm telling you, Diz, it just didn't feel right."

"Do you still have those pills?"

"Yeah, I've got them right here in my pocket."

Charlie took out the two Viagra pills, now showing signs of wear and tear from being nervously rubbed back and forth together. Diz couldn't help but wonder if there was enough chemistry left between them to get the job done.

"Well, use them before they get run through the goddamn wash or crumble away into powder. If you don't screw Crystal pretty damn soon, she's going to think you're gay or some damn thing."

"I ain't gay, Diz."

"Well, you're acting gay. You spend months trying to hook up with this exotic dancer and, when it finally happens, all you can come up with is having fricking ham and eggs in Hinckley, or Oliver or Moose Lake. What the hell's wrong with you?"

Charlie didn't answer. He took a long hard pull on his Black Russian and set it back on the bar without saying a word. He knew Diz was right, but it didn't change anything. He wanted to lay Crystal, but when he was beside her he felt so fat, so unattractive. Then, to make matters worse, Charlie had a massive case of performance anxiety. He hadn't been with a woman in so long he thought he would probably have an orgasm within the first five seconds. He wasn't even sure he would be able to hold off until penetration, which would really be embarrassing.

So they talked. Crystal drove like a NASCAR driver on crack cocaine while Charlie kept praying they wouldn't get killed or come across any state troopers as they roared down I-35, hitting every Denny's, Perkins, and 24 hour truck stop north of the Twin Cities. Oddly enough, Crystal was delighted in the fact that Charlie was behaving like a gentleman. She was tired of sex in all its curious manifestations. Crystal had been the object of desire for years—her fake tits, her long legs, her ass, her lips, her long bottle-blond hair, her blue eyes, her mouth, her calves, her toes, her hands, her pussy, her arms. Her every move had become entangled in an industry devoted to all things sexual. She was sick and tired of it.

Crystal loved the Monte Carlo speeding down I-35 at a 110 miles and hour. and she loved hash browns, cooked to perfection and smothered in ketchup. The more the merrier. And oddly enough, she was starting to have a crush on this Stupidnski guy. He was kind of cute, and he was so nice to her. Last Monday, when Charlie had skipped the buffet in order to dine with Crystal after work at a Perkins in Superior, Crystal insisted on picking up the tab.

She liked talking to him. He liked listening. Over time, Crystal told him her entire life story. How she had wanted to be a teacher. How she had once wanted to have children but she felt it was better to have her tubes tied than to raise kids in an environment that included the likes of Sugar Daddies, Jimmy Cortese, and the seedy crowd of eternal midnight. She was happy, she said, but not really.

Charlie, taking the high road, didn't want her to think that he was just after her to get laid. True, he was originally attracted to Crystal for the same laundry list of desires all men carry around with them—her fake tits, her ass, her blond hair—but there was something deeper now. Charlie was lonely. Crystal was lonely. Together they were less lonely. Maybe that's all love is.

Diz broke Charlie out of his daydream. "When are we going to Deadwood?"

"Soon."

"Are you still thinking about asking Crystal to come along?"

"I asked her last Tuesday."

"And?"

"She's thinking about it. She thinks it would be kind of weird to go the Black Hills with two guys. I think she's afraid of something kinky, who knows. She asked me to ask you if you had given any thought to taking a date along."

"Taking a date along?"

"Yeah, you know, another girl."

Diz took a second to think about it. "I suppose I could ask Rita. She just got fired from the Piggly Wiggly. She might want to see the Crazy Horse statue."

"Well, taking Rita along would make it a foursome, I think Crystal would feel a lot more comfortable heading to Deadwood as two couples. Can't say I blame her."

"Are you going to pay for both of us?"

"Yeah, I suppose I'll have to but it shouldn't be a problem."

"Why's that? It's going to take a shitload of money, hauling all of us to the Black Hills and back."

"I hocked the car."

"You what?"

"I took a loan out against the Monte Carlo. I don't have a job or anything, but Crystal took me over to her credit union and they said they'd lend me five grand on the car, provided I got insurance on it. So I bought an insurance policy for a year, which cost me almost a grand, and that leaves me just under four thousand, plus my nickel winnings. We're all set in terms of money. Hell, even if it were the three of us, I'd have to get Crystal or you a separate room, so taking Rita along ain't going to make much difference, will it?"

"Wow, that's a ton of fucking money, Charlie!"

"Yeah, but I've got to pay it back or sell the damn car, so I'm being careful with it."

"We'll have a ball in Deadwood."

"Yeah."

The two finished their drinks and ordered another round. The bartender had figured they would try to squeeze in one more round before the bell rang, and sure enough, it was 5:57.

Diz was planning to head down to the casino to gamble after getting hammered at the Riverside for next to nothing, but he now decided to change his plans and drive back to the Rez to find Rita. He had only seen her once since the Viagra affair, but he thought it was a pretty cool idea to go on a road trip with Charlie and Crystal in the backseat of a brand-new black Monte Carlo to the sacred hills of the Sioux.

Since the trip—aside from gambling money—was going to be free, he didn't think he'd have any problem convincing Rita to tag along. Hell, if Rita didn't want to go there was always Bobby Bear's sister Ashanti or half a dozen other reservation girls who would jump at the chance of a free vacation.

Charlie was planning to take in the buffet, then work the slots all night. He wasn't going to see Crystal until Monday night, so it would to be business as usual at the Black Bear. He hadn't told anyone except Diz about the four grand, which was in his newly opened checking account at the credit union, so no one at the casino would be hustling him to move up to the dollar slots. He was still in the trenches, making every buck the hard way, five cents at a time.

He liked to think of it as squeezing every nickel until he made the buffalo shit, even though he rarely came across a nickel ancient enough to have a buffalo on it. On the rare occasion that he found one, he'd give it a good squeeze and then toss it down the gullet of some eternally hungry slot. Maybe it would bring him luck. Life was grand.

Chain of Fools

Chapter 10: The Fire

My father refused to allow his bride to meet Maggie Stupidnski. Ever. Maggie didn't come to their wedding—she didn't send Beatrice and Stanley a gift or even a card for that matter. Maggie had not gone to any of her children's weddings, any more than she would go to their funerals. Her maternal instincts ended the moment a baby cleared her vagina. The only child she had been fond of, probably because of his own truckload of issues, was Scarface Joe, and he was long gone. In this regard, One-Eyed Maggie, as a mother, was more closely related to the fishes than to mammals. Once she spawned, she swam off in search of a stiff drink, leaving her kids on their own. Alligators make better parents.

Because my father knew this, he didn't want his wife to learn anything about the crazy, drunken whore who had supposedly raised him. A little more than a year after their wedding, when the apartment fire prematurely ending Maggie's life, the possibility of Beatrice meeting Maggie was forever off the table.

Stanley attended his dead mother's funeral and took Beatrice with him. Because of the corpse's extensive burns, the casket was closed. The services were held at Saint Mary Star of the Sea up on East

Third Street in central Duluth. There were only a handful of people in attendance. One-Eyed Maggie's friends quickly deserted her. Unable to conduct any boot legging business, she wasn't any use to them dead.

The priest conducting the service struggled to find something decent to say. Maggie hadn't been to church since she was knocked up with her first illegitimate child, John Mishap, almost forty years earlier. Everyone in attendance knew she was a renowned bootlegger, a local whore, a gambler, and the mother from hell, so a glowing eulogy about a devout Christian's untimely passing wasn't in the cards.

Knowing these facts, the priest read some perfunctory passages from the Bible, poured as much holy water as he had on the casket (hoping it didn't spit and sizzle when it hit the marble), and wrapped the entire ceremony up within fifteen minutes.

There wasn't a soul at the funeral who thought for one second Maggie was going right to heaven. The priest, who didn't really know her, felt that after a couple hundred thousand years in purgatory, Maggie might eventually find her way through the pearly gates, but he was being kind. All the rest knew, without question, that Maggie Stupidnski was already burning in hell. Satan himself had had the foresight to take Maggie out, using some of her homemade vodka to get the fires of damnation started. Surely Satan had plans for Maggie, long-term plans.

No one cried at the funeral. George Bazon, the boarder who was with her the evening the fire broke out, failed to show. Had he been there, George might have cried, but in the end he was too busy changing the dressings on his burns and searching for another place to live. Stanley wanted to cry but wouldn't let himself stoop to it. So in the end Maggie's funeral was dry.

They buried her up the hill in the Oneida Cemetery, not far from the grave of her favorite son. No one visits either grave. Maggie vanished into the unspoken abyss that is the end of a tragic life.

Stanley and Beatrice, along with Beatrice's two illegitimate children, walked out of the funeral and moved on. On that chilly windswept day in November 1947, Stanley vowed never to become like Maggie and wholeheartedly believed this was possible. But the die was cast. The broken machinery of his childhood was already chugging away, soon laying waste to his plans for a wife, family, and a decent home. The demons instilled into Maggie as here father yanked the stick out of her eye were silently, insidiously, passing from Maggie to her son, just as they would eventually end up within me: a tale told and retold across desolate stretches of time, unbroken in a sad symmetry, this chain of fools.

The fifties were fast approaching. The explosive devices planted inside my father's tortured soul were ticking: quietly at first, then louder and louder, eventually exploding late in the decade in an encore of familial dysfunction. I was there to endure the shrapnel.

On the Road to the Dakotas

The vacationers left for Deadwood on a beautiful Sunday morning in early May. They were supposed to leave the week before, but Diz became sick again after another lost weekend with his cousins. Crystal didn't want to go without the other couple, so they waited out Diz's recovery. When he showed up that Sunday Diz was still faintly jaundiced but he insisted he was well enough to hit the road. He'd never felt better in his life. He was going to see the memorial of Crazy Horse.

They had Map Quested their route half a dozen times on Crystal's computer and settled on a blue-highway only itinerary, using the onboard GPS to pick and choose their route along the way. Granted, there would be a stretch near the end when they would have to use Interstate 90, but for the most part the journey to Deadwood was going to be on two-lane highways through towns so small that by the time Charlie located them on their backup road map they were already through them.

They went south to the Casino, and took Highway 210 west toward Brainerd. Crystal, who had been warned by Charlie to watch her lead foot, was the designated driver. Once she cleared the edge of the reservation and the tiny town of Cromwell, she announced to all concerned that she simply couldn't drive a mere sixty all the way to Deadwood.

There followed a heated debate about who was going to pay the speeding ticket should they get caught. Charlie wasn't at all surprised when, as soon as it was determined that if Crystal got a ticket for speeding, Crystal was going to pay that ticket, she dug into her handbag and brought out a brand-new, state-of-the-art radar detector.

Upon seeing his girlfriend set this sleek black device on the dashboard, with the $119 price tag still dangling from it, Charlie knew his lectures about speeding had fallen on deaf ears. Crystal had no intention of driving to Deadwood at the posted speeds. By the time they flew through the tiny town of Tamarac they were pushing ninety.

Rita and Diz, cozy as kittens in the backseat of the Monte Carlo, didn't give a damn. They hadn't even bothered to put on their seat belts, electing instead to squeeze together and wrap themselves in a half-dozen assorted pillows Rita had brought along for the trip.

"Just in case we get sleepy," she told Diz, as she tossed them into the car.

Pillows provide very little by way of protection should you hit a train trestle at a hundred miles an hour, but that didn't matter. Diz's internal organs were already on the brink of failure, Rita had just finished the first of the two dozen joints she would smoke before they hit Deadwood, and neither of them particularly cared if they crashed and burned anyway. It would just expedite Diz's forthcoming liver failure, and Rita, stoned beyond description, would think it kinda cool.

Of the four of them, only Charlie was afraid of getting pulled over by the police, or, God forbid, dying. Crystal, her heart racing with adrenaline as she swept around sharp turns at seventy, never took the time or had any inclination to even think about it. Going fast was it. Thoughts of crashing or getting caught doing sixty in a twenty-five-mile zone never entered her mind. She was forever hopped up on the rush that pushing a vehicle to the limit can produce. There were also traces of coke still coursing through her veins from the line she did after finishing her coffee that morning. Crystal was having a ball.

Amazingly, she and Charlie had yet to do it. She thought about that quite often and had decided that when they got to Deadwood she was going to do him, and do him right. Charlie knew nothing of Crystal's plans, but Diz had been duly informed. Rita knew as well, helping Diz to find half a dozen replacements for the two Viagra pills Charlie had rubbed to powder. Once pulverized, the pills had sifted through the bottom of his pockets and vanished.

With the pills gone, Charlie had developed a terminal case of performance anxiety. He thought about screwing Crystal virtually every minute of his waking life, but when the opportunities arose for him to make advances, he waffled. In the back of his mind, he too was hoping that something would change once they hit Deadwood, provided they survived the road trip and arrived alive.

After roaring through Brainerd, with Crystal having to slam on the brakes once because her detector started chirping as they entered the outskirts of town, they all decided to throw the road map in the trash. Charlie broke out a pint of rum and everyone, including the driver, started taking pulls on it. Now in the hinterlands of Minnesota, they started taking any road heading west, southwest, or south that showed up on the GPS screen and appealed to them.

"Let's take 371 into St. Cloud," suggested Rita. "I've never been to St. Cloud."

"Screw St. Cloud, let's take 27 out of Little Falls, then 71 South to Sauk Center."

The route changed every time they came to a new intersection. It was road trip by committee, and even when the direction debate became quite heated, someone always conceded. The Monte Carlo, via a stumbling route only four drunks could devise, was steadily wobbling toward the Black Hills of South Dakota.

Rita started passing her joints around after they cleared the underpass for I-94 and Charlie broke out a second pint he had tucked away under the front seat. They crossed the South Dakota line a little after two that afternoon. When they pulled into downtown Watertown half an hour later they were road weary, starving, stoned, and drunk. From the moment the waitress walked up to their table, she was on to them.

"Can I get you some coffee?" she inquired, within a minute of their sliding into the small town café's vinyl-covered booth.

"Do you serve liquor here?" replied Diz, his bloodshot eyes giving her that blank vacuum- inspired pothead stare.

"Not until after five, sir."

"That sucks," declared Diz.

"And you ma'am?" The waitress was speaking to Crystal, who looked like a call girl amid these other three.

"I'll have a large Coke, a cheeseburger—double cheese—and do you guys serve hash browns?"

"The best hash browns in South Dakota, ma'am."

"Then I'll take a double order, extra ketchup."

The rest of the crew followed suit. Only Rita broke ranks and ordered a turkey club instead of a burger. Within the hour they were all loaded back into the Monte Carlo, heading west out of Watertown on Highway 212 toward Redfield. Ten minutes later Rita and Diz were dead to the world, snoring loud enough to be heard above the blaring radio's generic country tunes.

Charlie started dozing but fought it off, wanting to be sure he kept Crystal company on these straight flat highways known for making drivers drowsy. But Crystal, unbeknownst to anyone but herself, had snorted another line of coke in the woman's can just before leaving the restaurant, and she wasn't about to fall asleep, at least not in the next five or six hours. She felt like talking.

"So why'd you walk out, Charlie?" she asked unexpectedly once she knew for certain that Diz and Rita were asleep.

"I guess I got tired of the bullshit."

"You had a great job, didn't you? I mean, with the accounting firm and all."

"Yeah, it paid OK. I hated it, though. It was so tedious. Same shit, day in, day out, week in, week out. There had to be more to life than that bullshit."

"Has your wife remarried?"

"Yeah. About two years ago she met some guy who manages the Super Value grocery up in Kenwood. I think his first wife died of cancer or something."

"That's nice. Do ya ever talk with the kids?"

"No, not really. They're doing fine without me."

"You ever think about getting married again?"

"Sometimes, but I don't ever want to be an accountant. I enjoy gambling too much."

"Maybe you could become a stockbroker. That's legalized gambling, ain't it?"

"Pretty much. I suppose I could become a stockbroker. I like playing the odds, taking chances, that kind of shit. My other life was too routine. I felt I was drowning in it, like I was in some kind of nightmare and I was the headless horseman. How 'bout you, Crystal, you ever think about getting married?"

Crystal shifted uncomfortably in the driver's seat. "I'm not the marrying kind. Besides, with my tubes tied off and no chance of having kids, a family life, all the regular crap people seem to get married for, I don't see any reason to tie the knot with anyone. I like being free, I really do."

Charlie didn't reply, and they both retreated back into themselves. Reflecting on their own lot in life while looking across vast, unbroken fields of winter wheat in the distance. All the while screaming across the plains at a hundred and five. They were on their way to Deadwood, where their luck would change.

*****

It was eight o'clock that night when the Monte Carlo rolled down Main Street. Crystal had covered the 400-plus miles from Watertown in just under five hours. Rita and Diz had slept for most of the run, only waking up in the last half hour as they approached Rapid City on I-90. As the sun set, the old facade-lined streets of Deadwood seemed to come alive.

"This is awesome!" Diz exclaimed as they drove slowly past historic buildings, old restored hotels, and gambling casinos with names like Hickock's Casino, Miss Kitty's, and The Gallows. Crystal, who was starting to crash from her coke high, wasn't as impressed.

"Where the hell are we staying, Charlie. I'm wiped out."

"The Deadwood Gulch Resort. It's somewhere on Main Street. I think it's down on the right."

Within a block they had found it and pulled off into the parking ramp. They were all washed out from the eleven-hour drive and wanted nothing more than to get out of the car, shower, and relax in their rooms.

Charlie had booked a pre-summer discount at the Gulch. He had made all the arrangements, using the Golden Gate's free Internet computer. Mohammed, the manager, had given him some tips on how to get the biggest discounts possible. Because the rooms were tied into the Gulch's casino and Charlie had hinted at being a big roller, the rooms were deeply discounted—all two of them.

They unpacked and checked in. It had been decided early on that each couple would share a room, Diz and Rita in number 105 and Charlie and Crystal across the hall at 104. Aside from grabbing a bite to eat at the restaurant, Charlie and Crystal decided to hit the hay early.

Diz and Rita, who'd slept most of the afternoon, elected to take a stroll down Main Street and check out some of the casinos. They left the others in the lobby and headed out, stumbling into joints that looked to be a hundred years old, bearing classic casino names like Mustang

Sally's and Cadillac Jack's. Diz slipped a few nickels into a handful of slots, but he was too road-weary to do any serious playing. Rita drank rum and cokes and watched as Diz fed the slots.

Charlie and Crystal, alone in a motel room for the very first time, were having an awkward time of it. Crystal had made a serious commitment to do Charlie on this trip and still wanted to keep to her plan. But not tonight. Her two lines of coke had taken the wind out of her sails, and the all-day drive had left her in anything but an amorous mood. Her comments took Charlie by surprise.

"Charlie, I know you're expecting something from me this trip—"

"No, Crystal, I didn't bring you along just to bang you. I mean, if it happens, great, but—"

"—not tonight, Charlie. My ass is dragging from driving all the damn day, and I've got a headache that just won't quit."

"Then get some sleep and we'll take in the sights tomorrow."

There were two queen beds in the room. Charlie had considered taking a room with a single king but felt strange about it. In the end he decided it would be easier if both of them had their own beds, and that way, if things didn't go well, they could each have their own space. Charlie felt incredibly self-conscious about his weight whenever he was alone with Crystal. She was a dancer, with a sleek well-toned body. He was an alcoholic, with a bizarre diet that consisted of one meal a day at a buffet operation that loathed him and thousands of additional calories from alcohol piled on for good measure. He was pushing 260 pounds. Crystal weighed in at just over half that.

In an effort to feel less exposed, Charlie had brought along a large white bathrobe to cover himself when he walked between the bathroom and the safety of his bedspread. It made him look like a sumo wrestler in training. Training for what was the question.

Crystal couldn't help but giggle a little as he scurried from the shower over to the security of his covers. He was such a goofy guy, she thought to herself, so unlike the boys from Hinckley, who not only loved strolling around a motel room naked but filmed it from every conceivable angle.

Within the half-hour both of them were fast asleep, though it took Charlie longer than Crystal to doze off. He couldn't help but think about her, lying in the bed next to him. His thoughts had caused him to get an uninvited erection. He played with it for a little while, thinking about taking care of it on his own, then dismissed the idea as just too weird. She was just six feet away, for chrissake. He'd waited for Crystal a long, long time. He could wait one more night.

*****

Monday morning sucked. Crystal woke up first, stiff, washed out, and dazed. She had one of those moments when, the very instant you wake up, you panic. She looked around and realized she was in a motel room someplace. Was she dreaming? The feeling was over in seconds, once she caught sight of the huge bulk lying in the other bed. Then she remembered everything.

It's just Charlie, she thought, and we're in Deadwood. This isn't so bad. She grabbed her purse and headed to the bathroom. It was a nice bathroom, she decided at first glance. It had replica fixtures, with the toilet tank hanging way up on the wall and ornate radiators and a lovely ball-and- claw bathtub in the corner. Not bad, not bad at all.

She sat down and went pee. At the same time she opened her handbag and dug around until she found a little makeup kit at the bottom. There was absolutely no make up in the kit, just a small mirror, a flat-edge razor, a thin blue straw, and a tiny vial of fine white powder. Before she flushed the toilet, Crystal was buzzing.

She came out and decided it was time to tease Charlie awake. She was up to her old tricks once again and it was a sport she was good at. Crystal could tease an erection out of a box of cremation remains. She had spent the past seven years of her life teasing men, so this snoring walrus she was standing beside would be a piece of cake.

Careful not to wake him, Crystal got down on her knees beside the bed. She stealthily slipped her right hand between the bed and the top sheet midway down Charlie's body. She was going in and looking for it. Within seconds she hit the first obstacle, Charlie's underwear.

Never a problem. She slipped her hand, slowly, almost insidiously inside his loose-fitting boxers. Charlie rustled a bit as she continued on her way.

Please, please don't roll over now, you big oaf, prayed Crystal as her hand continued south,
Charlie settled back down. The sound of his snoring grew louder.

Crystal had it in her hand. It was a little on the small side—no surprise there—but it would have to do. She started to play with it, just a little. Charlie, still sleeping but unconsciously aware, was now parked comfortably in a sex dream and wasn't in any hurry to wake up.

Oddly enough, Charlie wasn't dreaming about Crystal but about Candy—Candy Cotton to be exact—and in his dream Candy was all over him. They were in the backseat of the Monte Carlo, parked in the rain overlooking Mount Rushmore. There was a movie playing—*Little Big Man*—on the faces of the four ex-presidents, and Candy was touching him down below.

In real life it was Crystal touching him and doing a damn fine job of it. Charlie was, to put it mildly, fully extended. Crystal was now thoroughly engaged in her skill set. She knew, at this point, she might be able to get him to go all the way if he didn't wake up first. And if he did, hell, she'd shed her panties and be on him before he could lock himself in the bathroom.

For a coked-up exotic dancer, it was a fabulous plan.

Charlie, in dreamland, was thinking it would be great if Candy let go of his unit and jumped on top of him because he needed—

Then he woke up. Still only half awake and startled by this person beside him, Charlie sat up in bed as though he had been zapped with a taser. Crystal screamed, not loudly but loud enough. Her hand shot out from under the covers faster than a retreating cobra. Charlie, quickly realizing it wasn't a nightmare but a goddamn dream come true, sat there silently and stared at this incredibly beautiful girl kneeling beside his bed, in Deadwood, via his new Monte Carlo, with $4,000 plus in his bank account and the biggest erection he had ever woken up with. He lay back down and smiled.

"What on earth were you doing, Crystal?"

"Nothing."

"Do you call that nothing?"

Charlie chuckled a bit and pointed to the one ring circus tent being held firmly in place by his penis.

"No, that's something. Something I can fix."

Charlie moved over in bed and said, "Then you'd better fix it."

Crystal went to Plan B. Slowly. Leaving the teddy on, she reached around and unsnapped her bra. It fell to the floor. Her breasts looked better freed. Her nipples were as firm as 24 karat gold, her tits the best money could buy.

Charlie knew what she was up to: Crystal was stripping for him. No pole required.

Next she slithered out of her panties. She did so shyly, as if she had only just noticed this man watching her every move. Her pubic hair, which Charlie had only glimpsed along the edge of her G-string, was much darker than her dyed-blond hair. It was neatly shaven along the edges and formed a perfect **V** between her lovely thighs.

Now only her sheer teddy remained. Crystal slid one strap down a little, and the loosely tied garment fell across her bare shoulder. She lifted up her right hand and untied the knot with a little flip.

All the while she made a cooing, squeaky noise that Charlie had never heard before, noise every man on earth wishes he could hear. As she giggled a little, the teddy fell gently to the floor. Feigning shyness to a fault, Crystal tried to cover her private parts, her right arm over her breasts and her left hand shielding Charlie's eyes from her womanness.

"I'm cold," she said, standing there looking like the *Birth of Venus*.

"Want to come in under the covers?"

"Do you mind?"

"What do you think?"

Crystal climbed in beside Charlie. As she did so her right hand went right back to where it had been a few minutes earlier. Charlie let go a sigh as she grabbed him. "Ahhhhh."

"Does that feel good?" Crystal purred as she started stroking.

Charlie couldn't speak. From this point onward there were no words left to explain how it felt. He had not had an orgasm, aside from a handful of self-induced moments of weakness, in four long years. The last orgasm he had experienced with a woman was a business transaction. An oral contract, so to speak.

Now Crystal—yes, the very same Crystal he was enamored of, was grabbing his cock at 10:23 A.M. in a motel room in Deadwood, South Dakota. Words were useless to describe what Charlie was experiencing.

Crystal didn't stop there. Silently, in a liquid motion she moved from being beside him to being on top of him. As she did so, her hand slid away, her body rolled up and over Charlie, and her ass slipped deliciously south. Before he knew what had happened, he was inside her. It was the absolute best moment of his life.

Wrapping the covers around her head, arms and shoulders like a squaw in the Black Hills, Crystal lifted her body up, leaving only her lovely breasts fully exposed.

As Crystal started working him, Charlie's breathing hastened. As she placed her hands next to her knees, the bedding slipped off her body, giving Charlie a full view. She closed her eyes, focusing on the motions that were taking him to the edge.

Charlie started squirming restlessly beneath her. It would only be a matter of minutes before he would have to let go. Time was moving too quickly, he realized. He wanted time to stop. He wanted everything to hang suspended in this delirium of pleasure.

By this time the room was awash with the midmorning sun. It poured through the sheer curtains of the only window and illuminated the room. Crystal's skin radiated the light, making her appear like a goddess, not a mortal. Charlie couldn't take his eyes off of her as she knelt on top of him, doing the dance of lovemaking.

Try as he might to delay the inevitable, he could not. In just a few more moments, Charlie exploded. It was not an orgasm, it was an avalanche. He arched his back, lifting Crystal up as he did and released. Crystal moaned and then cried out, softly, "Yes, oh, yes!"

Everything went white: the beige walls of the motel room, the curtains, the paintings, the TV: the world itself turned a pure burning white. There were no thoughts left in Charlie other than pleasure—pure white pleasure.

Crystal, caught up in the moment and delighting in Charlie's pleasure, found herself on the verge of orgasm as well. She kept on feverishly, until she too let go. It had been years since she had experienced an orgasm with a man. She had faked them a hundred times in the past, but this was no fake. Amazed at what was happening, she cried out as she came.

Crystal opened her eyes and looked at Charlie, who was grinning from ear to ear. Her long blond hair, hanging down past her shoulders, was wet and tangled. Her breasts were covered with fine beads of sweat, bearing beautiful witness to the passion of her dance.

"You are unbelievable," said Charlie.

"You're not so bad yourself, Mr. Charlie," Crystal said, falling away to lie beside him like a discarded rag doll. The room smelled of sex, a musty, faint, but pleasurable scent.

"Do you feel like showering together?" Crystal asked.

"Give me a few minutes, but yes, that would be great."

"Take your time. I'm not in any hurry today."

"Neither am I, Crystal, neither am I."

Chain of Fools

Chapter 11: My Birth

I was born in 1954. Lucky, lucky me. I had an older brother, and because of my father's ill-tempered drinking, my mother lost a set of twins in 1952. I was born during the height of the cold war, when the Russians and Americans were busy building H-bombs, Eisenhower was president and suburbia was all the rage.

We lived on Michigan Street the year I was born, in the Helm Street neighborhood, not two city blocks from Maggie's old haunts. After the war, my father had taken an apprenticeship with Youngquist Brothers Plumbing Company and worked his way into the union by 1951. At the time Stanley—I'll call him Stauch like everyone else—was doing mostly residential plumbing: cleaning clogged drains, setting and resetting old toilets, unplugging backed up sewer lines, leaking sinks, and overflowing tubs.

It was the kind of work where you smell like shit when you get back home at the end of the day, and a stiff drink helped to take the edge off. Over time, one drink after work became two. Eventually, two drinks led to three and after three it was more or less a free fall. By the time I was born, in October 1954 Stauch was downing a liter of vodka a day. He was a drunk.

Stauch had told Beatrice he needed to drink to help him cope with the constant ringing in his inner ear. Tinnitus was unknown back then, and the doctors never found a thing to verify his complaint. In a pitched battle of vodka versus sirens in the head, vodka always wins.

In my father's case, the vodka won big. Within a few years, Stauch no longer waited until one of the Youngquist Brothers knocked him off for the night at six o'clock, he started hiding pints among his tools and uniforms in the service truck. The owners knew Stauch was drinking on the job, but good plumbers were in high demand and my father was a good plumber in spite of the drinking. Besides, the Youngquist brothers were also alcoholics, so their moral high ground wasn't very high.

Stauch worked like a dog. He was often on call, leaving our house after midnight to fix frozen pipes in the throes of an icy merciless winter. Sometimes they would station him up on the iron range for a week or two to help plumb the new homes in the mining towns that were booming near Eveleth.

I was too small to know what the hell was going on. Like most children born to parents who spend most of their time screaming at each other, I thought screaming was normal. By the time I was four I was sure my father's first name was Son-of-a-bitch. In the constant arguing, the fights, the debacle that was my family life, everyone, from Grandma LeBlanc to my older sister Anna, called him that, and his mother, Maggie, didn't care; she thought her son's new nickname was kind of cute.

To make matters worse, Stauch was an angry drunk. He had a chip on his shoulder from the moment he woke up, hung over and ornery, until he passed out again at the end of the day. He must have studied swearing at Maggie's school of advanced profanity and graduated with honors, he could swear you straight to hell if he wanted to. And he oftentimes did.

My poor mother, who hardly drank and seldom to excess, was demonized by this lost soul. No matter who ended up with Stauch, even had he married a Johns Hopkins psychiatrist, it would have been ugly. Stauch had had his childhood stolen from him, he had seen too much death during his four years fighting the Japanese, and he didn't know where to start as a parent. With One-Eyed Maggie deserting Paul as a role model, it was amazing any of us made it out of the Helm Street neighborhood alive.

Most of my childhood memories are gone, victims of selective amnesia. What little I do remember was put in this tattered scrapbook of memory with a soldering iron: burned in, red hot, without benefit of painkillers.

I wasn't there when the twins were lost in 1952, but the story was passed down to me even before I was old enough to grasp its gravity. My mother was five months pregnant when she miscarried. My father, by this time, had a major—no, make that five-star general—drinking problem. He had always held the illegitimate births of the two earlier kids over my mother like some kind of trip-wire guillotine. In the twisted logic of a hateful alcoholic, it was always her fault.

"I should never have married you, you little tramp," went Stauch's diatribe, late into those terribly long nights.

Beatrice, insecure and defensive, didn't know how to respond. Most of the time she simply put up with it, but on this particular night she decided she wasn't going to stand for Stauch's hateful comments any longer. She knew he would come home drunk that night, just like the night before, but this time Mom locked the doors and put chairs against the handles, so even if Stauch had his key with him he wouldn't be able to get in.

He came home late, spending the last two hours at one of the nearby bars, a bar with no amenities aside from a well-stocked supply of nameless liquor brands and ice-cold beer. Bars to get drunk in.

When Stauch came home late that evening and found the doors fastened against him, he became enraged, screaming at Beatrice to let him in. In this burst of anger, he added that once he did make it in he was going to kill her and all the goddamned kids.

Most mothers don't react well to comments like this, and Beatrice was no exception. She refused to let him in and told him she would call the cops if he didn't leave this instant. He left but not for long. He drove up to his brother's place in New Duluth where he kept his 30/30 deer rifle. When he returned later that night, Beatrice had no time to call the cops. Using the butt of the rifle he broke out the back-door window, reached through the open pane, moved the chair that was leaning against the door handle, and walked in and sat down at the kitchen table, loaded deer rifle in hand.

Beatrice didn't know what to do. Stauch told her to sit down or he would shoot her. She sat down, but the trauma soon proved to be too much for her womb to handle and she started having contractions. Stauch, somehow remembering the twins inside of his wife were his and not those of strangers, awoke from the nightmare he had crafted and put his rifle down.

It was too late. He rushed his anxious wife to the hospital where she gave birth to two boys, but they were premature and died shortly after birth. Stauch never forgave himself for being such a fool, but this led him to drink more to forget his own misguided anger. He had recklessly killed his own unborn children.

The police were never told about the incident. Families kept things like this to themselves back then, not wanting any trouble. Stauch promised he would cut back on his drinking shortly after the incident, a promise that lasted about as long as this paragraph.

He never beat my mother, at least not that I know of. His was more of a constant verbal assault. That's how I remember him as a child, telling me and my brothers that we would never amount to anything, we were little fuckups, losers, worthless pieces of shit just like our mother. It was all about control, though he had no idea as to what needed controlling.

It got worse. By the late 1950s the relationship had descended into a sadistic, masochistic ritual: mother the victim, father the victimizer. My oldest sister, who was now in her teens, saw what was happening and moved in with Grandma LeBlanc to escape the madness. My oldest brother, who was big for his age, started standing up to this raging drunk but, more often then not, ended up being swatted across the face and sent to his room bleeding.

I remember my father, sometimes late at night, telling my mom that he was going down to the basement to build her a coffin. She would just sit at the kitchen table and weep. Sometimes, when she was feeling bold, Beatrice would reach for the phone and call the Duluth police. If my father had time, he would rip the phone off the wall before she could get to it. The phone company hooked our phone up so many times they once threatened to disconnect us for good.

The handful of times my mother actually got a chance to call the cops, my father was always smart enough to get out before the police arrived, so he was never once locked up for domestic abuse. But he was arrested repeatedly, outside the house, for DUI, resisting arrest, drunk and disorderly conduct, and failing to provide child support. None of the charges were serious enough to merit prison, but on more than one occasion he would do a sixty or a ninety day stint on the Saint Louis county work farm. The same place his father and mother had done stretches in. The Stupidnski name is a familiar one in the work farm's ledgers.

There was another miscarriage some years after I was born, though this one wasn't caused by anything Stauch did. Eventually I had two more little brothers and, finally, a little sister in 1959: a total of six. One half sister, one half-brother, and three siblings. Catholic schools, Catholic services, and, most importantly, Catholic guilt.

Deadwood, South Dakota

Diz and Rita woke up around noon. They had stayed up late, come home and had sex, drunken and weird sex, and fallen asleep together. In the morning, seeing this woman sleeping beside him, Diz felt strange, as someone else were on this road trip, not he.

After the drunken roll in the hay, Rita had fallen fast asleep. She felt fine. She was glad to have been fired from the Piggly Wiggly, allowing her to be able to take a long-overdue vacation. She hated that job anyway, scanning canned goods and pork chops and calling the manager every so often for a price check on cabbage. To make matters worse, they paid minium wage, which was like having to work for nothing. Being fired for Rita had turned out to be a blessing.

Rita wasn't so naive as to think she was in love with Diz Nelson, even remotely. For Rita, this romp to the Black Hills was just that: a week-long adventure off the Rez in a brand-new car with an old friend and a couple of white people who were footing the bill. When she returned to Fond du Lac next week, Rita's plans were to start a house cleaning business with a girl friend. They planned to clean homes in Cloquet, Duluth, and Superior. All they needed to get started was enough cash to purchase a used vacuum cleaner, some scrub brushes, soap and bleach. Of course, just like Rita's wild rice business, apple pie crust business, and beauty salon, her cleaning business would never make it to square one. She would be applying for work at the Super Value grocery store within the month, conveniently failing to mention anything about being fired from Piggly Wiggly in her application.

Diz was operating on much the same wavelength as Rita when it came to their relationship. It was a romp, a road trip, a week-long sojourn with another warm body. The sex was fine but, unlike liquor, Diz could take it or leave it. Diz had been married once, long ago, and at this point in his life, as a sick and hopeless drunk with no job, no plans for a job, and very little money, the chances of his doing much of anything were minimal. He lived simply, from tribal allotment check to tribal allotment check, spending his money and time with either his two favorite cousins or his best friend, Charlie Stupidnski. His was the KISS method of existence—Keep It Simple, Stupid—with the emphasis on *simple*, though one could argue the emphasis was really on *stupid*.

Diz had grabbed one of Rita's bare tits to wake her up. They were not particularly attractive tits either, the kind of breasts that were best kept in confinement. Once set free they were all over the place, spilled out across the chest like two huge fried eggs, sunny side up. Diz didn't care. He felt himself lucky just to be getting laid. Hell, two years ago he had gone to bed with a woman who was a cancer survivor and, to put it crudely, she was breastless. *Any port in a storm* was Diz's plan with women.

"What are you doing, Diz?" Rita asked, realizing this man lying beside her had his right hand wrapped around her breast.

"Do you want to shower together?"

"No, not really."

"OK, then I'll shower first."

"Fine. Jerk yourself off while you're in there."

"You're such a sweetheart, Rita."

"Thanks, but let me take a piss first, I drank way too much beer last night."

"OK."

As Rita, naked as the day she was born, made her way to the bathroom, Diz kept up the conversation. "I wonder if Crystal's jumped Charlie yet."

"I'll bet you a five-spot she has," Rita shouted back from the can.

"Dumb bet. I think you're right. She's going to sink her grappling hooks into him, and she probably got started last night."

"No, she was too tired. She probably did him this morning."

"We'll find out soon enough."

Rita came back into the room, crawled into bed, still buck naked, and turned on the TV. Some useless soap opera came on but Rita, who hated soap operas, didn't bother to change the station. It was all the same to her.

"What's our plan today? Are we going to see the Crazy Horse statue?"

"Nah. Charlie and I thought it would be nice just to hang out here in Deadwood today. Take in some casinos and the sights and shit, then go see the statue tomorrow. I'm not in the mood to hang out in the car again all day long."

"We going out for breakfast?"

"No. Charlie found an all you can eat buffet at one of the big casinos. He's planning to take us there for brunch, then we'll just bum around. It'll be fun."

"But I'm starving."

"Put some clothes on and head down to the lobby: they probably have rolls or something downstairs, you know, a continental breakfast. Grab a couple for me too. I'm going to shower."

"Shit, that means I have to get dressed."

"Yeah, chances are they won't serve you naked."

*****

Monday flew by. They had lunch at the Gallows, where the staff soon learned they were dealing with professional buffet busters. Everyone there hoped they weren't planning to stay in Deadwood for long. Only Crystal was civil, with the other three going directly to the tray-only technique perfected by Charlie at the Black Bear. The brunch cost Charlie fifty-five bucks but they consumed over eighty dollars' worth of food. Rita had never tried the tray method before, and she swore that from now on, whether it was at Sweet Tomatoes, Ponderosa Steak House, or China City, she would never bother with those annoying little plates again. With her turkey gravy literally spilling up and over the edge of her bright orange tray, Rita was a convert.

Rita and Diz both knew Charlie had gotten laid. When they first met in the lobby it was impossible not to note his changed behavior. Crystal was the exact same woman she was the day before, likable but professional. Charlie was smiling ear to ear. By the time they made the lobby Charlie had enjoyed multiple liaisons with his newfound love: the first time in bed, the second in the shower, and then on the small sofa just before hitting the road. If there was ever a happy man on earth, Charlie Stupidnski was that man.

His day ended in much the same fashion as it began. No sooner did they close the motel room door behind them than the two lovebirds were at it again. By the time he fell asleep Charlie realized he had experienced more sex than he had ever had before in a sixteen-hour period, whacking off included. He slept well.

Plans were on to visit the Crazy Horse Memorial on Tuesday. Diz was ecstatic. All his life, ever since he could remember, he had wanted to see the carving. Now, with the face done and the hole under Crazy Horse's arm carved out, the stone mountain was beginning to take shape. Thinking about it kept him awake half the night. Unlike Crystal, Rita was dishing out her action as if Diz were on some kind of sex diet. Once and only once was the sum total thus far, and unless Diz could get Rita drunk again, one might be the number he went back to the Rez with.

It's not a big deal anyway, thought Diz, as he lay awake beside her thinking about Crazy Horse. It's not like liquor, which is something you actually need to survive. Sex, in Diz's mind, was a luxury, liquor a necessity.

*****

"How far is it?" Diz asked, after they all got situated in the car.
"About forty miles or so," Crystal said.
"How long?"
"An hour, maybe an hour and a half. You have to take a little winding highway to get down there, according to the GPS."

Charlie was keeping quiet. He hadn't really spoken much at all in the past two days, happy to remain silent and content. He was not in Deadwood, but in heaven. Crystal had been good to him, to put it mildly.

The minute the Monte Carlo cleared the city limits, Crystal dug out her radar detector, set it up on the dashboard, and roared down Highway 385 like a NASCAR test driver who'd overdosed on human growth hormones. The road was winding and the curves dangerous but Crystal never once fell below sixty. Unlike the ride from Scanlon to Deadwood, Charlie didn't mind Crystal's incessant speeding. If Charlie died in a fiery crash on this trip, he would die happy.

No one was drinking. Diz had made it clear that there would be no alcohol allowed on the day they stood before the stone mountain that was slowly, methodically becoming a monumental tribute to a great Sioux warrior. In true character, Diz didn't exclude marijuana, so Rita had brought along a few freshly rolled joints and everyone was high as a kite within ten minutes of leaving town. Rita felt it was as if they were all just taking hits from a peace pipe and not in any way sacrilegious to the memory of Crazy Horse. Diz, stoned beyond measure, tacitly agreed.

They got to Avenue of the Chiefs in under an hour. The weather was sublime: perfectly clear sky, temperature hanging just around 70 degrees, and winds light and variable. It simply could not have been a better day to visit the memorial.

Diz, who typically was the last person to do such a thing, insisted on paying admission for everyone. "This is my treat, Charlie. You promised to bring me here, and you kept your promise; now I'm going to pay for everyone to see this monument and experience this glorious day."

Diz was well aware that admission fees help fund the memorial. He knew that Korczak Ziolkowski, the man who conceived of and designed the colossal carving, had refused to take any government funds to complete the work. Two separate times the federal government had offered Korczak and his family ten million dollars to help in the completion of the work, but both times the Crazy Horse Memorial Foundation had turned the money down.

This was going to be a statue built one admission dollar at a time by the people who came to see it. A statue built by the people and not by any government. Korczak had learned how to carve mountains while working with Gutzon Borglum, the man who designed and carved Mount Rushmore. Korczak brought many of the same techniques he had learned from Borglum with him to Thunderhead Mountain, where the image of Crazy Horse was slowly taking shape.

As they pulled up to the admission gate, Diz dug out his worn leather wallet.

"How much is it to get in, ma'am?" Asked Crystal as they pulled up to the entrance gate.

"Twenty five per carload, or ten dollars a person, whichever you would prefer."

Diz dug out two twenties and handed them up to Crystal. She took note of the forty dollars and handed it to the young Native American woman working the booth.

"Here's your change, ma'am,"

"No, keep the change and use the extra money to finish the statue," Diz hollered out from the back seat.

"Thanks," said the attractive Indian girl, bending down a bit to get a better look at the two Chippewa huddled together in the backseat of the car. "Thanks a lot."

She handed Crystal an admission ticket and smiled. Crystal pulled away, careful not to speed while driving up the Avenue of the Chiefs, fearing Diz would think it some kind of transgression. It was around noon as they reached the visitor's center. When the road curved they could catch glimpses of the immense carving in the distance.

"Wow, look at the size of that statue!" Rita exclaimed from the backseat.

"It's huge," added Diz.

"Hey, Stupidnski, is this Korczak guy related to you?" Rita asked.

"I don't think so, but he's got one hell of a last name: Ziolkowski. That's a whopper."

"He's dead, ya know. He died in 1982. But I think his wife is still alive and I know a couple of his kids are still involved with the project." Diz filled them in as Crystal looked for a parking spot.

"How long before it's finished?"

"No one really knows. They completed the face of Crazy Horse in 1998, and they're working on the horse's head right now. When it's done, the stallion's head will be twenty-two stories high. The statue itself is already the largest free-standing statue in the world."

Crystal parked and the four of them got out and made their way to the visitor's center. The interior of the Monte Carlo reeked of marijuana, so they were careful to leave all the windows rolled up before leaving the car. Rita took two joints with her, in case they could find a quiet out-of-the-way spot to light up later in the day.

Within minutes they were standing beside a large stone replica, comparing it to the completed work on the mountain nearly half a mile in the distance. Crystal dug out a little digital camera she had brought along and took a photo of Rita and Diz standing beside the scale model of the finished carving, one thirty-fourth of its actual size. Diz was so happy to be at the memorial there was almost an aura around him. It was his life's dream come true, to be so close to this monument to his hero, Crazy Horse.

Diz was well aware that the project had its detractors. Russell Means, Native American activist and actor, had always opposed carving a sacred mountain into the likeness of an Indian who never allowed anyone to take his photo. Lame Deer, a Lakota medicine man, thought the idea of making a beautiful wild mountain into a statue was a pollution to the landscape. But everyone had also hated the Eiffel Tower when Monsieur Eiffel conceived of it. Diz was keenly aware of the fact that all great endeavors stir a certain amount of controversy.

But as Diz and Rita stood there, with Crystal snapping pictures and the visitors' center filling with tourists, many of them Native Americans, Diz knew that Chief Henry Standing Bear's letter to Korczak in 1939, which put the entire process in motion, had plenty of supporters. The letter was in response to all the attention being given at that time to the ongoing carving of Mount Rushmore, a mere nine miles away. In it, Chief Standing Bear wrote, "My fellow chiefs and I would like the white man to know that the red man has great heroes, too."

Crazy Horse, the Lakota warrior who had led the charge against General Custer in the Battle of the Little Big Horn, was just such a leader. Diz couldn't take his eyes off the immense statue in the distance. After staring at it for ten minutes, he made his way over to a clerk working in the gift shop.

"Is there any way we can get closer to the statue?"

"Yeah, depending on the blasting schedule and stuff they run, sometimes a bus shuttles to the base of the mountain from the parking lot. Hang on a second, and I'll check to see if they've got one going today."

The clerk picked up the phone and called the main office as Diz waited anxiously for the news.

"You're in luck. They finished blasting Monday, and they're just drilling new holes for the next set of blasts, so the bus is running. It leaves at two. Do you want to buy some tickets?"

"Yeah, we'll take four."

"That's sixteen dollars."

Diz handed the kid a twenty. "Keep the change, it's my donation to the project."

"Thanks."

Over the next few hours the four of them made the rounds. They dropped in to visit the Native American Museum and Educational Center and had lunch overlooking the mountain at the Laughing Water Restaurant, where all four of them ordered Tatanka Stew and split two Native American tacos. Thus far it was the perfect day.

The bus was right on schedule. Diz was so excited that he seemed more like a child at the county fair than a grown Native American heading to the base of a granite mountain. But this was his day, his dream, and the others respected it.

"I can't wait to see it up close," said Diz to Charlie, as they boarded the bus.

"Me either, Diz. Hey, thanks for winning the Monte Carlo, for pulling the handle of the Big Bertha and shit. Without you, we wouldn't be here."

"Thanks for keeping your promise, Stupidnski. You must be related to this Korczak fellow, since both of you seem to like us Injuns."

"Hell, Diz, he might be my uncle for all I know. My family tree's a mess."

The bus crawled down the dirt road toward the base of the mountain. Ten minutes later, the bus driver advised everyone that they could disembark and warned everyone to avoid the piles of rubble that lay everywhere around the bottom of the carving.

"That's loose rock," he said. "Even when they're not blasting, we get plenty of rock slides from all the loose rock along the edge of the carving. We don't want you to get hurt."

"I'm going to walk around and take a look at his face." Diz said to Charlie and Crystal.

"That's fine. We'll just hang around here."

Diz and Rita made their way around the bottom of the mountain toward a vantage point where they could look directly west into the face of Crazy Horse. As they walked, Diz explained the tale of Crazy Horse's death and the fact that there is no authentic photo of the great warrior.

"You see, Rita, no one knows what Crazy Horse really looked like because he would never allow anyone to take his picture when he was alive. He felt that photographs might somehow steal his spirit, so he avoided all cameras and sketch artists during his brief lifetime."

"How did he die, Diz?"

"They killed him. They stabbed him with a bayonet on September 5, 1877. It happened at Camp Robinson, Nebraska, under very suspicious circumstances. They said he was resisting arrest when a guard stabbed him. He was only thirty-seven years old, much too young to die. He helped defeat Custer, Rita. Crazy Horse was a great hero."

Within minutes, Rita and Diz were standing in front of the monument, looking straight into Crazy Horse's beautifully carved face. Diz said nothing.

After a few minutes of silence, Rita turned to say something to Diz but stopped before she uttered a word. Diz was crying.

She saw the tears rolling down his cheeks, across his ruddy complexion, and onto the small granite outcropping they were standing on. A sadness radiated out from him, making the blue sky above seem cloudy, making the death of Crazy Horse a hundred and thirty years ago seem as if it had happened yesterday.

To Diz, this warrior's death represented everything that was wrong with the world. As an example of how the white man had come to destroy the life and livelihood of the red man, it stood for all the massacres, the broken treaties, the lies, and the ravaging of their lands.

After a long silence, Rita spoke. "Why is he pointing east?"

"He points east saying, 'My lands are where my dead lie buried.' He's right, Rita, Crazy Horse points east to where the white man first came from and where he enslaved and murdered our people. Where Jefferson stole the concept of democracy from the Iroquois, then took from us the corn, the potato, and the foods that feed most of the world. We have suffered at the hands of the white man, Rita. Will our suffering never end?"

Rita didn't respond. Their suffering would never end.

Diz became quiet from that moment on. It was an epiphany he experienced at the base of that statue. Someday, when it was completed, it would be more than two football fields in length and nearly two football fields high. But it was an awakening of sadness, not of joy. That broken, alcoholic Chippewa took on the weight of 500 nations that afternoon, a weight he would never shed.

Diz and Rita made their way back to where Charlie and Crystal were standing. Crystal had taken a half dozen shots of the mountain and a few of Diz and Rita as they stood in the distance staring up at the face of the memorial.

"It's something, isn't it," remarked Rita.

"You can really get a feel for how big it is when you're up close like this," said Crystal.

"Yeah."

Within a few minutes the bus driver had crawled back into the driver's seat and honked the horn several times to let everyone at the base of the mountain know it was time to head back. The four Minnesotans loaded onto the bus along with a couple of dozen other paying customers. No one had been disappointed in seeing Korczak and Standing Bear's dream up close and personal. It was an amazing accomplishment that would in time, Diz prayed, become one of the wonders of the modern world.

When they got back to the parking lot, everyone knew it was time to head back to Deadwood. As they drove down the winding Avenue of the Chiefs, Crystal put on the radio to fill the silence that permeated the Monte Carlo. When they hit the highway, Charlie turned around to Rita and Diz. "We're less than ten miles from Mount Rushmore, and they stay open until six. Do you guys want to head over and see that monument as well?"

"Never," answered Diz. Then, almost as an afterthought, he added, "Only if they let me piss on it."

Charlie figured the National Park Service would probably not allow Dismount Moose Nelson to urinate on Mount Rushmore, so he told Crystal to skip the right at Mount Rushmore Drive and continue north to Deadwood.

The mood was sullen. Little was said as the radio played country and western tunes and the sun vanished in the west. Every now and again, while glancing in her rearview mirror, Crystal caught glimpses of Diz, quietly weeping. She drove slowly, as if in some unnamed funeral procession. Shadows grew long and darkness gathered. Such moments are the death of dreams.

*****

The next few days in Deadwood were strange. After the visit to the Crazy Horse Memorial, Diz's mood changed. That Tuesday night he started drinking early and kept drinking until he was sick again. On Wednesday he told Rita he felt terrible and asked her to tell Charlie and Crystal he'd be staying in bed all day. When she asked if there was anything she could get for him, he said yes, a bottle of brandy.

Seeing that he was already having trouble with his liver again, she bought him a half pint, knowing even that much liquor was a bad idea. Rita felt sorry for him and hoped Diz would snap out of his funk before they left for Minnesota on Saturday morning. Rita had even offered herself up to Diz that same morning, only to have him tell her he wasn't in the mood for sex. Seeing the statue had had an effect on Diz exactly opposite from what everyone thought it would have. Instead of inspiring him, it weighed on him as heavy as the piles of broken rubble lying around its base.

Charlie would normally have been more responsive to the plight of his best friend, but he was too enthralled with Crystal and the amazing things she could do with her body. They had been experimenting with various positions and techniques during the past few days. Charlie's back was sore, but it was a pain he could live with.

Crystal found herself falling for this big, awkward guy. After the sex they would settle back into long, lazy hours of pillow talk. They always had a bottle of something or other beside the bed and, between the liquor and the sex, defenses softened on both sides. Charlie was sweet, and Crystal had a weakness for sweetness.

Rita, aside from nursing Diz's bout with depression, was having a ball. Charlie had given her $200 for spending money, and oh-my-God, was she spending it. She played black jack, roulette and the slot machines, and even tried a few hands of Texas Hold'em. For someone who wasn't much of a gambler, Rita's luck was incredible. By 3 A.M. Thursday morning, she had doubled her money and then some.

When she got back to the motel room, Rita found Diz fast asleep. He was snoring louder than a hibernating grizzly as she crawled in beside him. Rita noted that his skin tone was slightly jaundiced again and knew the rest was good for him. Maybe tomorrow he would snap out of it, Rita prayed, as she fell asleep. Maybe tomorrow.

*****

Diz woke up rested. "So what did you guys do yesterday?"

"The usual: gambled, drank, ate lunch at a different buffet. All you can eat. You know how Charlie is. We ate like royalty. "I was on a big winning streak last night, Diz, look at this." Rita took out a fat wad of twenties, held tight by a rubber band, and tossed them over to him.

"Wow. How much is this?"

"I think about four hundred and fifty bucks."

"That's a bundle."

"How you feeling today, Diz? You looked like shit when I came to bed last night."

"I feel better now, Rita. I've got a plan."

"A plan for what?"

"You'll find out soon enough. Can I borrow about fifty off ya. I've got to go do some shopping, and I'm running low on cash. I think I dropped too much money at the memorial. I've got to go to a hardware store before we get rolling today."

"A hardware store? What the hell for?"

"Like I said, you'll see soon enough."

Diz tossed the roll of twenties back to Rita and she peeled off three and handed them back. "Keep the money, Diz. Without you I'd never been asked to make this trip, and I'm having a blast. I just wish you were feeling better. What's got you so down?"

"It's this Indian shit, Rita. You know, Pine Ridge, Wounded Knee, Wind River—all the crap our people have suffered through."

"Well, feeling sorry about it ain't going to change history, Diz; get on with your life. We're talking about driving down to Custer State Park today for a picnic. You want to join us?"

"Sure, as soon as I get back from the hardware store. I've got to pick some things up before Friday."

"OK. See you in a bit. I'm going to take a shower and get ready."

Diz got up, still a bit under the weather, and got dressed while Rita headed into the bathroom. Long before Rita was finished with her shower, Diz was out the door and heading down Main Street in search of a hardware store and, by the time he returned, Rita was dressed. She was just about to knock on Charlie and Crystal's door when Diz walked in carrying a large canvas duffel bag. He set it down in the corner and, as he did, the contents rattled.

"What on earth's in that bag?"

"I'll tell you tomorrow, Rita. Let's just keep it between ourselves, because I don't think Charlie would approve."

"Approve of what? What the hell are you planning to do?"

"Tomorrow, Rita, I'll tell you all about it tomorrow. Let's just kick back and enjoy today. What I've got going isn't going to happen till tomorrow, so let's not even talk about it today, especially around Charlie and Crystal. Promise?"

"OK, I promise. But I don't understand what you're being so secretive about. Do you have some kind of present in there for Charlie?"

"No." Diz paused a moment, smiled in a devious fashion, and added, "Well, maybe he'll think it's a present."

Rita could tell he wasn't going to discuss the duffel bag any further. She shrugged her shoulders. She would just have to wait find out what it held.

"I'm going to wake up Charlie and Crystal."

"I think they're already awake. I heard some thumping and moaning sounds through the door as I came down the hallway. You'd think those two might have the decency to keep it down, but no, they want the whole damn world to know how much they love each other."

"You didn't put your ear to the door, did you? You scoundrel."

"Trust me, Rita, you don't have to."

Rita walked over and opened up their front door, which was located almost directly across the hallway from Charlie and Crystal's room. Even from the threshold, Rita could clearly hear the sounds of two adults enjoying a morning interlude.

Rita smiled, chuckled a little, and turned to Diz. "Should we call the office and make a complaint about the racket coming out of Room one-oh-four. That'd be funny as hell."

"No, it'd be mean, Rita. Let's just wait a few minutes until those two lovebirds are through. They can't keep that pace up for long."

"Yeah, I suppose you're right."

Rita closed the door and walked over the bed. She sat down beside the night stand, then picked up the remote, and flipped on the TV. There was some kind of infomercial on about a new vacuum cleaner that could pick up dirt from a mile away, or so it appeared. Rita found it entertaining. Diz went into the bathroom to take a piss. Five minutes passed.

Rita cracked her door again and listened. All was quiet in 104.

"They must be over."

"Sounds like it."

She walked across the hallway and knocked.

"Who's there?" Charlie hollered from inside.

"It's me, Rita. Are we ever going on that picnic or what?"

"Yeah, we're going. Give us a few minutes."

"We already have."

Inside the motel room Charlie blushed. "Those assholes must

have been listening," he said.

Crystal smiled, noting how embarrassed Charlie was. Crystal didn't mind at all that they had listened. Hell, she thought, if I had known they were out there I would have turned up the volume. Once an exotic dancer, always an exotic dancer. For Crystal, it was always Showtime.

Within the next half hour, all four were squeezing back into the Monte Carlo. The weather outside was holding, which was rare for the Black Hills in the spring. No one complained. As they headed out of town, Crystal was digging out her radar detector and everyone was looking forward to seeing the park and enjoying an afternoon in the countryside. Rita broke out a joint about the same time Charlie dug out a liter of sipping rum he had brought along for the occasion. By the time they were five miles out of Deadwood all four of them had bloodshot pothead eyes, and the rum was making quick headway on a carload of empty stomachs. It was Crystal who started up the conversation.

"So Diz, Charlie tells me your real name is Dismount Moose. That's a goofy name."

"My father named me. Well, his friends suggested it because of what had just happened to him."

"What had just happened?"

"My father's Native American name was Wind Rider Nelson. He loved to ride things, but not your normal things. He liked riding weird things, like trees, animals or soap box derbies. Things no one else would even think of riding. Hell, I don't remember hearing that he ever rode normal things, like a horse or a motorcycle.

"The year I was born, just a couple of months before my first birthday, he and his buddies decided it was time for my father to ride a moose. He had already ridden a deer and a bear and they weren't having any luck finding an elk, so they decided it was time Dad rode a moose. This was in the fall and the males were all carrying these huge racks, so it was going to be very dangerous and very interesting. My dad loved life that way, dangerous and interesting."

"How on God's earth can you get on the back of a moose without getting killed?" said Crystal, already swept into Diz's tale.

"These guys were smart when it came to wild animals. Believe it or not, getting on a moose is easy as hell. It was staying on the moose for the necessary seven seconds that damn near killed my dad. First and foremost, they had to find a moose. Back in the early sixties there were still plenty of moose just north of Island Lake, which is up on Highway four out of Duluth. There are a ton of peat bogs and tamarack swamps north of the lake. You can still find plenty of big moose up that way today and back then there were tons of them."

Diz reached up and took the liter of rum from Charlie, taking a long drink to wet his whistle. Then continued his story.

"Of course, everyone knows moose swim, and they swim quite a bit. Finding one that was swimming across a large bay was the problem. One of my father's brothers at the time had a small aluminum Lund with a twenty-horsepower outboard on it, and once they finalized the plan the four of them asked if they could use the Lund for a few days to go walleye fishing.

"They only had one fishing rod between the four of them and my uncle should have been alerted to the fact that you don't normally go walleye fishing with one fishing rod and two deer rifles on board, but you know how it is. He wasn't using the boat much and whatever these guys were up to he didn't give a shit one way or the other. Besides, they were paying for the use of the boat with some bootleg whiskey, so it was a fair trade.

"Anyway, they towed the Lund up Highway Four, launched it, and motored around the lake, keeping their eyes peeled for two straight days, looking for a big honking bull moose swimming lazily across one of the countless bays. And sure as shit, on the third day out they found one, and he was a brute.

"The plan was simple. Once they caught up to it in the Lund, they would pull alongside the moose and match its swimming speed in the water. A moose that big could tear a little boat to pieces on land, but in the water they're pretty harmless. All the guys had to do was get close enough for my dad to jump from the Lund over to the back of the moose, where he could hang on to his horns until the animal made it to shore."

"That's one crazy fucking plan, Diz," remarked Crystal, who was presently doing ninety- five down some twisting blue highway in the Black Hills.

"You bet your ass it was a crazy plan, but that's my dad. Well, it all went fine to start with. My dad jumped into the water and got on top of this fifteen-hundred pound animal's back, and the first thing that happened was that the moose became absolutely pissed off. I'm sure he was asking himself what kind of crazy goddamned monkey would climb on back of a seven-foot moose, and he made certain that my dad understood that, given the chance, he would grind him into dust on shore. The moose grunted, snorted, and picked up the pace.

"Now, the rules were that my dad, to make the ride official, had to ride the moose, not on water, but on dry land, for seven seconds."

"Why seven seconds?" Rita asked, equally engrossed in the story.

"Who the hell knows where they came up with the seven-second rule, but they did. Wind Rider had to go by the rules."

"Did he make it?" Crystal was impatient.

"I'll get to that in a minute. So anyways, the moose huffs and puffs, grinds its teeth, and generally gets meaner and meaner as it swims along, but so long as it's in the water it can't do jack shit about shaking this crazy Indian off its back. After a few minutes of swimming in circles, bucking and trying to dunk him under, the moose decides the best thing to do is get back on track and head for the nearby cedar swamp.

"It was a good block away and as they got near, the two guys with guns loaded and cocked their rifles, figuring if things got out of hand they would have to shoot the moose before it killed my father."

"What happened once it hit the shore?" interjected Rita.

"Let me tell you, things got out of hand quick. Everyone kind of figured that the moose would try to buck my dad off his shoulders the minute it hit the shore. The plan was that if my dad could hold on for seven seconds during the bucking they would then fire a couple of shots over the head of the moose and spook him off before he had a chance to stomp my dad to death.

"But it didn't happen. Instead of bucking, the moose, once its giant hoofs found bottom, immediately broke into a flat-out sprint into the nearby cedar swamp. The moose planned to use the low-hanging tree limbs to brush this asshole off his back. Once he hit the tree line, he ducked his big antlers down and started running straight into the forest. They both disappeared from sight within a few seconds so the guns were useless.

"My dad's crew quickly ran the Lund up on shore and hopped out, rifles in hand, but all they could hear was the sound of limbs snapping and my father screaming like a banshee in the distance. Thinking the worst, one of them pointed his rifle straight up and fired off a couple of rounds.

"That was my dad's lucky break because by this time the moose had found just the perfect branch and my dad had been scraped off this brute's back like a some kind of drunken wolverine. The moose, realizing his tormentor was now lying on the ground and writhing in pain, had spun around and was just about to pound my father into oblivion with is massive hooves when the two gunshots sounded.

"Having been hunted all his life, the bull moose took one last longing look at my helpless father lying there, snorted as loud as a rhino, and bounded off into the cedar swamp, never to be seen again."

"Was your dad OK?" Crystal asked.

"Not really. The branch he hit had broken his collarbone, but he was lucky it didn't break his damn neck. He was pretty bruised, but even though no one had bothered to keep the official time, they gave him the moose riding award anyway. He never did find an elk to ride, though.

"Two months later, just after I was born, one of them suggested they call his new son Dismount Moose, in honor of my father's crazy ride. My mom thought it was kind of cute and ended up giving me my nickname, Diz."

"Great damn story!" Rita exclaimed, breaking out a second joint.

"Yeah, great story." Crystal added, now securely drunk and high as a kite.

Charlie had heard the moose riding story a dozen times before. Sometimes Diz would tell it at the Black Bear Casino, other times at the Riverside. Charlie always loved to hear it though and, on this beautiful day in the Black Hills of South Dakota, he thought it was the best rendition yet.

Dismount Moose Nelson, the son of the seven-second Injun, had done his father proud.

Chain of Fools

Chapter 12: Paul's Passing

In an ironic twist of fate, Paul Stupidnski, the husband who walked out on Maggie and his family in 1924, died on Maggie's birthday. Maggie probably orchestrated it from her command center in hell. Since Paul had already made a confirmed reservation in the eternal inferno, God let the whole thing slip through without so much as batting an eye. The devil's allowed to have some fun now and again, especially when it comes to future tenants.

Paul's death was anything but easy. The accident that eventually killed him took place on New Year's Day, 1955. Paul was seventy years old when he passed away, and he was still working the backwoods of northern Minnesota, cutting pulpwood near the town of Cotton. Cotton is, even to this day, little more than a few lumberyards and a convenience store with a set of gas pumps in front.

Paul was working a skidder, a tractor-like piece of logging equipment designed to drag logs out of the forest, when the accident happened. Somehow, he got between a huge log pile and his skidder when the chain holding the logs together snapped. The pile came tumbling down, fracturing Paul's fifth and sixth vertebrae. Paul survived the accident but probably wished he hadn't.

In 1955, broken necks and the paralysis that accompanies them were far less treatable than they are today. At seventy, with a host of other health problems from years of chain-smoking cigarettes, hard drinking, and even harder living, Paul probably wouldn't fare much better now than he did back then, but he might have survived a few more years.

My father did go down and visit his father a handful of times between January 1, the day he entered Saint Mary's Hospital, and the day he died there two months later. All Paul did during his stay at Saint Mary's was deteriorate. His final cause of death wasn't the broken neck but the ulcers and sores that eventually covered his body. Paul more or less rotted to death, though because of the paralysis he couldn't feel the sores that eventually killed him.

Before the accident Paul had stopped by to visit Beatrice and Stauch quite a number of times. The only stipulation that my mother had when Grandpa Paul came around was that he wasn't allowed near my older sister. Paul was known to have a yearning for young girls, and Beatrice wasn't taking any chances with him. Even though their relationship was anything but rosy, Stauch agreed with his wife on this issue. Paul could visit, but he would be under constant supervision while in the house and never be left alone with young Anna.

There are no police records confirming Paul's preference for young girls. The truth being that, unless it was completely outrageous, pedophiles were seldom prosecuted back then. In Poland, where Paul was raised until he was sixteen, it wasn't at all uncommon for girls to marry as young as thirteen. Maybe Paul never really understood why Americans had such an aversion to child brides.

In any event, for the most part, the authorities didn't pay much attention to underage sex back in the 1950s, especially when it was consensual. And, although Paul was known to prefer younger women, my understanding is that he never raped or molested them. Most of the time, he simply paid for their services. In the backwoods of northern Minnesota, amid the 3.2 beer joints, remote lake cabins and subsistence farms, there were always young girls looking for extra spending money.

Stauch took his father's death harder than expected. He had only been four when Paul walked out, but over the decades he had grown close to this tough old man. As my father disintegrated into drinking, poker playing, and infidelity, he found a certain comradery—a kindred spirit—in his father. On rare occasions when Paul would come into town to sell his pulp to one of the local mills, they would even go out drinking together.

By mid-decade my father's drinking was crowning. By noon—hell, sometimes by 7 A.M.—he'd be drinking. There were even mornings when he'd pour a shot of vodka directly into his coffee to jump-start his day on the job. He hid liquor everywhere.

Sometimes, down in the basement, Mom would find a gallon of screw-top wine tucked away behind the furnace. On other days she'd find a pint hidden under the sink, a fifth stashed under the bed, or a half-finished quart behind the washing machine. Whenever she or one of the kids found a bottle stowed away somewhere, Mom would always dispose of it the same way—she'd take it to the sink, open it, and ceremoniously pour the booze down the drain. If Stauch came in while she was doing this he would curse a blue streak, telling her it was money she was pouring down that drain and not just the liquor.

The truth was that it was neither. It was Stauch's life she was pouring down the drain. By the end of the decade, life at home became indescribable. Dad was constantly drunk and things began to turn violent. Divorce was inevitable, but it would take a few more ugly years before Beatrice could face the fact that her marriage was over. Catholics have a way of living with pain. They suffer through it, guilt-ridden by the mere thought of divorce. *Till death do us part* came too close to reality in our family, far too close.

Custer State Park

The picnic in Custer State Park was glorious. Crystal found a deli in the little town of Custer, and they picked up potato salad and some fried chicken for lunch. After that they found a local liquor store and bought a case of beer before driving east into the main section of the park. Since it was so early in the season, the campground they had their picnic in was all but empty.

After enjoying lunch, the four of them went for a long beer drinking, laughing, and pot-smoking hike through the surrounding pine forests. Diz, Crystal, Rita, and Charlie all took turns swapping stories about everything and anything. As the sun started tumbling down in the west, the four of them, tired and for the most part wasted, crawled back into the Monte Carlo for the drive back to Deadwood.

Diz and Rita fell fast asleep in the backseat within five minutes of pulling out. As soon as Crystal heard them sleeping, she reached over and grabbed Charlie's pants, then winked at him provocatively. Charlie couldn't believe that Crystal was thinking about doing what she was actually starting to do.

With her left hand firmly gripping the wheel and the Monte Carlo hitting eighty down a winding park road, Crystal's right hand methodically unzipped Charlie's pants. A few minutes later, quickly succumbing to the concept, Charlie's cock was out and being carefully manipulated by Crystal's adept fingers.

They were out of the park now and onto a highway heading north back to Deadwood. Charlie was breathing heavy, clearly enjoying Crystal's skillful hand job. To reciprocate, Charlie reached over and slid his left hand down between Crystal's thighs, whereupon Crystal said softly, "No, Charlie, not while I'm driving. It's too distracting."

As Crystal sped along at a hundred and five, she stroked Charlie's cock until he simply couldn't hold back any longer. A few minutes later, Charlie was using a few of the extra napkins left over from the picnic and zipping himself back up. Crystal was a wild child, but Charlie didn't mind.

Diz and Rita slept soundly through the entire event. They rustled a few times during Crystal's session, but not enough for her to break it off.

God this girl is great! thought a very relaxed Charlie as they continued on into Deadwood. This is the best damn trip I've ever had.

*****

The picnic had taken its toll. That night all four of them decided to stay inside and avoid the sirens forever beckoning them to visit the casinos along Main Street. Diz finished off the twelve-pack and Rita smoked another couple of joints while Charlie and Crystal effectively barricaded themselves into their room with a second bottle of sipping rum, a full tube of KY Jelly, and two Viagra pills Diz had persuaded Charlie to try. What happened in that motel room that evening is best left to the imagination. Suffice it to say that nothing, absolutely nothing, went unmolested.

The next morning, the last day of their stay in Deadwood, started out pretty much the same as all the others had, right around the crack of noon. The weather had turned wet, cold and rainy, but no one seemed to mind. They were leaving town tomorrow. What was one rainy day out of a perfect week?

Plans were to kick around Deadwood all day, then pack that night for an early start back to northern Minnesota. Respecting Diz's request to keep it on the Q.T., Rita hadn't brought up the duffel bag during the picnic, but shortly after waking on Friday she was back to badgering Diz about its contents.

"OK, it's Friday now. You gonna tell me what's in the bag or not?"

"Not yet," said Diz, still half asleep and nursing a soggy beer hangover.

"If you don't tell me now, I'll just get out of bed, walk over, and open it up to see for myself."

"Go ahead. It won't help."

Rita jumped out of bed and walked directly to the big black canvas bag. She unzipped it and looked inside. What she saw didn't make a bit of sense to her.

"What the hell is that big thing?"

"It's a bolt cutter."

"What on earth do you need a bolt cutter for?"

"See, I told you it wouldn't help."

"And then there's this duct tape, vice grips, and rope. What the hell are you planning to do, Diz, rob a goddamn bank or something?"

"I'll tell you everything after we finish going to the buffet this afternoon. I don't want you to start freaking out, so don't ask me any more questions."

"You're weird, Diz, just like your father."

Rita was right. Diz *was* weird. What he was thinking about doing was just as insane as riding an angry bull moose through a cedar swamp for seven terrifying seconds. Maybe even weirder.

*****

They went back to the Gallows for brunch. The staff recognized the four of them immediately as the same bunch who had decimated Monday's profit margins. Regrettably, under the rules of engagement, there was nothing to do but seat them, act cordial, and treat them like any other paying customers. Behind the swinging doors leading into the kitchen there were death threats, talk of rat poison, and even a suggestion that they use the dead roaches held in a secret get-the-customer-from-hell-out-of-here jar, stashed behind one of the coolers. In the end the staff behaved. Reluctantly.

One of the waitresses serving them overheard Crystal talking about taking a different route home on Saturday and she immediately reported the encouraging news to her manager. They were leaving. It might take the Gallows a month to recover, but the worst was over. They celebrated the waitress's report just as Charlie reloaded his black serving tray with three dozen spicy buffalo wings and the entire container of blue cheese dressing. Where on earth did these heathens come from? The hostess asked herself. The answer was Scanlon, Minnesota.

After brunch, Charlie and Crystal announced that they were going to go back to their room and spend some quality time together. This was code for another sex-fest. They still had a quarter tube of KY left, and the effects of the Viagra, much to Charlie's surprise, had yet to wear off. Charlie's announcement lent itself perfectly to Diz's plan, but no one aside from Diz knew that.

"Hey, Charlie, do you mind if Rita and I use the car while you two are in your room. We want to go up to see the view of Deadwood from Mount Moriah before we head out tomorrow."

Rita looked at Diz suspiciously, not having heard a word of visiting that nearby peak from him earlier in the trip.

"In the rain?"

"Yeah, what's the difference? It's our last day here, and they say the view is great."

"No, I don't mind. When do you think you'll be back?"

"Oh, around four or so."

Charlie had no objections to Diz's using the car. Hell, thought Charlie, he was the one who had actually won the Monte Carlo anyway. The timing was good too, since Charlie figured he had time to bang Crystal once or twice and then take in a nap before they went out for their last night of drinking and gambling.

"Sounds great. You two have a ball," said Charlie, as he tossed Diz the keys.

They all walked back through the drizzle to the Deadwood Gulch Resort and went their separate ways. Once inside their motel room, Rita was all over Diz.

"What the hell are you talking about, Diz? We never talked about going up to Mount Moriah this afternoon. I don't want drive up to some viewing area in the pouring rain. What do you think I am, a goddamn moron?"

"We're not going to Mount Moriah, Rita. We're going to Mount Rushmore."

"What?"

"Yeah, you're going to drive me down to Mount Rushmore and drop me off there."

"What's this about, Diz."

"I can't really tell you, Rita, because if you know anything more than the basics it might get you in trouble. All I'm asking is that you drive me down to Mount Rushmore and then return to Deadwood."

"Without you? You mean I'm going to leave you there? How are you going to ride back to Minnesota in the morning with us if you're forty miles away? You're not planning on walking back, are you? It's one long hike back to the Rez, Diz."

"Look, Rita, don't ask me any more questions because, like I said, I don't want to get you in trouble. You'll find out what I'm up to soon enough but, if I don't tell you anything now, you won't have to explain what you did or didn't know later."

"Who's going to care about what you did or didn't do later?"

"Oh, they'll care. Trust me on that one, they'll care big-time. Now, let's get going. I'm not going to say another word."

Diz walked over and picked up the duffel bag. He set it on the bed and opened it up, rummaging through its contents looking for something. A few seconds later he said, "Oh, good, here it is," and pulled out a small plastic bag that held a cheap throwaway rain poncho. "I had a hunch I might need this," he mumbled, while stuffing it back in with the other items.

As promised, Diz let Rita drive. She had yet to get behind the wheel of the Monte Carlo and was secretly thrilled at finally having a chance to give her a spin. It was the nicest car Rita had ever driven and it still had gone less than 2,000 miles, even after the long drive to Deadwood.

Within half an hour they were barreling down U.S. 385 toward U.S.16. Then the route took them over to A-16 and south toward Keystone. When they hit South Dakota 244 they took a right toward Mount Rushmore. As the Monte Carlo barreled down 244 Rita took a moment to ask something that had been bothering her since hearing the moose-riding story the day before.

"Hey, Diz, I know I'm about ten years younger than you, but I don't remember ever seeing your dad around the Rez when I was growing up. What happened to him?"

"Oh, he died."

"I kind of figured that. Did he have a heart attack or something?"

"No, he died riding."

"Another moose?"

"No, a Norway pine."

Rita's curiosity kicked in and even though she could tell Diz wasn't in the mood to talk, she pushed on. "How do you ride a Norway pine."

Diz knew Rita wouldn't stop badgering him until he told her the whole story, so he reluctantly dove into his father's tragic ending.

"Well, after the moose ride, and not being able to find any elk around, my dad decided he needed to try riding something else. After a long weekend binge when I was three or four, he and his friends came up with the idea of riding trees."

"How on earth do you ride a tree, Diz? Trees don't move."

"Oh, yes they do, and damn quick, too. All you have to do to make them move is chop them down. You ride them as they're falling."

"That's total bullshit, Diz. That's, like, super dangerous."

"Yeah, it was pretty damn crazy, but that was my father's way of dealing with the world. He loved coming up with crazy shit like that.

"They started out small, which was smart. I think the first tree my dad ever rode down was a big old spruce. My uncle tells me it wasn't a huge tree, maybe forty feet tall at most. My father climbed up as high as he could, then told the two guys down below to chop it down. As it started to fall, his plan was to work his way quickly around until he was on the side of the tree that landed right side up.

"Well, the spruce was easy. They're so damn bushy that when they hit the ground all the branches break the fall. My father managed to work his way around to the upper side and landed without a scratch."

"That's just nuts."

"Yeah, it was nuts. The next tree he decided to try was a white pine. It was about a month later and they were all too damn drunk to be thinking straight. The pine was a good sixty feet tall, but damn near as thick the spruce was. Playing it safe, Eddy climbed only halfway up this time, figuring there would be less of an impact than if he climbed all the way to the top.

"When he got into position he yelled down to his buddies, 'Go ahead and chop 'er down!' which they did. It didn't go nearly as well as did the spruce, and this time my dad ended up breaking his jaw in the fall. He should have stopped there, 'cause tree riding was one stupid-ass idea.

"A year later, long after his jaw had been reset and healed, the four of them got drunk again one night and Eddy decided it was time to tackle this big Norway pine just south of Big Lake. This was probably one of the biggest damn pines in Pine County at the time, and one of his buddies outright refused to be a party to chopping it down. He got pissed off and went home, but the other three drove down and found the tree, even in the dark."

Rita knew where this story was going, but felt compelled to continue listening.

"This pine was huge. I've been told it stood almost ninety feet high and was three feet across at the base. Unlike the other two trees, it didn't have nearly as many branches and those it had were high up on the crown of the tree. It was real bad tree to pick for riding.

"My dad, drunk as hell, climbed up near the very top and once again yelled out to his buddies to chop 'er down. They did, but this time Eddy didn't get around in time. The tree landed on him and broke him up real bad. He died almost instantly."

"I'm sorry, Diz. I never knew."

"Thanks, Rita. It was a stupid thing for him to do, to ride trees. I was seven when he died so you weren't even born yet. That's why you never saw him around the Rez. He died tree riding. He was thirty-eight."

Rita, as Diz was telling his story, started thinking about the bolt cutters, the duct tape, and all the rest of the items in the black bag. Diz was up to something weird. She knew, that whatever it was, it wasn't legal and it wasn't good. He was his father's child, she concluded. Knowing he'd probably get his ass arrested for whatever he was planning to do, Rita realized Diz was right. The less she knew the better. At least there weren't any guns or knives in the bag, so whatever the hell his plans were, they apparently weren't lethal.

They arrived at the memorial about the same time Charlie and Crystal fell asleep back at the motel, a little past four. When Rita signaled to go into Mount Rushmore's expansive parking lot, Diz piped up.

"No, we're not going into the parking lot. Just keep driving about half a mile or so."

"What?"

"Rita, remember: Don't ask, don't tell. Just drop me off down the road a spell, but drive real slow so I can spot the landmarks I'm looking for."

Rita flipped off her turn signal and continued heading west on 244. It soon made a sharp turn to the north, following the contour of Mount Rushmore as it did. Once up the road a bit, Diz told Rita to pull over and let him out. He took his duffel bag and grabbed the liter of vodka they had picked up at a liquor store on the edge of Deadwood, then he headed toward the nearby woods.

"Where on earth are you going, Diz?"

"You'll know soon enough. Now get on back to Deadwood and make it quick."

Rita, half blocking Highway 244, knew Diz was right. Whatever in hell he was up to, she wanted no part of it. It had something to do with the memorial, but not finding any dynamite or explosives in Diz's duffel bag made her think it had to be more of a prank than anything drastic. Besides, Diz wasn't the violent kind, thought Rita. How much damage can you do with a pair of bolt cutters?

*****

Diz had been planning this part of his Black Hills adventure since the night they won the Monte Carlo. It was something he had wanted to do ever since he was a boy. Today was his day.

The spot where he had Rita pull over was familiar to him. A few weeks back Diz had gotten on the Internet at his cousin's place on the Rez and contacted some Lakota Indians about the old trails that wound their way through what was called the Six Grandfathers, long before it became the namesake of some New York attorney who "discovered" it in 1885. Diz knew all about Charles E. Rushmore, and he despised the white man for stealing the Black Hills from the Sioux and then changing the name of this sacred Lakota mountain.

As Rita sped off toward Deadwood, Diz spotted the two large Ponderosa pines mentioned in the last e-mail he had received. Right between them, he saw the faint trail heading northeast along the base of the mountain. According to that e-mail, this trail would lead him up the back ridge of the Six Grandfathers to where the Feds had installed a high-security chain link fence protecting the monument from intruders or terrorist attacks.

Back in 1971 a group of Lakota Indians, led by the holy man John Fire Lame Deer, took this same path up to the top of the mountain to plant a staff that formed a symbolic shroud over the president's faces. Lame Deer insisted his magical staff would keep their faces dirty until the United States honored the 1868 Treaty of Laramie, which granted the Black Hills to the Native Americans forever, a treaty that was broken with the discovery of gold in the

Black Hills in 1874. Diz knew, just as John Fire Lame Deer, that the Lakota considered the Black Hills to be "axis mundi," the center of the world, for their people.

Being out of shape, Diz found that the scramble up the mountain wasn't easy. His plan was to get up to the edge of the fence by 5 P.M., and remain there until darkness. He had to be careful not to get near the fence as there were infrared cameras, along with other high-security devices, that, if activated, could ruin his plan. When he made his move, shortly after nightfall, he would have very little time between cutting through the fence and reaching the edge of the monument.

Half way up the 2,000-foot rise, Diz sat down to take a rest. Luckily it had stopped raining, but it was still overcast and threatening. He found a small outcropping, sat down and looked back down the trail to make sure he wasn't being followed. He wasn't.

He cracked the bottle of vodka and took a long hard pull. He would need liquid courage to make the final mad dash to the cliff, but he was careful not to get too drunk. The information he had received from his Lakota friends was that the top of Six Grandfathers was rugged and dangerous. He remembered Cary Grant's mad dash to the face of Mount Rushmore, but knew damn well that it was filmed on a set and not on the actual mountaintop. From the photos he had studied on Wikipedia, along with the other information he could gather, the trip across the top of the rugged granite mountain was not going to be an easy one, especially in the dark.

Diz opened up the duffel bag and rummaged through its contents, making sure the flashlight was still intact and operational. It was. Diz was glad he had had the foresight to replace the cheap store batteries with alkaline batteries before leaving the hardware store. He took out the smaller headlamp flashlight to make certain the fit was tight. Sitting there with a bottle of vodka, in his dirty blue jeans, flannel shirt and tennis shoes, his headlamp on his head, he looked like a drunken Indian coal miner. He was ready.

After a few more shots of distilled courage, Diz continued up the mountain. As he huffed and puffed he kept thinking about the sad history of the Black Hills and the Lakota people. He remembered the Battle of Wounded Knee, a massacre that happened in large part because of the broken treaty and the white man's rush for gold. He knew that the man who carved the faces of Mount Rushmore, Gutzon Borglum, was reputed to be a member of the Ku Klux Klan. Hell, thought Diz as he struggled to catch his breath, the statue Borglum was working on before carving Mount Rushmore was in Stone Mountain, Georgia, a bas-relief of the Confederate leaders carved on the face of one of the largest granite outcroppings in the world.

The whole monument was designed to represent the one principle that drove Dismount Moose Nelson mad: Manifest Destiny.

"Fuck Manifest Destiny," mumbled Diz to himself as he worked his way skyward. "Who the hell gave white men the right to think they're any better than red men, or black men—or yellow men, for that matter. We're all just men. We're all equal in the eyes of the Great Spirit."

These thoughts comforted Diz as he grew weary from the climb. Three quarters of the way up he stopped to smoke a cigarette and take a few more shots of vodka. The view from this height was spectacular. The sun was breaking through the clouds and lighting up patches of the spring green aspen and bur oak below. Diz was now almost twice as high as the Empire State Building and the road beneath him looked like a black ribbon slicing through an endless forest. In the distance, he swore he could see the statue of Crazy Horse.

No, the KKK were wrong. Borglum was just another racist asshole carving white men's faces on a sacred mountain, thought Diz, as he rested, finished a smoke, and sipped some more vodka. That's why I'm going to do this and that's why I don't give a damn what anyone thinks or what the hell happens to me afterward. This is my one chance at setting things right, for myself and for all the Native American people whose land has been stolen and whose people were kept warm with blankets infected with smallpox.

This is for the 500 nations, whose land is and always will be North America, thought Diz, as he studied the beautiful landscape surrounding him. That's why I'm doing it.

After resting awhile, watching the sunlight make patterns of shadow and light on the landscape beneath him, Diz left his headlamp on, picked up the heavy duffel bag, and continued his ascent. Within half an hour he was at the top. Looking toward the south, he easily spotted the large chain link fence with coils of razor wire stretched atop it. He found a lone stunted spruce tree and sat down beneath it, trying to keep a low profile in case they had any surveillance cameras scanning the area. This is where he would wait it out. It was six-thirty now; it wouldn't be full dark for another hour or two. It was time to take a rest, have a couple of smokes, and enjoy a few more shots of vodka before he made the mad dash to the edge. Once he cut through the fence and set off all the alarms, he would have to leave everything behind except his headlamp, the bottle of vodka, and his backup flashlight. They would be on to him in minutes, and it was almost half a mile to the edge of the monument from the fence.

*****

By this time Rita was approaching Deadwood. She couldn't help but wonder what she was going to tell Charlie and Crystal about Diz. He had specifically told her not to mention their destination that day, but he hadn't given Rita a clue as to what kind of tale she should come up with regarding his disappearance. Rita was never good at lying. As she entered the outskirts of town she had resolved to simply tell them the truth: She had dropped Diz off on the backside of Mount Rushmore, though she had no idea what in God's name he was going to do there.

And that's exactly what she said, after knocking on their motel room door, and apparently interrupting yet another lovemaking session. After a two-hour nap, the lovebirds had found themselves horny as ever and had started having at it again within minutes. Charlie's penis was developing calluses.

"Rita, is that you?" Charlie shouted from the bed.

"Yes, I've got some news about Diz. Can I come in?"

"Wait a minute."

Charlie wrapped his oversized body in a sheet, leaving Crystal wrapped in the bedspread, undid the deadbolt, and opened the door, allowing Rita to come inside. The odor was distinctive and, unless you were involved, a bit offensive.

"Where's Diz?"

"He's at the monument."

"Crazy Horse? You took him back to see Crazy Horse?"

"No, he's at Mount Rushmore. I dropped him off there with a duffel bag full of bolt cutters, ropes, flashlights—shit like that. Whatever the hell he's planning, it's not good. I don't think he'll be heading home with us tomorrow, so I thought you two should know."

"Shit. Diz is going to do something stupid. Why didn't I see it coming? He's probably going to try to pull off some anti-patriotic pissed-off Indian crap, and if they catch him he'll be in a shitload of trouble."

Crystal saw that Charlie was very worried. "What do you think he's going to do?"

"I don't know. He probably wants to desecrate the monument somehow. Did you see any explosives in his stuff? A gun, some dynamite, anything?"

"No, just some duct tape, a big pair of bolt cutters, and some other stuff. He had a bottle of vodka with him. Maybe he's planning to make a Molotov cocktail."

"No, Diz would never waste vodka on a Molotov cocktail. Besides, what harm could that do to four faces carved out of granite. The worst that might happen is that they would have to pressure-wash burn marks from the stone. No, my guess is he brought the vodka along to drink, not to throw."

"What should we do?" Crystal asked.

"Nothing for now. By the time we could get down there it would be pitch black. We can't call the police: they'll learn soon enough about whatever the hell Diz is up to. I suppose the only thing we can do is to wait to hear from him. I'll go downstairs and extend our stay until we find out what's happening."

"Yeah, that's a good idea, Charlie. We can't just up and leave Diz somewhere in the Black Hills."

"No, I wouldn't even think of it. I'll go fix our reservations, and then the three of us can get a bite to eat. We'll hear something by morning, I'm sure."

Chain of Fools

Chapter 13: It Gets Bloody

Just before the divorce in 1963, things had gotten clinical with my parents. We had moved from Michigan Street to a shack on the outskirts of Duluth, right next door to Stauch's sister, Lizzy. My mother thought that if we could somehow get Stauch to stop frequenting the West End bars he might slow down his drinking. She was, like thousands of women before her and thousands yet to come, wrong to think this.

Stauch did stop going to the White Front, the Western, and the other bars that catered to budding alcoholics in that part of town, but he quickly replaced those joints with carbon copies down the street in Hermantown, West Duluth, and Lizzy's place, not two hundred feet from our front door.

Lizzy was married to Fred Schultz back then, and both of them were confirmed drunks. Lizzy and Fred had one son who ended up dying in prison, not unlike her younger brother, Scarface Joe. Lizzy was overweight and had bad teeth, with equally bad breath. Naturally, Lizzy and Fred drank like fish. Fred was a taxi driver who drank only after his shift was over. All I can remember about him was his face, always flushed because he suffered from permanent high blood pressure, around 320 over 140. Fred ultimately died from a massive stroke.

Stauch seldom went to bars once we moved to Haines Road. With Lizzy and Fred's joint so close, driving to a bar was unnecessary. He could walk next door, get drunk, and then stumble back home and vent on his family. No DUIs to concern yourself with and the added luxury of living a dozen miles or more from the nearest police station.

It was on just such a night, amid the storm of violence that had overtaken our family, that I was nearly killed. It wasn't my father who wielded the cast iron skillet that hit me, but my older sister, Anna.

Stauch had come home drunk from his sister's place. It was in the dead of winter, when darkness comes just past four in the afternoon. Christmas was over, but no one had bothered to take down the tree or put away the decorations around the house. There weren't many gifts exchanging hands that Christmas—there hadn't been for years—but my mother always wanted things to look the part, even if the giving had all but ceased.

Stauch was always pissed off about something. Anna had moved back in from Grandma's for a short while, but she was soon to leave home for good, driving off to California with her cousin in search of some level of sanity. On this particular night, sanity was absent.

Within minutes of returning home, Stauch and Beatrice started in. Beatrice told him that if he didn't stop swearing and screaming she was going to call the cops and get his drunken ass thrown in jail. Following standard procedure, Stauch immediately ripped the goddamn phone off the wall and threw it outside.

Anna, who was upstairs in her room, had finally had enough. She was going to kill that lousy son of a bitch and she was going to do it tonight. Gary, my older half-brother, was by now able to hold his own against Stauch, and more than willing to help. Anna came downstairs and while Stauch and Beatrice got into a shouting match, she grabbed a cast-iron frying pan from the top of the old gas stove, and started swinging.

I was in the living room when the melee broke out, playing with one of the few toys I had received for Christmas, a small duck pull toy whose feet went round and round as you dragged him behind you. One of my uncles had made it for me and I loved it.

Most of the time, things never became physical with Stauch.

But *most of the time* didn't apply that terrible night. Gary was punching Stauch, Beatrice was standing in the kitchen telling everyone to stop, and Anna was trying to hit him in the head with the skillet. She was going to kill him if she could just land one solid blow to his skull.

Little did they realize that I too had joined the battle. I had snuck into the kitchen and crawled under the kitchen table. Using my pull toy as a trip wire I was attempting to wrap the string around my father's legs while he struggled with Gary and Anna. I never saw the cast iron skillet that hit me.

All I remember was that when I finally came to, the kitchen floor was covered with my blood. The others didn't even notice that I had been hit on the head with the frying pan until they started sliding around on the linoleum floor. Beatrice, seeing that what they were slipping on was actually blood, let go a scream that stopped the madness in a heartbeat. All three combatants looked down at me, and the sight of this child collapsed on the floor with blood pouring out from the top of his head made them cease and desist.

Anna, in one of her many swings with the heavy metal skillet, had missed my father but connected with me. Initially they thought I might have been killed.

I was unconscious for a long time while my mother held me, pushing down on my wound with a dishrag to stop the bleeding. When I finally came around, I was disoriented and groggy. As is often the case with domestic abuse, there are just too many questions to answer when it comes to life threatening injuries. They talked about taking me in for stitches but never did. Instead, they clipped away most of the hair around the wound and used half a box of Band-aids to pinch the skin together and stop the bleeding. Stauch left the house and drove five miles back down to the West End to start drinking again, clearly shaken up by the near death of yet another of his kids.

Anna left for California a few weeks later, returning to Duluth decades later, and Gary told Beatrice that he would kill that bastard if he ever set foot in the house again. To this day it's impossible to know how severe the injury was. Though I was very, very tired afterward, my mother wouldn't let me fall asleep for hours, fearing I had a concussion and might never reawaken. I lost a lot of blood that night, but I was young. Within a week I was back in school with a bandage, a cover story about a bike accident, and a home without a father.

The divorce papers were filed in 1963. They should have been filed a decade sooner, but no one wanted to deal with it. Stanley was now Maggie, albeit in a different time and a different set of circumstances. The chain of fools was linking itself to the past, just as it would to the future.

They say that 60 percent of all the families in America today are dysfunctional. If that's true, the other 40 percent are in denial.

Atop Six Grandfathers

Diz looked around him and decided it was dark enough. It wasn't pitch black yet, but he felt that waiting until total darkness might not be a good idea. From all the photos he had seen, including the aerial shots from Google Earth, it was going to be quite the exercise in mountaineering to get from the fence to the top of President Washington's head in just a few minutes, and complete darkness would not be any help at all. At least the rain had stopped and the sky had broken up from a monolithic grey to patches of clouds and starlight. He didn't need the poncho and was glad for it. The rain would have made the granite top of the mountain even more slippery.

Deciding it was now or never, Diz grabbed the bolt cutter, the rope, and the duct tape out of his bag. He walked toward the fence, knelt down and lightly prodded it with the tip of the bolt cutters, praying it wasn't electrified. It wasn't.

With the large bolt cutters he cut a sort of doorway large enough for him to squeeze through, and without a second's hesitation he crawled through this opening to the other side. Using a small piece of his rope, he tied the flap to the uncut section of the fence. He had thought he might need the duct tape to cover the sharp edges but the bolt cutters had handled the chain links so easily it wasn't needed. Diz knew this was the only fence between him and the presidents, but he had figured all along that the government would have the area under constant surveillance, either with infrared body heat detectors, night-vision cameras, motion detectors, or a combination of such devices.

Diz was right. Within seconds of his entering the security zone, the twenty-four hour monitoring system kicked into gear. Two night guards, unused to seeing anything other than bobcats and deer with the high-tech infrared cameras, were shocked to see an image that clearly resembled a two-legged hominoid, not a four-legged animal.

"Hey, Chet," said one of the guards, watching the monitors in the basement of the Memorial Museum. "Take a look at this."

"What the hell. That's a person, don't you think?"

"It ain't no damn deer, that's fer sure."

"We'd better call security and get someone up there. It might be a goddamn terrorist."

In a drill they had gone over a hundred times in practice but never done in earnest, Chet picked up the phone and dialed the police in Rapid City, some fifty miles away. The monument had only minimal staff to secure Mount Rushmore and the plan had always been to notify the SWAT team in Rapid City in the event of a terrorist attack such as the one they apparently were witnessing.

"Hello? This is Chet Sadler with the Mount Rushmore security staff. We've got a situation."

"This is Sergeant Wilson. What's up, Chet?"

"We've got an intruder on the mountain."

"You're kidding me, right?"

"No, we picked him up on the infrared camera. He's inside the fence, heading toward the carvings."

"Oh, my God, he's probably planning to blow up the statues. Can you pick him up on the night-vision cameras yet?"

Chet flipped a couple of switches, and the monitors above them changed from red and yellow images to a strange glowing whitish-green light. On one of them you could plainly see a solitary man wearing a headlamp and carrying two objects.

"Yeah, we got him. He's just walking along, heading directly toward the edge. He's carrying something, but I can't make out what it is."

"Shit. We've got to scramble the Black Hawk. Stay calm and keep your eye on him. We'll be there in ten, maybe fifteen, minutes max, and we both know that working his way across that broken granite is going to take him all of that. Go to Channel 19 and we'll stay in constant communication."

"Will do, Sergeant. Switching to Channel 19 and standing by."

On the mountaintop, Diz had walked right by a camera of some kind, mounted on a tall metal post, and noted that the camera had followed him as he hurried past. Obviously, by this time, some three hundred feet into the security zone, they knew he was up there.

Diz realized he was going to get caught. He had no emergency escape plan, no helicopter tucked away in Keystone waiting for his secret password. This wasn't exactly high-end espionage. Nor was it a secret plot to blow up one of the most visited destinations in the United States. All Diz wanted to do was to piss on George Washington's nose, nothing more, nothing less.

When Diz realized they were on to him, he broke into a trot. However, from decades of doing little more than drinking and smoking cigarettes, Diz was already exhausted from the climb up. Running was out of the question, given his physical condition; the best he could muster was a kind of limping trot. He had pulled a muscle on his right side scrambling up some broken rocks near the end of the trail, so as he ran it seemed as if he had already taken a bullet on one side. There was no mistaking Dismount Moose Nelson for James Bond.

The first part was easy, mostly scrub brush, some stunted Ponderosa pine, scattered spruce, and patches of bare, flat granite. The tough part was coming up. Diz was genuinely concerned that he wouldn't have enough time to make it to George Washington's bust before they got to him. As he started climbing onto the deeply creviced section of the mountain, still some distance from the edge, he was startled to hear a loudspeaker.

"Whoever you are up there, please halt immediately! You are trespassing on government property. You must put down your weapons and stop now!"

"GO TO HELL!" the laboring Indian shouted as he picked his way southeast toward the four stone faces.

Of course, Chet, who was on the loudspeaker, couldn't hear Diz's reply. No one had thought to install a microphone on the series of loudspeakers the federal government had installed shortly after 9/11 but, even if they had, they wouldn't have been exactly thrilled with this Indian's response.

"Put down your weapons and surrender now!" continued Chet on the loudspeaker, noting from the monitors that his commands appeared to elicit absolutely no response from this intruder.

"*I don't have any fucking weapons!*" Diz yelled in response.

Then, with a glimmer in his eye and a smile on his face, Diz retracted that statement. "Yeah, I do have a weapon and I'm getting it out right now."

To the astonishment of the Chet Sadler and Bruce Olsen, the second security guard on duty that night, they watched in disbelief as this intruder, glowing in the eerie pale-green light, unzipped his barn door and took out his penis. Thinking at first he was simply going to take a piss and continue onward, both men were utterly confounded by the fact that this man, whoever he was, had bared his penis without pissing a drop, and continued onward toward the statues.

"What the hell is this lunatic up to?" Chet quizzed his co-worker.

"Damned if I know. I hope the SWAT team gets here before he makes it to the edge."

"What is that thing he's carrying? It looks like a bottle of liquor."

At the same moment that Bruce had correctly identified Diz's vodka bottle, Diz, as if on cue, stopped and took a long steady pull.

"Yeah, it's got to be a liquor bottle. Look, all he seems to have in his other hand is a flashlight."

"OK, let's think about this. Unless he's wearing some kind of explosive vest, this guy isn't heading to the monument to destroy it. What the hell is he up to?"

"Damned if I know. Listen."

Bruce kept quiet for a few seconds. In the distance they could clearly hear the sound of a large helicopter.

"Wow, that's what I call a quick response team if ever there was one."

"Holy shit, it hasn't been fifteen minutes since we called them."

"These guys are good."

"They're the best damn SWAT team in America, Chet."

The triple shot of vodka had put a newfound fire into Diz. He was making steady headway toward the edge when he too heard the distant sound of the approaching helicopter. He had expected it, realizing weeks ago that the only quick method of getting up to the top of Six Grandfathers was by chopper. He would have to pick up the pace, even as the terrain continued to deteriorate.

With the vodka kicking in and the chase on, Diz mustered all the physical energy left in him to make it to the top of George Washington's head. As the helicopter approached a large spotlight shone down from the sky and started heading toward him. He flipped off his headlamp and ducked into a nearby crevice.

The chopper swooped in close as the spotlight worked over the area. Diz was still a five-hundred feet away from George Washington's hairline. For a brief instant, the spotlight went right over him and Diz was glad he had decided to wear his black jacket. They had not seen him.

As the chopper dipped to make another pass over the mountaintop, Diz got out of the crevice and continued running. It was too dangerous for him to continue toward the edge without the aid of his headlamp. Besides, the chopper was behind him for the moment. As long as he didn't look back, they might not catch the dim light of his solitary headlamp in the distance.

As he ran he heard the sound of police behind him. Not wanting to give his position away he struggled not to look back.

Behind him a few hundred yards the helicopter was hovering still. The surface of the broken granite was simply too dangerous for the chopper to put down on, so the only solution was to have the seven member SWAT team rappel to the ground via two long ropes presently dangling from either side of the Black Hawk. It looked like a scene out of a Bruce Willis movie. The team members were carrying assault rifles, stun guns, Mace, night-vision goggles, headsets, bulletproof Kevlar vests, and helmets with spotlights mounted in them, virtually every known high-tech military gear known to western man.

Diz, on the other hand, had abandoned his backup flashlight, flipping it on and setting it upright as a diversion, and was continuing on with his pecker out and only his bottle of Petri vodka in his right hand. The discrepancy between the two adversaries was astounding. Clearly, the SWAT team had the upper hand.

Once they got the seven members of the team safely on the ground, the two pilots took off toward the precipice and the running suspect. One of the pilots noted the solitary flashlight shining upward, but seeing it wasn't in motion and the other, dimmer light was, the pilot decided it was a decoy and didn't bother with it.

Diz was presently scaling down the last steep granite ledge that lay directly above Washington's skull. Having to use both hands to work his way down, he had taken one final drink of the vodka and abandoned the bottle at the very top of the mountain. He was careful not to break it in hopes that should he somehow miraculously escape the SWAT team, he could pick it up and take it with him on the way back down. It was a long shot, but then again, he hated to waste vodka.

Within a minute Diz had climbed down the solid rock bluff and was standing on a small pile of broken scree that lay behind Washington's head. The pile had formed during the blasting period in the thirties at the same time the immense pile of broken rock had formed in front of the monument. These rock shards were smaller, almost gravel size, and formed a nearly flat surface for the next fifty yards to the crown of Washington's skull.

Just as Diz was making his final dash, the chopper's spotlight found him. The pilot had a two-way radio permanently connected to the commander of the SWAT team and was on that radio the instant he found the intruder.

"Captain Morrison, this is Black Hawk, do you read me? Over."

"You're coming in loud and clear, Black Hawk. What is the status of the terrorist? Do you have a visual?"

"That's affirmative. He's heading toward George Washington right now, approximately one-hundred feet away, a white male, approximately six foot or so."

"Is he armed?"

"No, sir, he does not appear to be carrying any kind of a weapon, but he may have explosives hidden under his jacket. Wait a minute."

The chopper pilot took a long studied second look. It just didn't seem right.

"Come back, Black Hawk, come back."

"Captain Morrison, do you still read me?"

"Yes, sir, what's up? We've just about caught up to him. Do you want us to take a shot?"

"No. Don't shoot. I don't know how to put this, but he appears to be running with his dick out."

"What are you telling me, that his dick is exposed?"

"That's a ten-four. His penis is hanging out of his blue jeans, and it's taking somewhat of a beating from the looks of it."

"Why on earth is his dick out?"

"Who knows? I think this guy is some kind of nut job."

"We'll hold our fire for the moment, but we'll be on him in less than five."

"I'll keep the spotlight on him and stand by."

"Ten-four."

The pilot held his position. Far below the crest of Mount Rushmore, a small crowd had gathered to watch the incident. The two security guards were now outside, glad they weren't up there, scurrying along that rugged mountaintop. Some janitorial staff, having heard the helicopter and wanting to see what was happening, had also wandered out into the night to try to catch a glimpse of the action.

Along with those people, half a dozen automobiles had pulled over along Highway 244, several of them with binoculars, all trying to figure out what on earth was happening on top of Mount Rushmore. What they all saw will never ever leave them.

With the choppers brilliant spotlight illuminating the path between the granite rubble and the top of George Washington's huge head, the rest of the journey was a piece of cake for Diz. Feeling the effects of his final shots of vodka, and having needed to take a piss for the last two hours, the rest was equally easy.

Diz made it to the top and looked behind him. He could see the seven SWAT team members not a hundred feet away, running with their hand guns drawn directly toward him. He then did what he had wanted to do since he was a little boy.

Diz took his right hand, grabbed hold of his penis, and took the biggest, baddest piss of his life. From a distance, using an expensive pair of binoculars, one of the tourists who had pulled over to see what all the commotion was about thought this lunatic was pouring something on George Washington's head, like an acid or some kind of liquid explosive.

As he focused his binoculars on Diz, the reality of what this man was doing suddenly dawned on him. He was taking a piss; his bright yellow stream, illuminated by the chopper's spotlight, was impossible to miss, even from a quarter mile away. In the calm, damp night air, the urine was landing directly on Washington's granite nose.

Diz was in seventh heaven. Ever since high school, when Diz had learned about the racist principle of Manifest Destiny, he had wanted to do something to repudiate it. He tried the debate team but was kicked off the team within a week because of his swearing. He wrote several letters to the *Cloquet Lumberjack* newspaper but the editors never published them. They were more like rants.

In the end he had decided to discredit the concept of Manifest Destiny, a concept still very much alive today, in two distinct ways. One was to go into a tirade on the subject whenever he got drunk. The second was, given the opportunity, he would piss on the nose of George Washington, the father of their country.

Charlie, his two cousins, and almost every other drunk in Carleton County had been privy to Diz's inebriated Manifest Destiny speech. But George, our founding father so to speak, aside from some workers who pissed in his ear several times over the years it took to carve his likeness, had never been so insulted. While pissing on a statue's nose won't do a thing to rewrite the history of the sad, ethnic cleansing of Native Americans over the past five-hundred years, it did wonders for Diz's sense of self-esteem. The chopper's spotlight added just the right theatrical touch, he thought as he whizzed away. He was hoping and praying they were getting all of this on camera. They were.

In the last few seconds of his lengthy urination, the SWAT team caught up to him. Seeing what he was up to, and with a sense of blind patriotism that seems to dovetail well with the premise of Manifest Destiny itself, one of the SWAT team members disobeyed orders and just as the captain yelled, "Hold your fire until he's through!" this young man, originally from Oklahoma, ran the last fifty feet up to the top of the president's head and tackled Diz from behind.

It was a miracle that they didn't roll off the bluff, bouncing once off George's pee-stained nose, then plummeting to their death hundreds of feet below. Diz, knowing that resisting his imminent arrest would only complicate things further, did little to oppose this policeman's attempt to save the dignity of the United States of America. His job was done. What happened from this point forward was of little concern to him.

Once he was tackled to the ground and safely subdued, it was apparent to everyone that it was a Native American they had apprehended and in all likelihood not a terrorist. They could smell the fact that liquor was involved. Diz's lengthy interrogation began immediately.

"Why did you just piss on George Washington?" The Captain of the SWAT team asked as the Oklahoma boy brought him back to his commander.

"Because the bastard deserved it."

"What did George Washington ever do to you?"

"He kept slaves and helped steal this land from us. So did Jefferson, in case you're interested in American history."

"You're in a hell of a lot of trouble. You know that, don't you?"

"It comes with the territory. I've got no regrets for what I did."

The captain asked Diz to please put his penis back into his pants, and Diz, smiling all the while, did as requested. Then the captain, while reciting the Miranda rights to Diz, went about the business of frisking this solitary Indian atop Mount Rushmore, finding nothing by way of plastic explosives, knives, guns, or any weapon other than the penis itself. Even though the captain realized this probably represented more of a personal prank than any kind of imminent danger to the famous memorial, he followed protocol and handcuffed Diz's hands behind his back and, in keeping with the new requirements of arrests under the Patriot Act, placed a black cloth sack over Diz's head. Within minutes, Diz looked more like a prisoner at Gitmo than a drunken Indian atop the Six Grandfathers— the irony being that, according to the Treaty of Laramie, the SWAT team members were the ones who should have been arrested for trespassing, on *Indian* lands. So much for honoring treaties. So much for the lure of gold.

The captain radioed in the Black hawk, which had been hovering at a distance, and within a few minutes the helicopter was two-hundred feet above them. They lowered a rescue basket and Diz was placed into it, lying face down and heavily secured by nylon straps. A minute later he was winched into the belly of the chopper.

The members of the SWAT team, one by one, were likewise hoisted up, and ten minutes later all but two of the team were heading toward the landing pad in Rapid City. The two left behind had been ordered to retrace Diz's path from the base of the mountain to where he was tackled, in hopes of finding dynamite or some kind of explosives. What they found was a half-empty bottle of vodka, a broken flashlight, and a pair of bolt cutters lying beside a freshly made cut in the chain link fence.

The helicopter pilot went much slower than he had an hour earlier, during the scramble to Mount Rushmore, and little was said on the long ride back. Although Diz was terribly uncomfortable, no one bothered to remove the prisoner from the lifting basket, thinking they would transport him via ambulance to the police interrogation room in the same device. Diz bitched at them several times to at least free up his arms so he could breathe, but the SWAT team members, who were unanimously appalled at what this Indian had just done, had no sympathy for him.

When they finally took Diz off the stretcher at police headquarters he was clearly in pain. That's when things went from bad to worse, as incidents like this often do.

Two detectives, Lieutenant Bruce Rodgers and Sergeant William Malcomb, both of whom had recently undergone two weeks of training at the CIA's antiterrorist complex just outside of Langley, took the suspect into their custody shortly after Diz was booked. From the onset, neither man bought Diz's story. They wanted to know who else was involved in this plot to deface, possibly destroy, Mount Rushmore. They were convinced there was more to this story, and to get at the truth they were going to utilize all the various interrogation techniques they had recently learned at Langley.

It was approaching midnight when the two of them took Diz into the basement of the Rapid City police headquarters and led him into the interrogation room. The room was equipped with massive loudspeakers, brilliant halogen light banks, and padded walls. There was a single folding card table and three plastic chairs in the room. High in one corner a single camera videotaped everything for the record, although if things went badly everyone knew the tapes would be destroyed.

Naturally, what these two officers had been trained in was torture, but at Langley they had masked their techniques in more user-friendly jargon. Terms such as *sleep deprivation,* and *forced standing* among other non-torturous-sounding words were used. The detectives soon found it was a lot easier to attend the antiterrorist training camps and study various interrogation techniques than it was to find any terrorists in windswept South Dakota. At best, there were a few hundred Muslims living in the entire state and thus far, none of them showed any inclination toward following the practices of Osama bin Laden or al-Qaeda. While there had been several uprisings at Pine Ridge Indian Reservation in years past, nothing of late had been stirring in that arena either. These two detectives, still pumped up about their recent training, were going to use some of what they had just learned, come hell or high water. Diz's timing could not have been worse.

The video tape started rolling at 12:15 A.M. Saturday morning. What transpired afterward will never be known, because when Diz went into organ failure twenty-seven hours later, the tapes went conveniently missing. To began with, the two detectives took turns asking Diz questions that had no connection to his motives. Things like "Who's behind this?" "Where did you get your funding?" "Are there any more subversive acts such as this planned?" "Are you a member of al-Qaeda?" "Have you ever been abroad? To Iran? Afghanistan? Iraq?"

Diz, terribly out of shape and weary from his ascent of The Six Grandfathers, was in no mood to cooperate with these two assholes. He told them it was just a harmless prank, but as they kept badgering him he started going into one of his tirades about how the United States

Government had screwed over the Indians and the whole lot of them could go to hell. They immediately sensed an opportunity and took a different tack. "Are you a member of AIM?" "Do you want to violently overthrow the United States of America?" "Who put you up to this?"

It was all about fear, and Diz was sick and tired of fear. The government of the United States had been selling fear since the day of its inception, thought Diz, and his interrogation was just another version of it. Fear of ruthless heathen savages who would scalp you in a heartbeat. Fear of black men, freed slaves, Mexicans, Cubans, yellow Japs who attacked us at Pearl Harbor. Fear of Nazis, Koreans, Communists, Vietnamese and the fear du jour: Middle Eastern terrorists. Everyone was out to destroy the United States of America, and Diz, somehow or other, was in on it.

Once the men were sequestered in that tiny interrogation room, the questions went on for hours. There was a second room across the hall with two small beds in it, and the detectives would take turns napping or, sometimes, simply leave Diz standing, his hands tied high above his back, until, exhausted, he leaned forward and started to choke. At the CIA training facility, this form of torture, called Palestinian Hanging, was a particular favorite; Bruce and Bill were thrilled to give it a try.

Neither detective considered the fact that they were dealing with a run-down, burned-out, middle-aged alcoholic with a history of liver trouble. They didn't care. They were more interested to learn if Hamas or AIM was involved. Diz kept trying to convince them that he didn't even know a single Arab and that all he wanted to do was to piss on Washington's nose because of Manifest Destiny.

The two officers would have no part of it. It was too simple and too obvious. There had to be more to the story.

"Who transported you to the memorial?" "Where are your co-conspirators hiding?" "Were you carrying any explosives?" "Where did you hide them?"

After twenty-seven straight hours of questioning, the stress overwhelmed him. At 3:27 Sunday morning, Diz collapsed. Bruce and Bill were clearly disappointed. They felt he was just about to break and tell them everything he knew about the dangerous sleeper cell operating out of Deadwood, South Dakota.

Two days later, after slipping into an irreversible coma, Diz was dead.

"What do you mean you can't tell me anything!" Charlie screamed over the phone.

"This is a matter of national security and we are under strict orders not to disclose anything about the incident. Not to you. Not to anyone."

"Just tell me where you're keeping him."

"No."

"When can we see him?"

"After the interrogation is complete. And I must advise all of you not to leave town, since I'm sure the detectives will want to speak with all three of you very shortly."

"Who are these detectives? Can we get in touch with them?"

"They'll be contacting you. You're lucky you're not already under arrest. No more questions. We'll be in touch with you. Be advised that you are currently under surveillance."

Charlie hung up, disgusted. The security staff at Mount Rushmore was stonewalling. There was no news coverage of the event, and they refused to give Charlie, Rita, or Crystal any details. They did confirm that they had a suspect in custody and he was being interrogated. They didn't confirm that it was Dismount Moose Nelson, but Charlie knew it had to be Diz. They refused to say where they were keeping him, what he was charged with, or when he might be released.

The Patriot Act and the post 9/11 paranoia had helped to turn a silly act of civil disobedience into a convoluted plot of international terrorism. Under these new rules of engagement, the powers that be were under no obligation to disclose anything to anybody until they were authorized by their superiors to do so. Everything was secretive and scary.

It was one thing for Islamic terrorists to call America the Great Satan, but it was quite another when Americans started behaving like devils, Charlie thought to himself, as he hung up the telephone in disgust. Maybe the Islamists were on to something, he wondered.

"It's no use, Rita, they won't tell us a thing. I don't know what on God's earth Diz did last night, but I do know they've arrested him and they're keeping him somewhere. The idiots suspect he's a terrorist."

"Shit, Diz, ain't no terrorist. He's harmless as a fly. There wasn't anything in that duffel bag that could seriously hurt any one of those four faces and they know it." Rita was irritated.

They knew something had gone awry on Saturday morning, when Diz failed to return home. Charlie had called the security staff at Mount Rushmore to see if they had any news of what was happening. They refused to confirm who they had arrested. They did go so far as to tell him there had been an *incident* at the memorial late Friday night, but they were not at liberty to discuss any of the details.

The three of them spent the rest of the afternoon calling all the local small-town police stations to see if they could find out anything more about the whereabouts of their friend. When they called the Rapid City police headquarters around four that same day, they were told that, yes, they did have someone in custody, but they were not going to disclose any information regarding the prisoner or the nature of his crime because of national security issues.

On Monday Charlie started calling lawyers to see if one of them might be able to help. By the time one of them got back to Charlie it was too late. On Tuesday afternoon, Charlie received a phone call from the Hospital in Rapid City that put him into a state of shock.

"Hello, is this Charlie Stupidnski?" The woman slaughtered his last name.

"Yes. Who's calling."

"My name's Clair Delany, and I'm with the public relations staff here at Rapid City Regional Hospital. I'm calling you because the authorities have informed me that you knew an individual by the name of Dismount Moose Nelson, is that correct?"

"Yes, we all know Diz."

"I'm afraid I have some bad news for you, Mr. Stupidnski."

Charlie could tell immediately from the tone of her voice that the news wasn't just bad, it was devastating.

"What's happened to him?"

"I'm sorry to have to tell you that he's passed away."

"What?"

"He died this afternoon at one-forty-four P.M. Death occurred due to complications resulting from liver and other organ failure."

Charlie froze. He pressed the phone into his ear to the point where it became painful and remained silent. He looked to Rita and Crystal, who were sitting on the bed beside him, and his look told them everything.

"Oh, my God, no!" exclaimed Rita, as she broke into tears. Crystal buried her face in a nearby pillow and wept.

Charlie started to cry too.

"Sir, are you still there? Sir?"

"Yes, I'm here. Can we come and see him?"

"I don't see why not. We found your name in his wallet, and the police told us they had already been in contact with you. Do you know where we might be able to reach his next of kin?"

"He has a couple of cousins back at the reservation in Fond du Lac, but his mother and father have both passed away. It won't take much to let everyone know."

"Do you have their names?"

Charlie, still weeping quietly, went about the business of informing this woman where she might be able to reach Diz's two cousins. He was having a hard time concentrating. He had so many questions. What had Diz done at the memorial? What happened at the police station? Why was Diz dead? For God's sake, why was Diz dead?

*****

The long ride back to Minnesota in the Monte Carlo could not have been more different than the crazy trip to Deadwood they had taken two weeks ago. Crystal didn't place her radar detector on the dash; she didn't feel like speeding. Rita sat in the back alone while what remained of Diz, an eight-pound box of bone and ash, sat amid their luggage in the trunk. Rita sobbed most of the way home.

The past four days in Deadwood had been painful. After seeing Diz for the last time in the refrigerated viewing room in the basement of the hospital where he died, everything went into this surreal state of suspended animation. Nothing, absolutely nothing, was real.

Charlie, Rita, and Crystal were all interviewed by two Rapid City detectives, one of whom had helped interrogate Diz after the incident. After hours of questioning all three were exonerated from having anything to do with what had happened. Halfway through Rita's interrogation the detectives finally divulged Diz's crime to her: Diz had urinated on George Washington's nose, an act of extreme distaste and possible sedition. After two hours of questioning, they reluctantly concluded that Rita, who drove Diz to the monument, had no idea what he was up to and was not a co-conspirator. You cannot arrest someone for giving a friend a lift to the base of a mountain, though both of them were aching to take Rita back to the same interrogation room where they had effectively tortured Diz to death.

- 213 -

After the cousins were informed of Diz's untimely demise, there was another day of long-distance deliberations as to what to do with his remains. There was some talk of burying him at the Pine Ridge Indian Reservation not far from Deadwood. A few phone calls were made and in the end it became too complicated. Diz was Ojibway, Pine Ridge was Sioux. There had never been any love between these two tribes, and even though the tribal council appreciated what Diz had done atop The Six Grandfathers it was clear to Charlie and Rita that they would prefer that Diz be buried elsewhere.

It soon became apparent that getting Diz's body back to Minnesota intact was not going to be cheap. In fact it would more or less wipe out all of Charlie's loan against the car and, after several long conversations with Diz's cousins, everyone agreed it was economically unfeasible to transport Diz's remains back via ambulance or hearse to Fond du Lac.

In the end, cremation became the only viable option. On the following Friday, one week from the day Rita drove Diz to Mount Rushmore, a local mortuary incinerated Dismount Moose into a pile of bone chips and ashes. Charlie picked up the plastic lined cardboard box containing his remains at 5 P.M. that afternoon and took care of the bill out of his cash reserves. He cried when the mortician handed him his best friend in a cardboard box. He was still crying in the passenger seat as they sped along Interstate 90 toward the Minnesota border.

The two detectives, during the interviews, had more or less outlined what had happened to Diz, bits and pieces at a time. They told them about the pissing incident, about Diz's rants on Manifest Destiny, and the fact that he collapsed late Saturday night. They didn't admit that they had kept Diz awake for twenty-seven hours or that they had employed numerous torture techniques on him during his nonstop interrogation. They failed to mention that they had killed him.

Charlie had contacted several lawyers, including a local representative of the ACLU, but the consensus among them was there was little or nothing they could do. Had Diz survived there was a chance he could have filed a complaint against the Rapid City Police Department, but he hadn't survived. Lacking his testimony and given the culture of secrecy and denial that was the brave new world of America, the lawyers felt that the best thing to do was let it go. Besides, fighting it would mean staying on in Deadwood, possibly for years, and no one had the heart for that.

No, it was better to take Diz's ashes back to the reservation, hand them over to his two cousins—who planned to take them to the Saint

Louis River and set them free—than it was to spend years trying to find out what had happened after Diz was tackled atop George Washington's head. The only solace the three of them could draw from the incident was that Diz had indeed pissed on the first president's nose—that was something, under the circumstances, that everyone could be proud of.

Saturday evening, after dropping Rita off with Diz's remains in her arms and kissing Crystal good night around ten-thirty, Charlie pulled into the Golden Gate Motel and went to his room. He set his luggage in the corner and flopped back on his bed like a warrior who just had witnessed his heart ripped out and shown to him. Deadwood had not turned Diz's luck around at all.

Life sucked.

The next morning, in a nihilistic mood, Charlie finished his book. This was what he wrote:

Chain of Fools

Chapter 14: The End

Diz is dead. He always wanted to be in my stupid ass book and now he's in it, even though he won't ever know. You don't know Diz because we're not related. No, that's the wrong thing to say. Diz and I *were* related. We were blood brothers. For the past year we've been the best of friends, sharing the ups and downs of temperamental slot machines, happy hours, and drunken celebrations that sometimes ran till dawn.

They killed him. All he did was piss on the nose of a statue carved on a sacred Indian mountain in the Black Hills, and they killed him for it. They did everything but waterboard the poor bastard, and Diz fell apart. Hell, he was so near the edge the night they took him into custody that someone should have seen it coming. Someone in that police department should have been able to tell the difference between a drunken Indian and a terrorist. But they didn't.

They kept him awake too long, kept him standing, grilled him about co-conspirators who never existed, and eventually he crumbled. Given what they put him through, I probably would have crumbled as well. Most of us would.

He always wanted to be in my book, so now he's in it. We're all in it. We're all a bunch of fucked-up victims of science. The detectives from Rapid City, Diz's cousins, Diz's dad, Rita and her drunken, abusive father, One-Eyed Maggie, my own screwed up father—hell, there isn't a person out there who doesn't have some kind of moldy skeleton hidden away. It's the chain, the unbroken connection from one messed up generation to the next, that binds us all together. The gill net of fate and family.

So this is my last chapter. There isn't anyone who's ever going to read my book, because as soon as I'm finished typing this I'm going to throw my goddamned laptop into the river, a few days behind Diz's ashes. When it hits that cold rushing water, every word I've written will be erased. Erased—just as we are all erased from the blackboard of time.

Yeah, that's what we are. We're just chalk, a momentary statement written on a blackboard the size of infinity. Diz is dead—just as I am dead—just as you who will never read this are dead. Nothing is everything. Everything is nothing.

I know how I'm going. I like to put it bluntly; I'm in my pre-cancerous stage. With the smoking—the cigarettes and pot; hell, opium if I could get my hands on it—lung cancer is as certain to find me as it did my father.

As for the rest of my story, here it is in a few paragraphs: I graduated from high school and made it on to college; the University of Minnesota at Duluth is my alma mater. I majored in accounting. I got married. We had three kids. I started drinking after the second child was born. By the time the third kid was five I was a drunk.

My wife and I started having trouble after I had an affair with one of the secretaries at work. She divorced me. Our kids are turning out like shit from what little I hear about them. Like I gave a rat's ass. I walked out of work nearly a decade ago, and I'm glad I did. I kept drinking—with newfound determination, I might add.

The secretary ditched me shortly after I quit my job. She was years younger, and as soon as I left my wife and kids she started talking about marriage and having kids, and I thought, Shit, I just walked out on all that bullshit; why on earth would I walk right back into it? So I told her I didn't want any more kids and that was it. Hell, I was running out of money and she didn't like the look of it. She left me a Dear John letter and ditched. I'm not going to blame her for it.

I bounced around doing freelance accounting until I discovered slot machines. I started playing them on a regular basis at the Fond du

Luth casino downtown for a year but finally decided the town was too full of ghosts for me. I kept running into some of my old fellow workers from the firm, bumping into my ex-wife's relatives, seeing people I went to high school or college with and, to top it off, the sheriffs were always trying to serve me with papers for not paying child support, so I moved to Scanlon, keeping all my winnings in untraceable cash.

That's where my book ends. Actually, it ends a half hour from now in the bottom of the river, after I carry this cheap computer to the Riverside Bar and give it a hefty toss. Then, because it's almost four o'clock, I'll head right into the Riverside and get in on today's happy hour. By six, I'll be so fucking happy you won't even recognize me.

Maggie and her brood of misfits and miscreants will return to the oblivion they came from. The story of a bunch of drunks from northern Minnesota will remain as untold as the stories of all the drunks, drug addicts, and dysfunctional families spread out across America like fields of rotting wheat.

Because none of it matters.

My kids will probably grow up to be just as screwed up as I am. They'll be just as screwed up as my father and all the fathers and mothers before him. Life goes on. Like some speeding Monte Carlo heading toward a head on collision with an eighteen-wheeler, all we can do is to sit back and take the scenery in before the crash. That and smoke one of Rita's joints while finishing off a bottle of bottom-shelf vodka.

This is how my book ends, and yes, Diz, you finally got to be in it.

The End

The Golden Gate Motel

Charlie finished writing and flopped back onto his lumpy mattress. As always, he gazed up at the water stains and noted they were on the move again. It had been a wet spring in northern Minnesota, and the old leak had opened up again. The room had a damp, musty smell to it and Charlie could see where the stains were getting darker by the day. He had told Abdul about the new leak weeks ago and the manager said, "I'll get right to it."

Charlie knew better. Abdul had promised him that he would fix his noisy, leaking toilet the day after Charlie came into the office and complained about it, and that minor repair had taken two months to fix. Until the popcorn ceiling started falling, or the imaginary Amazon began dripping water on the cheap carpeting the roof leak would go unpatched. It was like staying in a motel in purgatory.

Charlie leaned over and took the Gideon Bible from the night stand drawer. He rifled through it quickly, trying to find a misplaced joint among Psalms or Romans. But the Bible yielded nothing but salvation, and salvation was the last thing on Charlie's mind.

He got up and opened the top drawer of the room's solitary dresser. He was in luck. Tucked away beside his unwashed T-shirts was a half-full pint of rum. He thought about taking his ice bucket outside, washing out one of his numerous stolen casino glasses, and buying a

Seven-Up at the vending machine beside the tiny lobby, but he didn't bother. He unscrewed the top and took a long, dedicated pull of the liquor miraculously saved for him.

It felt warm and cleansing as it slid down his throat. Charlie put the cap back on and went over to turn on the TV. He had accidentally shut it off earlier in the morning, and he wanted some company as he drank. Amazingly, the program that came on was *The Jerry Springer Show*.

"How timely," mumbled Charlie, as he headed back to bed to finish off the rum. Jerry was interviewing a young woman who had been abused by both parents as a child. The conversation was typical and everything was going well until Jerry, in true form, produced both parents from behind the stage in a kind of dysfunctional reunion that no one, least of all the abused daughter, really wanted. Things got weird.

Charlie found it amusing. He wondered if it might not be possible to somehow write Jerry Springer to see if he couldn't get on his show to talk about One-Eyed Maggie and his father and all the shit he had gone through as a child.

But as he finished off the last few sips of rum, Charlie decided he was too fat to be on TV. Besides, his ex-wife would probably get even more pissed at him if he started cashing in on what a mess he had made of their family. By the time the last few drops of the intoxicating brown liquid slid down his throat, Charlie had decided it wasn't worth the effort. Springer had all the drunks, bastards, abusive parents, neglected children he would ever need. Hell, reflected Charlie, there was so much dysfunction out there that Jerry's show could run for the next million years without ever running out of material.

With the rum gone and the clock pressing three-thirty, Charlie knew it was time. He got up and booted his computer out of Windows 95. As he did so, he realized it was out of force of habit. I'm going to toss the laptop in the river in a few minutes. Why on earth did I need to boot out at all? he asked himself, as he double clicked on the appropriate symbols.

After it shut down, Charlie quietly closed the old Toshiba and put it under his arm. He walked out of the motel room just as the daughter in the television show was trying to strangle her father. Springer's strong-armed bouncers were all over this angry girl as Charlie started toward the door.

"Welcome to my world," Charlie said to the television set as he shut his motel room door behind him. The rum was already having a marked effect on his empty stomach. Charlie knew he wanted to be as drunk as angels when he threw the computer away, so he was glad he had found the half-filled pint. The empty Bible was a letdown, though, as he would have loved to be high as well.

When he walked out into the mid-afternoon air, Charlie was overwhelmed with sunlight. It was absolutely gorgeous out. It had stopped raining just before noon and the sky had steadily cleared while Charlie had written the final chapter of his memoir. Now it was nearly cloudless, 70 degrees and a perfect spring day.

The sunlight annoyed him. He wished it were still cloudy and raining. Dreary weather would have been more to his liking. After all, he thought, I'm going to the funeral of my masterpiece. I might as well have the weather for it.

He started walking toward the Riverside with his laptop tucked under his arm like an oversized textbook. The cars on Highway 61 rolled by him as he stumbled toward the bar. They were having a SPRING BLOWOUT! at the used-car lot, and the entire parking area was decorated in balloons, banners, and brightly colored flags, all of them dancing and fluttering in the breeze.

An overzealous salesman, erroneously mistaking Charlie for a prospect, started walking up to him. The salesman stopped short when Charlie gave him a look that said, "If you come one step closer to me, asshole, I'll shove this fucking laptop up your ass."

The salesman backed off and headed back toward the office to sit around and bullshit with his fellows. He was new. The other salespeople knew about Charlie and his brand-new Monte Carlo and wouldn't dare approach him, especially when he was on his way to Happy Hour. They told the new guy he was lucky he had stopped.

When Charlie got to the parking lot of the Riverside Bar he caught a view of the river. It was still flowing strong, flustered by recent rains and the last few vestiges of melting snow lying deep in the muskeg and tamarack swamps that lay up along the headwaters.

Charlie walked over to the edge of the stream. The water was stained by the tannic acids flowing out of the swamps, looking dark as coffee as it tumbled toward Lake Superior. Lying behind boulders and along the edges were large, pillowy batches of foam, created by the rapids, and then trapped in the eddies and whirlpools. The cascading water made a constant ever changing din as it tumbled downhill.

The grass along the riverbank where he stood was already knee high, shimmering a brilliant green in the midday sunlight and accented by a handful of late-blooming dandelions and early-blooming wildflowers. Dragonflies and bees worked the edges of the river, while high overhead a flock of crows headed inland toward Cloquet, squawking and calling loudly as they flew.

The world outside was the antithesis of the world inside. In that world all was lost. Diz was dead, Charlie's memoir was soon to be drowned like some unwanted cat in a gunnysack, and even his relationship with Crystal appeared to be falling apart. It was cold and raining that morning for Charlie, and the bucolic scene around him seemed like an act of treason.

Charlie took the laptop out from under his arm and held it in his two hands for a second. He then lifted it up to his lips, kissed it gently, and threw it as far as he could into the rushing river. It made a large splash and then vanished. With the current running strong, the laptop continued to tumble downstream for miles, breaking up into a multitude of wires, transistors, and shards of plastic long before everything dumped out into Saint Louis Bay some ten miles downstream.

One-Eyed Maggie, Paul Stupidnski, Ted Ring, Stanley, and all the other miscreants vanished, along with the hard drive that had momentarily resurrected them. They returned to unread obituaries, court documents, and the reels of microfiche they would always belong to. Chain of Fools was gone.

For a brief moment Charlie thought about joining the laptop in the river. Tears welled up in his eyes as he realized the last year of his life was now being smashed apart by eddies and submerged boulders. He wanted to die. Then, like a faithful drunk, he realized that if he jumped into the river he would miss Happy Hour. Death would disallow him the luxury of drinking a few more rounds of two-for-one vodka Sevens. He knew in his heart both paths were suicide, but the one that offered him Happy Hour was easier and slower. He turned away from the river and walked into the bar. By six that night, Charlie Stupidnski was a drunk as any man can be.

*****

The first time the telephone rang, Charlie ignored it. He covered his throbbing head with his lumpy foam pillow and rolled away from the noise. It rang at least a dozen times before the determined caller gave up. That was around eleven in the morning. After coming home drunk from the Riverside the night before, Charlie was in no mood for conversation.

At noon the phone began ringing again. Charlie was still sleeping, nursing his elephant-sized hangover for as long as possible, exchanging one kind of pain for the other.

On the fifteenth ring he broke down and answered the call. It was rare for anyone to call him at the motel, and with Diz gone, Charlie had no idea as to who in hell it could be. As he reached for the phone he wondered if he had somehow forgotten to pay this month's rent. At the Golden Gate Motel all rents were paid in advance and in cash. Abdul was no fool.

"Charlie?"

"Yeah."

"It's me, Crystal. Where've you been? I tried calling you all last night but there was no answer. Abdul thought you might have left town or something. What's going on?"

"I went to the Riverside last night to have a few bumps. You know how it goes."

Crystal didn't respond. She knew how it goes.

"I've got some news, Charlie. I hope you're sitting down."

"I'm lying down and I'm hung over as hell, so make it quick."

"I'm pregnant."

Everything fell. The damp ceiling collapsed on top of the overweight fool lying hung over on his cheap mattress. The roof above the Sheetrock fell. The sky above the roof fell, and as if to accentuate the earthquake of Crystal's announcement, the bedrock the motel was built on started tumbling straight to hell. Charlie didn't know what to say.

"You're kidding, right?"

"No, I'm not kidding, Charlie. I'm six weeks pregnant."

"But your tubes are tied, Crystal. It's impossible for you to get pregnant when your tubes are tied, isn't it?"

"My doctor told me the chances are one in a million, or something like that. It does happen, though, and it happened to me."

"Shit."

There was a long silent pause. Charlie kept falling as Crystal waited for a better response than the word *shit*. That response never came.

"I want you to be on the birth certificate as the legal father."

"You're not really thinking about having this baby, are you?"

"Of course, I'm having the baby. It's a goddamn miracle, Charlie. I'm thirty-eight years old, I'm a stripper with my tubes tied, you're a drunk, and I'm having this baby. There is no negotiation here, Charlie. I'm just asking that you sign on as the father so the child isn't some kind of bastard."

The motel, the bed, and the collapsed ceiling tumbled clear of the bedrock and entered the hot molten core of the planet three miles below. Charlie, moments ago in the throes of a hangover from hell, found himself painfully sober and sweating profusely as the temperature inside the room climbed exponentially. He realized he was going to be a father again for the first time in seventeen years. He should have thrown himself into the river yesterday and spared himself this phone call.

"No. I'm not signing the birth certificate, and I'm not paying you a penny of child support!"

"I'm not asking you to pay any child support, Charlie. I know damn well you've been living like you do to avoid paying child support to your ex, and I don't expect you to change your ways now. I just want to give the kid a real father and a chance at having some kind of future."

"Just like Diz's future, I suppose."

"Look, Charlie, you can't keep blaming yourself for what happened to Diz out in Deadwood. He was the idiot who ran off and pissed on Mount Rushmore. His liver was all but shot anyway and you and I both know it was just a matter of time. Get over it, Charlie. You've got to move on with your life and stop feeling so damn sorry for yourself."

Charlie felt like hanging up. The last thing he needed was some unwanted psychoanalysis from a two-bit stripper from Esko. What he really needed was a joint and half a dozen aspirin. But he stayed on the line because, in the back of his mind, he knew Crystal was right.

"Let me think about it, Crystal. Just give me a day or so to think about doing what you're asking me to do. I'm not sure I want the kid to be born with a name like Stupidnski. Let's be honest with each other. I don't want to keep this damn genetic chain going on any farther than it already has."

"We'll use my real last name, Charlie. We'll call him or her Carlson, so you won't have to burden the kid with your screwed-up last name. But I don't want the kid to be a bastard. Even if you never see him again, at least he'll know he had a father."

Charlie wanted to use the famous one-liner that every man who gets this phone call wants to say: *How do you know I'm the real father, you little whore*, but he didn't. He knew he was the father. His thoughts, blurry as they were, went back to that first morning in the motel room at Deadwood when Crystal was kneeling beside his bed, waking him up. He knew she hadn't been cheating on him since then, and she hadn't gone out to earn any after hours money because he had given her a thousand dollars shortly after they had returned from Deadwood. He also knew he still loved her, whatever that was worth.

"Let me think about it, Crystal. I'll call you tomorrow."

"Stay sober, Charlie. Try to stay sober while you think about it."

"I'll try. Good-bye."

"Good bye."

Charlie hung up the phone, reached around and grabbed the remote, and flipped on the TV. The station was running a rerun of *Gilligan's Island.* Completely inappropriate.

"Gilligan's an asshole," Charlie mumbled to himself, as he got up to pee and search for some aspirin. "A first-class asshole."

Charlie took a long piss and found himself caught between laughter and tears. He found the bottle of aspirin and poured six of them into his hand, half tempted to take the entire bottle. He was going to be a father again. Who invented life? he asked himself as he washed down the pills with a glass of lukewarm tap water. Who the hell invented life, anyway?

*****

"I'll do it on one condition, Crystal. I'll sign the birth certificate provided you let me choose the name of the kid."

"What sort of name are you thinking about, Charlie?"

"I'm not going to tell you until the baby's born."

"That sucks. Why won't you tell me? You're not planning to name the baby some weirdo name like Moon Unit One or some shit like that, are you?"

"I might. I might want to name him Charlie if it's a boy, or Beatrice, after my mother, if it's a girl. Either way, my terms are simple. You get a real person's name on the birth certificate so the little bastard isn't a bastard, and I get to name the little bastard either way."

Crystal didn't like the tone of Charlie's voice but something, something indescribable, made her consider the offer. Charlie, despite his foul mood since Diz's death, had been more than kind to her lately and Crystal felt that his kindness, if she cut him some slack, might well continue all the way through her pregnancy.

"Let me think about it, Charlie. As long as you promise not to name the child something too strange, something that will make it hard on him when he gets into kindergarten or high school, I'll probably be OK with it. But give me a few days to think about it, will you?"

"Hell, Crystal, the kids not due for another seven months, take your time. I'm not going anywhere."

"I'll let you know in a week or so."

Crystal decided to change topics. "So how's the book coming?"

"You mean Chain of Fools?"

"Yeah, of course. Unless you're working on some other book I don't know about."

"It's not coming or going anywhere, I finished it."

"Wow, great. Can I read it?"

"No. I threw it in the river."

"You did what?"

"I threw the book—I mean the laptop that held the manuscript—in the Saint Louis River two days ago. It's flotsam and jetsam by now: gone, finished, complete, sunk, kaput. My book is lying at the bottom of Saint Louis Bay. Like an Italian mobster might say, Chain of Fools is swimming with the fishes." Charlie almost chuckled as he said this.

"Why did you throw it away? You've spent a year writing it."

"I can't write, Crystal. Even if I could, no one out there wants to read a book about a bunch of screwed up alcoholics who are long since dead and buried. Maybe Diz, Dena, and you might have read it, but it was really a piece of shit. It's better off in the bay."

"That's too bad, Charlie. I think a lot of people might have liked to have read it."

"They can dive in after it if they want."

Crystal refused to humor him. This wasn't a good sign. Charlie had already been fending off depression, and the loss of his one true passion wasn't a good omen. Lacking his manuscript to keep him focused, all that was left for her boyfriend was gambling and liquor. Not an endearing combination.

"I'm sorry you threw your dreams away, Charlie."

"I'm not."

"Do you want to come over tonight and have dinner with me?"

"Not tonight, Crystal, it's the seafood buffet at the Black Bear. I never miss it. Maybe I'll come over next weekend or something."

"That would be nice. I'll let you know then if I'm OK with your offer to name the baby."

"That's good. I'll talk to you soon."

"'Bye now."

"'Bye."

Charlie made the buffet that Monday night and ate even more than usual. The manager noted that his Indian friend wasn't with him but knew nothing of what had transpired in Deadwood. Whatever the reason for Diz's absence, the manager was glad for it. He had enjoyed a two-week hiatus from those eating machines, and profits were up. He wished only the worst for Charlie.

*****

"I still don't think it's a good idea, Crystal. What if you have a little girl and he names her Pussy or some sorry ass shit like that. What are you going to do then?"

"I thought about it. Hell, Rita, I'll just give the girl a nickname when she's old enough to talk. Crystal ain't my real name either, it's Lois."

Rita laughed out loud.

"What's so funny?"

"I just can't imagine you at Sugar Daddies with the announcer saying, 'And dancing next will be the pregnant Lois Lovelock.'"

"That's not funny, Rita."

"Yes, it is. You're going to have a heck of a time working the pole at eight months pregnant, don't you think?"

"I'll stop dancing when I start to show; you know that."

"Yeah, I know that. But I still think it's a bad idea to let Charlie name the kid. Even if you go with a nickname, the real first name will always be on the birth certificate, and later in life that could be a real problem. But hell, Crystal, it's your baby and it's your decision. You just asked me what I thought and I'm telling you. Don't do it."

Crystal appreciated Rita's input, but her mind was already made up. She wanted her child to have a real father. That was more important than some ridiculous name Charlie might come up with. The thought crossed her mind on more than one occasion that if her child was a boy, Charlie might well name him Diz after his deceased best friend. Oddly enough, Crystal sometimes hoped that would happen: she had become kind of fond of that name, odd as it might sound.

"Maybe he'll name him Diz if it's a boy."

"Yeah, he probably would do something like that. But I don't mind the name Diz all that much, Crystal. It kind of grows on you."

"It sure does. I miss that crazy Diz, Rita. Even if he was a drunk, he was a lovable drunk."

"I miss him too. Listen, Crystal, my cousin's coming over in a little bit with her two kids so I've got to run. Like I said, I wouldn't do it, but I'm not in your position right now, so it's really up to you."

"Thanks for your input, Rita. I'll let you know. 'Bye now."

"'Bye."

Crystal hung up the phone and started thinking about what to have for dinner. Charlie was coming over around seven and she wanted to cook something special. She knew how much he liked seafood, so she had gone down to the Piggly Wiggly earlier and picked up some jumbo shrimp. She was going to make seafood Alfredo. Knowing Charlie's appetite, Crystal planned on cooking for four.

Charlie arrived around six thirty looking like hell. He had been staying up later than usual, and between his lack of sleep and excessive drinking, his appearance suffered. Crystal could see he was gaining weight again, trying to eat himself out of his current state of depression. It didn't take long before the conversation focused on the unborn child Crystal was carrying.

"Have you decided yet? You know, about letting me name the kid?"

"Yeah, I have. It's fine, Charlie, you can name the baby."

"You know my other condition."

"About child support."

"I'm not going to pay a dime. You're going to sign an agreement stating that you will neither request nor expect any child support from me whatsoever. That I am only signing the birth certificate to verify that I am the biological father, nothing else. I don't want any complications, Crystal. I want you to be perfectly clear about that."

Crystal was reluctant to agree to the second condition, but if she objected, Charlie would walk and her child would be fatherless. Maybe once he sees the baby, she thought, maybe then he'll want to help. Infants can do that: they can change a person.

"I know how you feel about child support, Charlie. You've got a track record on that subject."

"Don't get pissy with me, Crystal. You're no fucking angel either."

Seeing their conversation was heading south, Crystal quickly changed the subject, hoping to avoid an all-out fight. She ignored his last comment.

"Do you know what day it is?"

Charlie glanced over at her, almost disappointed that she didn't take the bait. "It's Saturday."

"No, it's not just Saturday. It's my birthday."

Charlie, having totally forgotten, felt foolish.

"I never remember birthdays." Then, as an afterthought, he added, "Happy birthday."

"Thanks. I'm thirty-nine, Charlie. I'm thirty-nine years old and pregnant. Your child in me is my present and yes, it is a very happy birthday for me."

Dinner went well. They talked about the old days when Charlie used to come in for lap dances every Monday and Tuesday when the club was a virtual ghost town and they laughed out loud about how crazy it must have looked to the SWAT team when Diz got out his dick and pissed on the nose of George Washington. As the fettuccini settled in and the half-gallon bottle of white wine vanished into the evening, the two of them started touching each other like they used to.

Before long the conversation wandered from words to zippers. They soon found themselves in Crystal's bedroom with her on top and Charlie lost in the glorious moment that is sex. It had been weeks since they had slept together and their passions were running high. For a brief period in time each of them became lost in the musty fog of lovemaking.

Crystal looked gorgeous, thought Charlie, as he watched her throw her head back and arch her body back as she approached climax. She wasn't just a woman, she was an angel in the throes of lovemaking. She dissolved into the vacuum that is the essence of sex.

Charlie could not hold out a moment longer, and as he came, Crystal joined him. A moment later, she lay at Charlie's side, exhausted. Neither of them spoke.

Around midnight, after watching some television together in bed and sharing a large bowl of Neapolitan ice cream with strawberry jam spread on top, Charlie started a conversation that Crystal wasn't looking forward to.

"That was nice, but I've got to tell you that it feels weird having sex with you now, Crystal."

"Why?"

"You know, with the baby inside you and all."

"You're not going to hurt the baby by having sex with me, Charlie. It doesn't work that way."

"Yeah, I know, but it just feels wrong somehow."

"Well, if you got on top of me that might just be the case, but not the way we just did it. There's no pressure on my womb when we have sex like that, and I enjoy it, Charlie. Tonight, I really enjoyed it."

Charlie looked down at Crystal's stomach, trying to see if he could tell she was pregnant. She was lying on her back beside him with the covers pulled up tight over her naked body. As hard as he tried there was no way of telling Crystal was with child at this stage of her pregnancy. She was way too early on to be showing. The only indications that she was pregnant were her craving for extra strawberry jam over the multi-flavored ice cream and an occasional bout of morning sickness. Her stomach, a dancer's stomach, remained flat and as beautiful as ever.

"I don't know. We'll see."

Around one o'clock, with both of them half asleep, Charlie told Crystal he was heading back to the Golden Gate with the Monte Carlo. Crystal asked him to stay at her place but it was fruitless. Charlie closed her apartment door behind him and walked out to his car. He stuck the keys in the ignition, started to turn the ignition, then inexplicably stopped. He leaned back and started to weep. He didn't know why and he didn't care. He just wept.

Ten minutes later, Charlie started up his car and drove home.

*****

Months passed. Crystal started to show halfway through her second trimester, and when she did, Charlie stopped having sex with her. They tried it a few times but Charlie couldn't bring himself to the point where he felt comfortable having an orgasm. He knew Crystal was right about sex not hurting the baby but felt too awkward to do it. He announced that sex between them was over until after the child was born, and his decision was final. He told Crystal he did the same thing when his former wife became pregnant decades ago. Knowing that didn't help Crystal, who presently felt both physically and emotionally abandoned.

As the months wore on, Charlie also withdrew emotionally—withdrew into the liquid fog that is alcohol. He became his father, spending most of his time inside the confines of his tiny motel room, sharing what little space he had with his booze. All else faded into a lonely blur.

With the money he had left from his car loan, there were weeks on end when he never bothered to even start the Monte Carlo. He ate hot dogs from the nearby Erickson gas station and washed them down with vodka. He ate candy bars by the score and washed them down with rum. Aside from an occasional accidental meeting with Abdul, the motel manager, and worrisome phone calls from Crystal, he hardly spoke to anyone. He stopped walking over to the Riverside, even for Happy Hour.

He was now a complete, self-destructing alcoholic: a drunk, a dipsomaniac, a lush, a boozer, a victim of science curled up inside himself like some kind of dying, shell-less, overweight snail. The liquor formed the useless shell that held him. Life was emptiness.

As he drank, he gained weight. When he drank, his chain smoking reached absurd proportions. There was one day when he smoked five packs of Camels. His voice began to take on that raspy, deep-throated texture of the chronic smoker. The tips of his fingers, on both hands, became permanently stained a jaundiced yellow. His clothes sometimes went unwashed and unchanged for a week.

On more than one occasion Abdul thought about some kind of intervention. He had called several organizations—the Salvation Army, the Red Cross—but they said, as long as he was not harming anyone beside himself, there was little they could do. Abdul was afraid he might pass out with a lit cigarette and burn down the Golden Gate Motel. Abdul was right to be concerned. Twice in the past month Charlie had awakened to the smell of smoke—nearly dying Maggie's death a half-century later.

Life slipped away. Crystal moved closer to her due date just as certainly as Charlie moved further from joy. She was certain that if he continued on his present course he would be soon dead. He would die in a rush of sirens, twisted steel, and the sound of the jaws of life cutting him out of a rollover on Interstate 35. He would develop liver failure just as Diz did and perish slowly, drinking himself into the grave. He would suffer the heart attack that was long overdue from arteries clogged with bags of sixty-nine-cent potato chips, Snickers bars, and Camel cigarettes.

If he kept drinking the way he was drinking now, felt Crystal, death would find him. Crystal knew this as certainly as she knew his child was within her, kicking and stretching daily, waiting for that moment when birth brought a new life into the world. And as surely as she watched him fall, she felt his child reaching for the very thing he was fleeing, the ecstasy of living.

Her thoughts were as troubled as Charlie's, which wore on her. She had tried to make amends with her family, telling her mother over the phone about her miraculous pregnancy and forthcoming motherhood, but the family wanted no part of it. Only Rita and a few of the girls at Sugar Daddies stayed close. Rita became her best friend, attending birthing classes with her and helping her out around the house as she neared her due date. Little things, but important to Crystal.

They went to garage sales and Goodwill stores searching for baby clothes, cribs and high chairs. The girls at the club held a baby shower for and gave Crystal boxes of Pampers, milk bottles, plastic rattles, and adorable outfits that could be worn by either a boy or a girl.

Rita had asked Crystal to find out what sex the baby was going to be but Crystal refused to ask her pediatrician. The amniocentesis that was performed, because of Crystal's age, had established the sex of the fetus without question, but Crystal had told her doctor not to so much as hint at whether she was carrying a boy or a girl. It was to be as much of a surprise as the unknown name Charlie was going to be giving the newborn baby.

The pregnancy itself was going well. Her years of dancing had kept Crystal's body in perfect health. Luckily, her after-hours work had never resulted in any lingering STDs which might have compromised the health of the baby. Her doctor kept reassuring Crystal that she was much younger than her chronological age and need not worry about the approaching labor and delivery.

Crystal willingly stopped drinking and smoking in sheer appreciation of the miracle of her pregnancy. As the months went by, her womb swelled with life and Crystal anxiously awaited the day when she would hold the baby in her arms and not in her abdomen. She waited. She watched Charlie slide away. She cried. She became more and more beautiful with every passing week. She became the mother of us all.

*****

"Hello?"

"Hello, Charlie. My water broke."

"Your water heater?"

"Not exactly, Charlie. The other water, the water that surrounds the baby."

"Oh, shit."

"Can you come over and take me to the hospital?"

"Now?"

"What do you think, next week?"

Charlie was in no position to think. It was one in the afternoon on a generic Tuesday and he was still lying in bed, trying to avoid the hangover he faced almost every waking day of his life. He hadn't talked to Crystal in two weeks, having been preoccupied with finishing off a case of Popov vodka he had purchased on special at the One Stop. The last liter still held a few cups of the clear pain-numbing liquid in it, and his sole agenda was to finish it before the day, whatever day it happened to be, was over.

"Yeah, I'll be right over. I haven't showered yet."

"I don't think they'll be paying much attention to you at the delivery room, Charlie. I'm the one who's having the baby."

"You're probably right."

"Hurry, Charlie. My contractions are starting."

"OK, I'll be right over."

Charlie didn't need to get dressed. He had passed out with all his clothes on the night before, around 3 A.M., after getting back from a losing streak at the casino. The past few months had seen his nickel reserves dwindle to several hundred of the little alloy cameos. He didn't really give a damn, spending most of his energy trying to drown himself in a series of empty bottles. Winning or losing no longer mattered. Losing was easier.

He went into the bathroom to take a piss and brush his teeth. The mirror in the tiny bathroom told his story in discouraging detail. His hair was graying and disheveled, his stubbled face unshaven, and his eyes road-map bloodshot. His off-white long sleeve-shirt was so wrinkled it was all but impossible not to notice he had slept in it, and his unbelted blue jeans were stretched to the limit, still stained from yesterday's buffet-busting marinara sauce.

For the most part, out of habit, he ignored the reflection in the mirror. He brushed his teeth and tried to remember the last time he was called upon to ferry his wife to the hospital. That was the year Robbie was born, seventeen years ago. He hadn't seen Robbie in seven years and wondered how tall he might be today. He was almost a teenager when his father had walked out, now he was almost old enough to vote. Time flies when you're an alcoholic.

He wasn't looking forward to the birth of this next child either. He was fifty-four years old and not exactly a Norman Rockwell picture of fatherhood. By his calculations he would be in his seventies before this child graduated from high school. Realistically, Charlie figured he would be dead by the time the kid made it out of middle school, especially if he kept up his current pace. Like he gave a damn.

As he spit the last of his toothpaste backwash down the drain, he kept thinking about the list of names he had worked up and stuck in the Gideon Bible beside his bed. God, I've got to remember to take the list before I leave the motel. I'll be lost without it.

There were nine names on the list. Four of them were boy's names, four were girl's names, and one was capable of naming either a boy or a girl. He thought he would take a damn good look at the kid before deciding which of the names to choose. Some were actually nice names, while a few would stand out as clearly as would a cleft palate or a birthmark that covered half the kid's face. Names that would scar the child from day one.

Of course, Diz was one of the names if it was a boy and Maggie if it was a girl. Charlie was hell-bent on making sure the chain would continue, no matter what name he settled on. For a long, long time the name Link was on the list, but he had crossed it out two weeks ago as being just too obvious. Link was a switch-hitting name, capable of being used by either a girl or a boy.

Maybe I'll put Link back on the list, Charlie thought as he rifled through the Gideon's Bible, hoping to find an errant joint in Corinthians. There was no misplaced joint, so he settled on his piece of scratch paper, tucked safely in Romans. "Yeah, I think I will add it to the list. Link's a real nice name."

He grabbed his jacket to ward off the bitter cold that descended on northern Minnesota every February and headed out to his Monte Carlo. The car looked as rough as he did. The once shiny black finish lay buried beneath a crusted coating of road salt, dirt, and sand. Dark globs of frozen ice hung behind every wheel well, and the front windshield had a large crack in it from where a semi had kicked a rock at him two months ago, when he was driving back from the casino. He wasn't about to spend any money fixing it. At least, it didn't leak.

I hope the damn thing starts, he thought, as he sat down in the driver's seat and stuck his key in the ignition. It started reluctantly.

He waited for the engine to warm up a few minutes before putting it into drive. On cold days like this the Monte Carlo had been killing once he put it in gear so it was better to wait awhile. When he finally shifted it into drive it hesitated a bit but managed to keep running. He was out of the parking lot and heading toward Crystal's apartment in Cloquet within fifteen minutes of her phone call. That was as fast as she could possibly have expected him to move.

When he arrived, Crystal was in the middle of a contraction. She was doubled over on the couch and when she heard the doorbell ring the best she could do was to shout, "Come on in, Charlie." He heard her calling out and couldn't miss noticing the strain in her voice from the hallway that led into her apartment. He checked the knob and discovered the door was open. He approached her cautiously. It was clear to him from the moment he saw her that she was writhing in pain.

"Crystal, are you OK?"

"What do you think, Charlie? I'm having a baby and it hurts like hell."

"How far apart are your contractions?"

"How the hell do I know? I'm not exactly timing them. Just wait a minute or two and this one will pass. Then get me out to the car and over to the hospital as fast as possible. Can you do that for me, Charlie?"

"Yeah."

Charlie sat in the matching chair directly across from the couch Crystal was lying on. Both were worn and in need of replacement. Overall, the apartment looked good. As Crystal continued to moan on the couch, Charlie got up to look into her small bedroom. The used crib she and Rita had purchased at the Cloquet Goodwill was set up in the corner. Charlie looked behind him and saw they had moved her highboy dresser out next to the couch to make room for the crib. There was a cute mobile hanging above the crib with a dozen tiny stuffed teddy bears on it. They were attached to a musical wind-up mechanism that probably played some lovely melody like "Twinkle, Twinkle, Little Star."

"The room looks good, Crystal," said Charlie to no one in particular. Crystal couldn't make out that he had spoken at all, being far too absorbed in her pain.

Charlie could see that they had painted the ceiling a light blue and stuck those little Day-Glo moons and stars on the ceiling directly above the crib. It reminded him of another lifetime, one he rarely thought of these days, a lifetime that now seemed to have existed centuries ago. For an instant, he felt nostalgic, as if he missed it. As quickly as those feelings came to him, he dismissed them. He wanted no part of this.

As he counted the stars above the crib he heard Crystal cry out behind him. "This one's almost over, Charlie. Grab my bag next to the bed and let's get going."

Charlie couldn't miss the large bag lying at the foot of Crystal's bed. He grabbed it and headed back into the living room. Crystal had already sat back up, her stomach as huge as Charlie's and a worried look upon her face. This was her first child, and at thirty-nine she had a right to be worried.

Charlie grabbed her under the arm and helped to lift her up and off the sofa. As he held her he could feel her trembling. He knew that he would have to get her downstairs to the car before the next contraction set in or they would spend ten minutes in the cold, dark hallway.

They hurried down the stairs and out into the windy afternoon. Charlie opened the car door for her and helped her in. He felt odd in doing so. Still hungover, unshaven, and in his mid-fifties it was all wrong for him to be driving this young woman to the hospital with his child in her womb. He put those thoughts away as quickly as they entered his head. Yes, it was odd but there was no point in dwelling on it.

They hardly spoke as Charlie sped toward Cloquet Community Memorial. Crystal realized that today might well be the last day she would ever see Charlie and this might well be the last favor he would ever do for her. She knew he might choose the baby's name, say farewell, get back into his dirty Monte Carlo, and drive away, taking the same route south as he took years ago. She hoped it wouldn't happen but had no way of preventing it. There was no tomorrow to talk about, so little was said.

Charlie pulled up to the emergency room door and honked the horn. He was hoping it would draw some attention and help to get the staff out here with a wheelchair. About half a mile before getting to the hospital Crystal had gone into another contraction, and she was in no condition to walk from the car into the emergency room.

One of the nurses inside made note of the extended car honking and came outside to investigate. Being close to the Fond du Lac Indian reservation, they had all seen more than their fair share of gunshot and stabbing victims over the years and from the looks of this dirty Monte Carlo, that's probably what the nurse expected to find.

As she approached, Charlie hit the button on the electric windows and by the time the nurse peered into the car it was clear that no one had been stabbed.

"How long has she been in labor?"

"About an hour or so. This is her first baby. This contraction just started a few minutes ago."

"Any idea how far apart they are?"

"Five, maybe six minutes or so. Her apartment is just a few miles away."

"I assume you're the grandfather."

Charlie rolled his eyes. God, he thought, it's already started. I'm just too damn old for this shit.

"The father."

"Right. I'm going to get a wheelchair. Wait here."

The nurse ran back through the electric doors that opened into the waiting room, found a wheelchair and was back at the car within minutes. By the time she had arrived Crystal's contraction had settled down, providing a window of opportunity to wheel her inside while Charlie parked.

"Do you have a doctor I should call?" she asked Crystal.

"Yes. Please call Dr. Peterson. He's with the clinic."

"I know him. We'll notify him in a few minutes. It's going to be a while before we need him, though. I'm sure you're well aware of that. Your husband says this is your first child. Is that correct?"

"He's not my husband. He's my boyfriend, sort of. But yes, this is my first child. My tubes were tied years ago; this wasn't supposed to happen."

The nurse didn't respond. There was clearly more information in Crystal's comments than the nurse was ready to handle.

Charlie returned from the parking lot and all three of them went through the emergency room and headed down a long wide corridor toward another section of the hospital. The nurse wheeled Crystal into an elevator and pushed the button for the second floor.

"Where we heading?"

"To the birthing suites. There's no reason to tie up a bed in the emergency room for her. She's looks to be in fine health, and seeing this is her first child it might be a while."

Charlie nodded in agreement. It wasn't an emergency any longer. It was a mother giving birth and that was a far, far cry from a car accident or a stab wound.

Once they arrived on the second floor it was an equally long ride down another corridor and through a set of doors that opened into a brightly lit waiting room with four large birthing suites surrounding it. Two of the rooms were occupied. Two were empty. The nurse went up to the nurses' station, held a brief, subdued conversation, and came back to the wheelchair.

"Room two-seventeen, right over there." She pointed toward an open door not twenty feet away. "Please wait out here while we get her situated."

Charlie sighed. He was glad to stay in the waiting room. Hell, he didn't even want to be here, for that matter. Everything had gone so wrong since Diz died. Crystal had somehow gotten pregnant, his luck had gone to hell, he'd gained twenty useless pounds. Everything.

Hours passed. Sometimes Charlie would step over the threshold of her room to check on Crystal, while other times he would simply sit out in the lobby and listen to her moan. Rita had shown up and taken over in the father's supportive role. Rita had attended birthing classes with Crystal, and it was far easier to let her handle the ordeal than for Charlie to get involved.

Around 11 P.M., Dr. Peterson arrived. Rita had told Charlie a few minutes earlier that Crystal was fully dilated and the baby was on its way. Dr. Peterson checked Crystal immediately, and didn't find any complications. Crystal's health, despite her age, was working in her favor and she was holding up as well as any mother might in the throes of giving birth.

To kill time, Charlie would get out his list of names and run over them. At nine o'clock one name seemed to jump out at him, while at ten-thirty it was another name he favored. It became an obsession, something he couldn't define.

Crystal hardly spoke as the contractions became more and more severe. Rita held her hand, wiped the sweat from her forehead, and held an ice pack to her pelvis as the pain and pressure mounted. As the moment of birth neared, Charlie became less and less interested in being in the room. It seemed like some kind of slow-motion car accident. There was the blood, the screams, the moaning, and the systematic motion of nurses and doctors, orderlies and aides, all buzzing around the mother in this strange, surreal dance of life.

On several occasions Charlie was more than half tempted to get back into the elevator, head outside into the frigid air, and find himself a liquor store. If there was ever a day he needed a stiff drink, this was it. Yet as much as he wanted to go out and retrieve a pint of vodka, there was another part of him that wouldn't allow it. He felt a twinge of guilt every time his thoughts wandered in the direction of the nearest package store but, he couldn't muster up the heartless courage to do it. When Crystal's doctor arrived, Charlie realized he would have to make it through the night cold sober.

At exactly 12:23, with Charlie sitting nervously outside in the lobby, he heard the distinctive cry of a child come from behind the closed door of room 217. By this time, exhausted and bewildered by the sheer reality of Crystal's labor, he found himself unexpectedly proud upon hearing that sound.

Ten minutes later, Rita brought the baby out to Charlie. It was wrapped in a tiny pink blanket and still partially covered with the fluids of childbirth.

"Congratulations, Charlie, it's a girl."

Upon seeing the child, so small, so fragile, Charlie found himself unable to keep from breaking into tears.

"She's so little," he said.

"Yes. She's your little girl, Charlie. Do you want to hold her?"

"No, I can't hold her."

"Yes, you can. She won't break. The doctor has already looked her over. She's got all of her fingers and toes and is in excellent health. She's your little angel, Charlie. A real miracle baby, given the fact that Crystal should never have been able conceive her at all."

Charlie stood beside Rita and stared into the dark brown eyes of the infant. The child was wide awake, looking around but, like all newborns, unable to focus. Her hands were the size of quarters, thought Charlie, while her fingers appeared doll like and perfectly pink. Despite being newborn she had plenty of light brown hair and Charlie could see that she was going to have her mother's good looks.

"She's like a doll."

"She is a doll, Charlie. Here, take her."

Charlie cautiously extended his huge arms out toward Rita. The nurse who had wheeled Crystal in hours earlier, the nurse who was pulling a double shift that day because the hospital was running short-staffed, watched from the nurses station as this scene unfolded. She had witnessed this before, the melting of many a man at the hands of an innocent. She smiled to herself as this huge bulk of a man carefully held this tiny, beautiful child.

Charlie, not knowing quite what to do, gently rocked the infant back and forth in his arms, looking like some misplaced giant who had accidentally found a baby in a nearby snowbank. It was obvious to everyone that Charlie was deeply touched by this child.

"Crystal said everything's fine. She told me to ask you for her name. I guess you two decided you're going to name the baby tonight. Is that right?"

"Yeah. I'm supposed to name her. I've got a list."

"Where is it?"

"It's in my right front pocket."

"I'll reach in and get it for you, Charlie."

"No, wait. Give me a minute."

Charlie, all the while gently rocking the baby, turned around and walked off down the hallway a few feet. He wanted to be alone with his daughter. He needed some space.

Turning his back on Rita, he stopped and stood in the empty hallway, tears rolling down his cheeks. He thought of his list of names. There were four names for her on his list, three of which would mark this tiny child from this night forward. All of them carried a certain amount of freight. Names that in some fashion or another would do little more than help to keep the chain unbroken.

As Charlie looked down upon this glorious, innocent face, he found himself inexplicably hesitant to choose any one of the four, and Link was out of the question.

Why should I do this? he thought to himself, as he peered into this bundle of innocence resting in his arms. Why should I burden her with the sins of One-Eyed Maggie, my useless son of a bitch of a father, or any of the others. They're all dead now, dead and gone.

Maybe, just maybe she can do it. Maybe, like her mother, she's strong enough to break this endless cycle I'm caught up in. Maybe this little girl can get past it and move on. Have a husband who sticks around and builds a life worth living. Maybe, somehow, I can help.

Charlie turned around, walked back toward the birthing room, and nodded to Rita.

"I want to go in and see Crystal now. Is that OK?"

"She's tired, but I'm sure she'd love to see you."

Charlie gently handed the baby back to Rita, still uncomfortable with holding something so vulnerable in his lumbering arms.

He opened the door wide for Rita and looked inside the room toward the bed as he did.

Crystal was a wreck, but a smiling wreck. She had been sweating and her dyed blond hair was hanging down in wet strands across her damp hospital gown. The floor at the base of her bed was covered in smears of blood and the vestiges of childbirth. The room had a strange, acrid odor. None of it mattered.

"Isn't she beautiful, Charlie," Crystal said as Rita handed the child back to her mother.

"She's incredibly beautiful."

Once back in Crystal's arms the tableau was perfect. The exotic dancer was no longer an exotic dancer. She was the Madonna. The child in her arms would never be a bastard. The child was Charlie's little girl. Rita, caught up in the emotion of it all, started to cry, ever so softly.

"Have you given her a name yet, Charlie? I'll keep my promise if you do."

"Yes, I've chosen a name."

"What is it?"

"Angelina."

"That's a lovely name, Charlie. Was that the only name on your list for a little girl?"

"No. I had several others, but I lost my list."

Rita looked over to Charlie and wondered what he was saying to Crystal. He had just told her it was in his right front pocket a minute ago. She looked down at his pants more closely and saw the edge of a piece of paper sticking out. Clearly, reflected Rita to herself, he hadn't lost the list at all.

"Can I help raise her, Crystal?"

"Of course you can. She's your daughter."

"I'm kind of an asshole, you know. I mean, I've not been a very reliable father. And then there's the drinking, and—"

"Oh, shut up, you big oaf. You'll do just fine. Now come and give me a big kiss before I boot your butt out of here so I can get some sleep. I'm exhausted."

"OK."

Charlie leaned over and kissed Crystal on the forehead, his silent tears falling on Angelina as he did. Rita burst into tears too, suddenly feeling as though Diz was in the room beside them, watching this scene unfold.

"Good night, Charlie. I'll see you in the morning," said Crystal.

"Good night, Crystal. Good night, Angelina. And thanks for everything, Rita."

Charlie turned around and walked out of the room, unsure and apprehensive of what would happen next.

"Angelina's a nice name," he said to himself, as he got back into the elevator and headed back downstairs toward the parking lot and his unwashed Monte Carlo. "Little Angel. Angelina. A lovely name, really."

This book is dedicated to my mother,
Harriet B. Sobczak,
who taught me that love can break the chain.

About the Author

Charles Sobczak lives and writes on Sanibel Island, Florida. He formed Indigo Press, L.L.C. in 1999 with the publication of his first novel, *Six Mornings on Sanibel.* From the original print run of 3,000 copies the novel went on to become the best selling book on Sanibel. It is currently in its sixth printing with more than 23,000 copies sold.

His second novel, *Way Under Contract—a Florida Story,* published in 2001, went on to win the coveted *Patrick Smith Award for Best Florida Literature 2001.* It brought Sobczak's writing to the attention of readers across Florida.

After the publication of *Way Under Contract*, Sobczak put together a collection of award-winning essays, short stories, and poetry in a selected works volume titled *Rhythm of the Tides.* In 2005, Sobczak won the *Alliance of the Arts Writer of the Year Award* in Lee County, Florida.

His third novel, *A Choice of Angels,* was released in 2003 and went on to garnered a starred review in *Booklist,* the official publication of the American Library Association. It also won a **National Bronze Award** from *Foreword Magazine* for the *BEST WORK OF RELIGIOUS FICTION 2003.*

Changing directions Sobczak began work on the non-fiction book *Alligators, Sharks & Panthers: Deadly Encounters with Florida's Top Predator—Man.* The book won a **National Bronze IPPY Award** from the Independent Publishing Book Awards, Traverse City, MI.

Chain of Fools is Sobczak's fourth novel. He is currently writing a field guide to Sanibel Island titled, *Living Sanibel,* to be released in early 2010. It is a full-color handbook on flora and fauna of Sanibel Island, as well as a reference guide to all of Sanibel's bike paths, hiking and kayak trails.

Along with his writing, Sobczak also works as a Realtor with **VIP Realty Group**. He enjoys traveling with his wife, Molly Heuer, and their two college-age sons, Logan and Blake. Sobczak is a lifetime member of SCCF (Sanibel - Captiva Conservation Foundation), president of Lee Reefs, past president of Solutions to Avoid Red Tide and the Sanibel Island Fishing Club. He is also a member of PURRE (People United to Restore Our Rivers and Estuaries) and an avid offshore angler.

Six Mornings on Sanibel

Since its publication in November of 1999, *Six Mornings on Sanibel* has become an island classic. This engaging tale of the accidental meeting of two strangers on the Sanibel fishing pier has touched the hearts of thousands.

Carl Johnson, a wise, retired fishing guide from Sanibel, and Richard Evans, a young, stressed-out divorce attorney from Peoria, share more than snook runs and cold Cokes during their six mornings together. They share tales of love, suicide, and heroism. This tale is about knowing when it's time to die and when it's time to start living again. It is about something rare in this hurried age: wisdom.

"It was a wonderful story...Perhaps it was the simplicity and honesty between two men of different backgrounds that gave the book that specialness. Very much **Tuesdays with Morrie,** *this book provided thought and a good read."* Barbara Wilson, Barrington, RI

"A lifetime of wisdom in a one-week adventure."
The Book Reader, San Francisco, California

"I just finished reading **Six Mornings on Sanibel.** *It made me cry...It was not a simple tale though, it had a great deal to say and I wish just about everyone could read it."* Pat Janda, Fort Myers, Florida

"I found your book a good read. It reminded me a little of Hemmingway's **Old Man and the Sea** *and your characterizations are well drawn."* Bonnie Thomas, Moline, Illinois

"Each of Carl's stories of vanity, friendship, greed and survival deeply affect Richard, who begins to change...Sobczak captures the essence of Sanibel and the lives of his characters poignantly. He tells his story with humor, understanding and the voice of someone who lived it."
Harold Hunt, **The Cape Coral Breeze,** Cape Coral, Florida

"The book had so much to say about life and what really matters. I recommend it to everyone." Deborah Larson, Illinois

A Choice of Angels

This compelling novel was conceived and written shortly before the tragedy of 9/11/2001. Set in Istanbul, and Atlanta, Georgia, it tells the tale of the forbidden romance between the rebellious son of a Southern Baptist minister and the daughter of an Islamic family from Turkey.

Capturing the centuries-old conflict between Christianity and Islam and set against the backdrop of terrorist attacks, invasions, and the rise of religious fundamentalism, *A Choice of Angels* is a timeless tale of love, intolerance, and forgiveness. It won a **Bronze Award** from *Foreword Magazine,* and a starred review from *Booklist,* the official publication of the American Library Association.

"Each of Sobczak's characters rings true, and his every setting, whether a Turkish mosque or an Atlanta advertising agency, is compellingly detailed. He's funny, tolerant and unpreachy. And obviously, he's timely."   *Booklist Magazine*—starred review

*"**A Choice of Angels** holds a prism to the light and lets the love between two young people illuminate the political and religious dilemma in which the world has become entrapped."*
Priscilla Friedersdorf—*The Island Sun,* Sanibel, Florida

*"**A Choice of Angels** is not only a good read, but its message is timely enough to be required reading...it may help to free some minds from the vise in which their religion has imprisoned them."*
James Abraham, *The Port Charlotte Sun,* Port Charlotte, Florida

"Charles Sobczak's novel is about the greatest of themes—faith, hope and love. It's powerful, provocative and relevant. It's not just a story of our times, but for our times."
Michael Lister, Florida Author

*"**A Choice of Angels** reminds me of how I feel—that love does not know land or religion. Everyone should read it."*
Alia Islam

Rhythm of the Tides

From a blind Krazy-Glue peddler in the grand bazaar of Istanbul to a simple bicycle ride through Acadia National Park in northern Maine, these stories, like modern parables, explore the deeper meanings concealed in the most unlikely of settings.

Spanning more than forty years of writing, **Rhythm of the Tides** covers some of Sobczak's early works from the 1960s through several award-winning newspaper essays in the late 1990s. Along with the essays, which include *My Racoons, The Guests Are Gone,* and *I Could Learn to Love Kansas,* the book contains several short stories and a collection of poetry and lyrics. From humor to heartbreak, this short work of selected works will give hours of reading enjoyment.

"Each brief tale is only a page or two, but when you have read one, you just want to keep on reading—a difficult book to put down."
The Lake Wales News, Lake Wales, Florida

"I must admit I find a great deal of genius in this book, and madness with a purpose. There was a compelling need to see where Sobczak was going to send me next. Frivolous, loving, moral, salty, fishy, scary, thoughtful, crazy and wondrous are adjectives that describe Sobczak's work."
The Island Reporter, Sanibel, Florida

"Sobczak has a gentle touch and a wondering mind and obviously enjoys stringing words together, thus producing some enjoyable reading for us. A nice bedside or seaside book."
The Tampa Tribune, Tampa, Florida

*"**Rhythm of the Tides** certainly lives up to his previous books, although very different in content and style. Another ten out of ten!"*
Bob Jacob, Christchurch, England

Alligators, Sharks & Panthers

Deadly Encounters with Florida's Top Predator — Man

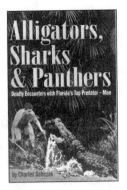

Released in November 2006, this nonfiction title explores the complex and often strained relationship between mankind and his fellow predators. Covering 26 fatal human/alligator and shark attacks that have occurred in the Sunshine State over the past 60 years, the book serves as a "what not to do" when encountering these creatures in the wild. The book recently won the 2007 *IPPY Bronze Award* for best regional nonfiction title. This national award is presented by the Independent Publishers Book Awards Group out of Traverse City, Michigan.

"A fascinating (if sometimes horrifying) and well-written look at the critters which sometimes turn the tables on the planet's dominant predator, us. It balances their sometimes less-than-friendly treatment of Homo sapiens with accounts of the grim impact people have had on them. A good book to read if you care about our environment and don't want to end up as dinner."
> Paul R. Ehrlich, PhD Stanford University /author of
> *The Population Explosion*

"The call to consider the other side of the 'predator' coin, combined with backed up research makes this book a must read. It contains an educational quality that would suffice to make it a required read in the nation's school systems."
> Susan Haley, Florida author, Sarasota

"Although he pored over hundreds of news documents for his research, Sobczak says he strives to not come across as a journalist...each fatal wild animal attack thus comes to life as a miniature story, sometimes not for the faint of heart.
Sobczak does not attempt to hide his fervent environmentalist politics, which jump out from within the book's very title. While alligators, sharks and panthers may well fit the category of predators, the distinction of "top predator" is awarded to man."
> Dave Garey, Staff Writer, *Port Charlotte Sun Herald* 2/12/07

"This book is both entertaining and educational, and it grabs your attention right from the start. It also offers profound judgements on what has happened to nature, and who is responsible. It deserves a wide audience."
> Patrick D. Smith/Florida author of *A Land Remembered*

Also by Charles Sobczak

Alligators, Sharks & Panthers:
Deadly Encounters with Florida's Top Predator - Man
(2007)
Paperback ISBN-13: 978-0-96761990-3 $16.95

A Choice of Angels (2003)
Hardcover ISBN 0-9676199-7-1 $24.95
Paperback ISBN 0-9676199-9-8 $15.95

Rhythm of the Tides (2001)
ISBN   0-9676199-1-2 $13.95

Six Mornings on Sanibel (1999)
ISBN-13: 978-0-9676199-5-8 $13.95

Questions regarding ordering information, readers' club discounts
and/or comments are encouraged and welcome via:

Toll Free Number:	877-472-8900
Local Number:	239-472-0491
Fax Number:	239-472-1426
Email:	indigocontact@earthlink.net
Web Address:	www.indigopress.net
Mailing Address:	Indigo Press, LLC
	P.O. Box 977
	Sanibel Island, FL 33957

- Visa or MasterCard Accepted -
Orders may be placed via our website, telephone or US Mail.